THE INNOVATION MILLIONAIRES

THE INNOVATION MILLIONAIRES

How They Succeed

Gene Bylinsky

Charles Scribner's Sons · New York

Parts of this book first appeared in *Fortune* magazine:

"General Doriot's Dream Factory" (August 1967)
"California's Great Breeding Ground for Industry" (June 1974)
"How Intel Won Its Bet on Memory Chips" (November 1973)
"Zoecon Turns Bugs Against Themselves" (August 1973)
"Visionary on a Golden Shoestring" (June 1973)
"KMS Industries Bets Its Life on Laser Fusion" (December 1974)

Illustrations:
Page 2   Georges F. Doriot (*Alan F. Lydiard*)
Page 24   E. F. Heizer, Jr.
Page 46   Frederick E. Terman (*Stanford University*)
Page 72   Kenneth H. Olsen
Page 94   Keeve M. Siegel
Page 120   Alejandro Zaffaroni (*Steve Rees*)
Page 142   Gordon E. Moore and Robert N. Noyce (*Roger Marshutz*)
Page 164   Carl Djerassi (*Robert A. Isaacs*)
Page 182   George N. Hatsopoulos (*Hutchins Photography*)
Page 204   Sam Wyly

Copyright © 1976, 1974, 1973, 1967 Gene Bylinsky

LIBRARY OF CONGRESS CATALOGING IN PUBLICATION DATA
Bylinsky, Gene.
    The innovation millionaires.
    Includes index.
    1. Success.   2. Inventions.   3. Venture
capital.   I. Title.
HF5386.B956   650'.12   75-43790
ISBN 0-684-14564-2

PRINTED IN THE UNITED STATES OF AMERICA

For Gwen, Tanya, and Gregory

Acknowledgments

This book had its genesis in a *Fortune* series on innovative science companies and their founders, as well as in other articles I have written for the magazine. Patricia Cristol, editor at Charles Scribner's Sons, deserves the credit for spotting the seed and enthusiastically encouraging its growth. The author is grateful to Charles Whittingham, *Fortune*'s assistant publisher, for arranging the release of the Time Inc. copyright, and to Robert Lubar, managing editor of *Fortune*, for arranging a leave of absence that allowed me to write the new chapters and bring the other material up to date. Many other colleagues on *Fortune* contributed. Special thanks for enterprising research are due to Lorraine Carson, Aimée Morner, and Wyndham Robertson, and also to Gwen and Carmella for transcribing notes and typing parts of the manuscript.

CONTENTS

ix

Contents

Scholars and Dollars

Our greatest natural resource lies six feet above ground—in the minds of our brightest scientists, engineers, and other technically oriented people capable of fusing science with business. At a time when the United States is exhausting its premium fuel resources there emerges an urgent necessity to capitalize on the brain power and the innovation potential of our scientists and engineers. One needs to recognize the national significance of the literally thousands of competent individuals, a few of whom will someday qualify in prestige with those selected for special attention by Gene Bylinsky. These men should be encouraged to assume risks in technological ventures, and society should make appropriate innovations to ease this risk-taking. In a very real sense science and technology constitute the new frontier for America as its territorial boundaries limit its natural resources.

Given the immense impact of applied science on the nation's economy, it is strange that scientists continue to play such a little role in politics. To be sure, men of great wealth like David Packard exert very significant influence in political circles, largely because of their fortunes and their inclinations. But the great mass of scientists remain aloof from the political process. I was personally struck by this fact back in the days when Sputnik seemed to circle everywhere about the planet except over the White House. Because of my involvement with Adlai Stevenson as an adviser on nuclear test ban policy, I had some contact with the Democratic National Committee and I took the initiative of writing a letter proposing a formal union of scientists and politicians to deal with problems of science and technology. This led to the founding of an Advisory Committee on Science and Technology, and as a result politicians rubbed shoulders with Nobel Prize winners and other illustrious scientists. The Democratic Advisory Council was responsive to proposals made by such luminaries as Harold C. Urey to create a National Peace Agency. I learned that presidential candidate John F. Kennedy thought that the Soviets had preempted the word *peace* and we reluctantly settled for the U.S. Arms Control and Disarmament Agency as the name for this brainchild of the council's scientists. Here was innovation on the part of scholars, not for dollars, but for the national good.

The thought occurred to me—sometime after JFK's election made the Democratic Advisory Council a political artifact—that scientists who were able to work together in a political context might be able to fuse their brains in a business venture. Accordingly, I joined an ingenious politico, Charles Tyroler II, in proposing that a number of us capitalize brain power in an organization called Quadri-Science, Inc. Tyroler had been the director of the Advisory Council throughout its existence. We acquired the physical assets of the council—JFK's Capitol Hill painting by Walton, a huge boomerang-shaped, cigar-stained conference table, files full of political memorabilia, and walls full of political cartoons. Harold Urey became chairman of our board and we set out on the road to corporate glory via the equity exchange route. My reason for telling this story is that one of the first companies in which Q-S acquired an equity position was the Institute for Scientific Information, whose founder and president was recommended to us by Nobel Prize winner Joshua T. Lederberg. The latter is one of the few scientists I have known who is instantly recognizable as a true genius, and he saw in Dr. Eugene Garfield, ISI's creator, a man with the qualities of the personalities selected by Gene Bylinsky for his book.

Garfield had a singleminded idea that consumed all his waking moments, namely, that he could assemble, process, and purvey scientific information that would be helpful to scientists and make a profit at the same time. When our corporate vectors lined up, ISI had annual revenues of less than $500,000, was not making money, and was generally believed to have little chance of doing so, but this did not disturb Garfield. He had founded his one-employee company in Philadelphia by obtaining a $500 HFC loan, matched by $500 from another HFC office across the Delaware River, and threw all his energy into selling science information to scientists.

One of Garfield's clever innovations was to collate title pages—tables of contents—from magazines in various scientific fields. He bound these pages into a publication, a sort of a sophisticated *Scientist's Digest*. A physicist, say, could then skim over the titles of the articles and order reprints from ISI. This has turned out to be a phenomenally successful idea, and Garfield has since expanded it to many scientific disciplines. His company also offers a number of computerized information services.

Accustomed to old-fashioned library browsing and to corridor conversation at conferences, most scientists frowned at the notion of paying for such information service, even though it could be shown to be highly cost-effective in terms of the scientist's use of his time. By battering at the doors of tradition and selling his innovative products the hard way, Garfield managed to keep his company going. Today ISI employs 350 people and in 1975 racked up sales of over $10.5 million with a tidy profit that other companies in the same sales bracket would envy. It is the world's leading company in its field.

Bylinsky's men, exponents of high technology, all seem to possess the Garfield drive and a sense of the market; all are highly sophisticated in their research and are a light-year apart from the days of woodshed inventors. There is, of course, some element of chance discovery, but modern innovators guide their work by the steady compass of good science and by the discipline of years of creative activity in the laboratory. Gene Bylinsky, however, demonstrates that scientists-innovators can be as comfortable in the arena of high finance as at the laboratory workbench. In the case of Alejandro Zaffaroni, he shows that the biochemist of Syntex fame could invade the jungle of drug financing and survive; in fact, he dazzled the drug business by raising $52 million for his Alza Corporation before marketing a single product.

Alas, for every Zaffaroni, a dozen scientists with bright ideas and high drive lose financial control of their enterprises at the troubled crossroads where finance and technology intersect. This is a pity because the really bright ideas appear to spring up in small enterprises. This is an area where the United States has yet to evolve a national pattern of support for technological innovation—to duplicate elsewhere the peculiarly attractive environment that radiates from the Stanford University campus and from Boston's Route 128 complex. The U.S. government agencies have spent fantastic sums for research and development—for example, about $60 billion for space research projects, with only the tiniest drip-out of technological benefits. The National Science Foundation has skirmished with the technological innovation problem, doing case studies of the cardiac pacemaker, steroid contraceptives, electrophotography, hybrid grains, tape recorders, and a few other such developments in an attempt to identify the critical events on the pathway leading from the bright idea to successful technology. I would draw one conclusion: the U.S. government spends the lion's share of its research and development dollars where there is the least likelihood of contributing to the national economy. Defense spending did at one time invigorate certain areas of our technical economy, but this DOD fertilization factor is now very low. The irony here is that countries like Germany and Japan who benefit from our defense hardware are free to divert their R & D dollars to products of consumer value. In effect, we subsidize our competition.

Bylinsky's prose pictures of our technological innovators invite us to speculate about many aspects of the tumultuous interface that exists between science and society, but they do more—they illuminate the human nature of the innovators. They emerge as flesh-and-blood creatures with vanities and peccadilloes—with humor and with pathos. But withal there is a sense of excitement—a thrill of the chase—that Bylinsky skillfully weaves into his narratives. Today's Magellans set out upon uncharted seas on subtle voyages of discovery where monetary rewards are more than matched by the immense payoff in human benefits.

Ralph E. Lapp

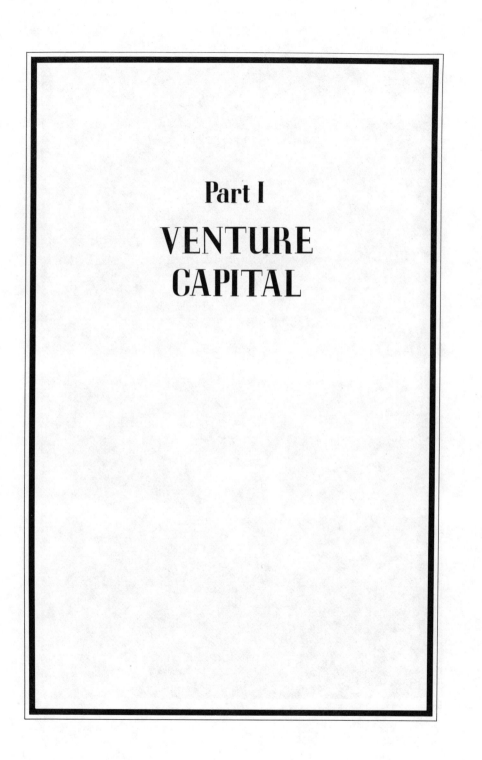

Part I
VENTURE CAPITAL

CHAPTER ONE

General Doriot's
Dream Factory

A hurricane of technological change has transformed American life in the past three decades. Suddenly laboratory curiosities have become highly successful products, bolstering the nation's economy, upgrading the quality of our lives, giving impetus to whole new industries: television, jet aircraft, digital computers, and a host of others. Yet, oddly enough, in this era of tremendous technological achievement there is still a mystery about the process by which new ideas can be translated into tangible products, business, and profits. Big corporations spend millions of dollars on research and development and complain about too meager results. On the other hand, brilliant technical men, eager to translate their knowledge into productive industry by starting companies of their own, often cannot find the kind of managerial support and encouragement they need.

Getting financial support is no longer the problem it once was. An army of venture capitalists—private individuals and groups, investment bankers, small business investment companies—has sprung up, ready to spread seed money in promising places. But the trouble with many of these investors is that they are impatient, they expect results too fast, and they don't understand the nature of technically oriented enterprise. In the words of one engineer industrialist, they tend to treat a science-based company as "just another shoe store."

It is a very special, sensitive kind of assistance these companies

3

need, and it isn't surprising that only a few backers of new ideas do well in bringing up such baby firms. Among the successful ones, probably the most astute, certainly the most unusual, has been Georges F. Doriot, until recently president of American Research and Development Corporation (ARD), the Boston-based risk-capital company.

For nearly twenty-eight years Doriot served as ARD's leader and guiding spirit. He retired in June 1974 but remains an ARD director. Doriot was born in 1899, but as he says, "Some young men are so damn old." He remains active, advising ARD, speaking before business groups, always looking into the future. Recently he jumped at the chance to fly, along with other dignitaries, aboard the French version of the supersonic Concorde from Boston to Paris. His accomplishments in pioneering the venture-capital business are striking, for Doriot created a legend in his lifetime.

General Doriot, as he is widely known (he won the rank of brigadier general as a U.S. Army Reserve officer in World War II), put much more than money into new companies and expected to get much more than money out. He had no use for easily attained wealth. He was much more concerned with guiding scientists-dreamers and keeping up their enthusiasm and hopes just when those hopes needed nurturing. He was, in short, not a man looking for a fast return on his money, but a nursemaid of dreams.

But as the driving force of ARD, Doriot demonstrated how a highly personal, patient upbringing of new companies can pay off in terms of money, too. Infant enterprises in which ARD has invested have pioneered in the manufacture of atom smashers and novel machines to desalt brackish water, have been among the first to make small transistorized computers, and have led in the design of pallets for air freight. While they were making their contributions to technological innovation, many of them have performed well—some spectacularly—in the stock market. And there are more promising entrants coming along to keep ARD's net-asset value climbing.

In the beginning, ARD's performance was anything but spectacular. In 1947, its first full year of operation, the company realized a net capital gain of $87; it lost $241,228 in 1950, made $138,414

4

the year following, and lost $1,436 in 1954. But since 1955, ARD has consistently reported gains, and it made a record $2,555,134 in 1966. Its net-asset value, just under $3.4 million at the end of its first year, zoomed to $93 million at the end of 1966 and continued to a remarkable $428 million by the end of 1971, when ARD was merged into Textron, Inc., the big Providence, Rhode Island, conglomerate. ARD had started as a publicly held company with $3.4 million in stockholders' money. In one way or another and at one time or another, ARD has involved itself in the affairs of more than one hundred companies. Today it has an interest in thirty-six. In only six of these does it list its investments below their original cost—a showing that most venture capitalists would envy.

It was typical of Doriot's approach, however, that he did not let himself be overwhelmed by good fortune. "Success is a very dangerous period," he is fond of remarking. "It goes to our heads." And in any case, sensational performance in the stock market is not his measure of success. Many other venture capitalists think in terms of getting a desired rate of return from their investments within a specified time. Not Doriot. He often referred to his companies as "children" (he is married but childless himself). "When you have a child, you don't ask what return you can expect," he says. "Of course you have hopes—you hope the child will become President of the United States. But that is not very probable. I want them to do outstandingly well in their field. And if they do, the rewards will come. But if a man is good and loyal and does not achieve a so-called good rate of return, I will stay with him. Some people don't become geniuses until after they are twenty-four, you know. If I were a speculator, the question of return would apply. But I don't consider a speculator—in my definition of the word—constructive. I am building men and companies.

"Your sophisticated stockholders make five points and sell out," he scoffs. "But we have our hearts in our companies, we are really doctors of childhood diseases here. When bankers or brokers tell me I should sell an ailing company, I ask them, 'Would you sell a child running a temperature of 104?' "

In applying this operating philosophy, Doriot constantly sur-

5

prised people. He impatiently dismissed the idea, which even preoccupied some of his scientists-dreamers, that a new company should show profits from the start. Sometimes a beaming young industrialist would rush in to trumpet proudly the news of early success—only to be knocked back on his heels by the soft, French-accented warning, "That may do you a lot of harm."

Something of an ascetic himself, Doriot worried that his "boys," the young scientists and engineers, would succumb to the temptations of early success. He feared that their efforts would slacken and that "they'll start buying twenty-cylinder Cadillacs, fifty-room mansions, go skiing in summer, and swimming in winter."

These fears, in most cases, proved spectacularly unjustified. In 1957, for example, when the Digital Equipment Corporation, of Maynard, Massachusetts, began to make money from the start, the general warned Kenneth Olsen, president of the company, to beware of the pitfalls of success. Today Olsen, a blunt, hard-working man in his late forties, is a millionaire many times over, but his way of life hasn't changed too much from the time when he was a researcher at the Massachusetts Institute of Technology's Lincoln Laboratory and Digital Equipment was just a dream he shared with a friend named Harlan Anderson. Olsen did buy a larger house, but he still cuts the lawn himself. One of the few concessions he has made to his new status is to buy a second canoe. "It's nice not to worry about smashing up a canoe," he says.

Digital Equipment has turned out to be one of those Cinderellas of the computer age. It has been riding the tide of the apparently insatiable demand for the fast, inexpensive computers used in scientific and medical research and increasingly in commercial applications. Started as a three-man operation crowded into one room of an ancient woolen mill, the company has grown to where it employs 20,000 people and has not only taken over most of that huge mill but also has built plants in eleven other locations. In its 1974 fiscal year, Digital Equipment reported sales of $422 million and a net profit of $44 million. That year it joined the ranks of *Fortune*'s top five hundred U.S. industrial companies. In fiscal 1975 the company's sales were expected to exceed $500 million—

6

making Digital Equipment one of the most successful post–World War II high-technology firms. ARD's original investment of $70,000 in Digital Equipment rocketed by the end of 1971 to an amazing $350 million when ARD distributed its Digital stock to ARD stockholders as it merged into Textron.

Of course, not all ARD-financed companies have done that well; a few have been painful disappointments. Some years ago ARD poured $1.6 million into the stock of a tape-recorder manufacturer called Magnecord, Inc. The company had management problems from the beginning, and some of the ARD people thought it should be sold off. But Doriot wavered for a long time. Eventually Magnecord was merged into Midwestern Instruments, Inc., which in turn became part of Telex Corporation. By the time ARD got out, it had lost more than a million dollars. The Magnecord situation, says Doriot, "was poorly handled." It was also a case of Doriot's becoming too enamored with a company, a failing to which he admits. "When is a hope no longer a hope?" he asks.

If Doriot's approach was unusual, so was the base from which he operated. When ARD was started by a group of pioneering Bostonians in 1946, very few investors were prepared to put their capital into venture situations. The chief founders—the late Merrill Griswold, long head of that venerable Yankee institution Massachusetts Investors Trust; Ralph E. Flanders, then president of the Federal Reserve Bank of Boston and later senator from Vermont; and Karl T. Compton, then president of the Massachusetts Institute of Technology—saw the need to furnish not only risk capital but also encouragement and advice to beginning enterprises. So they created a powerful team of financial experts, skilled business managers, and leading scientists. As technical consultants, they brought in some brilliant men from MIT, such as Edwin R. Gilliland, head of the chemical engineering department, and Jerome C. Hunsaker, head of aeronautical engineering.

Doriot, although no scientist (he did study mathematics, physics, and chemistry in college, however), was recruited at first as chairman of the board of advisers. He had originally been the

ARD board's choice for president, but he couldn't assume that job right away because he was still in the army. So Flanders acted as president until December 1946, when Doriot took command. At the Pentagon, Doriot had served first as director of military planning for the Quartermaster General, and later as deputy director of research and development for the War Department General Staff. He gained a reputation for spurring on researchers and production men to accomplish things they didn't think they could do. "When one little unit was in trouble, he'd spend three weeks on it and it would blossom," recalls a wartime colleague. He was an innovator, too. Under his supervision the army developed, among other things, new dehydrated foods and uniforms with new thermal properties and abrasion resistance. Adding a typical Doriot touch, the general also made suspenders, which he wears himself, an item of army issue.

Doriot himself says that during that time he "found out how brilliant people could be if their glands are stimulated. My people worked like slaves—and we had no stock options in the U.S. Army."

Stimulating people, inspiring them to delve into the future, often startling them with his seemingly unorthodox beliefs and techniques—these have long been Doriot trademarks. He was born in Paris the son of a pioneering automotive engineer. His father for a long time worked for Peugeot but later founded an automobile manufacturing company of his own. Georges Doriot's parents, both Lutherans, were strict disciplinarians. Says a friend, "I'm sure that when he came home in the afternoon, he was asked, 'What did you do today that was worthwhile?' And if it was worthwhile, he was told to get a good night's sleep so he could go out tomorrow and do it again." Doriot recalls that his father would spank him when he wasn't first in his class. "I am still scared, and have been ever since I was eight years old, of classrooms and professors."

Nevertheless, Doriot became a professor himself. After coming to the United States in 1921, he graduated from the Harvard Graduate School of Business Administration, became an instructor there, and advanced to the post of assistant dean. Along the way he acquired a number of directorships in companies and even served as president of McKeesport Tin Plate Corporation and chairman of National Can Corporation for a short time before leaving for the Pentagon. He managed to combine these business activities with teaching and remained on the faculty at Harvard until 1966. He taught so memorably and controversially that many old-time students who have forgotten other professors' names still remember Doriot vividly.

The course he taught was ostensibly about how to run a company. But in fact it consisted of a series of lectures expounding Doriot's views on life, business, and even on picking a wife. He hammered into his students' heads three main themes: self-improvement, attention to detail in daily work, and an active concern with the future. ("Understand the value of time, be intent on reaching a worthwhile goal, and drive toward it through infinite and coordinated attention to detail.") He drove his students hard, but their reports on technical and scientific developments to come, as well as on straight business subjects, attained a degree of fame and earned as much as $30,000 for some groups of students who published the reports on their own.

"He excited and interested a large number of his students," says former Harvard Business School dean George Baker. "He made their minds turn over. And he was able to transfer his imagination and verve to them." He instilled such a religious attitude toward the value of time in some students that one remarked ten years after graduation, "I've had a hard time relaxing. I learned from Professor Doriot how to spend each moment profitably and constructively and I can't break the habit."

His lectures were peppered with pungent remarks and pithy metaphors:

·"The intelligent man doesn't use the 'standard' method of action."

·"The smart man knows how to make money on what he has today, but he keeps an eye on the future."

·"Always remember that someone, somewhere, is making a product that will make your product obsolete."

·"The banker is your friend in good times; in bad times he remembers he is a trustee of someone's money."

·"An auditor is like a tailor; he can make a fat man look thinner or taller or younger."

·"You will get nowhere if you don't inspire people."

·"Be friendly but not chummy with your lawyers."

·"Always look relaxed when you are very tense inside. Never look mad unless you need to."

·"Never have more than two cocktails on any occasion. If any information is to be exchanged over whiskey, let us get it rather than give it."

·"A good talent is to know whom to go to for advice, help, or people to do a job. When one needs help, he is likely not to find it. Therefore, begin a list of persons on whom you may call for help at some later date on some unknown matter."

·"A committee is an invitation to do nothing. Very few committees can perform better than the weakest man. You can't drive a locomotive with a committee."

·"We should give beauty and dignity to the word *work*."

Doriot himself maintained a work pace that would have tired a man forty years younger. He was up at seven and soon could be seen walking briskly from his home on Beacon Hill across the Public Garden to the stately John Hancock Building, where ARD had its offices on the twenty-third floor. During the day he talked with investment bankers, university professors, patent lawyers, hopeful would-be industrialists, and coached his staff on dealing with people and problems in affiliate companies. He usually ate lunch in the cafeteria in his building. ("You can eat there in ten minutes and then come back to work. Even important people don't mind eating there.") At night he took papers home to read and occasionally painted with a palette knife when he couldn't sleep or didn't feel like working. He ordinarily went to sleep at eleven but regularly woke up at two "to worry" and would start scribbling notes on a blue pad in the dark. "He isn't a fellow who makes snap decisions," says a former colleague. "He'll go home and think about it all night. Then he'll come in in the morning and ask to review the bidding."

Venture Capital

The decisions Doriot was called upon to make required plenty of contemplation. First and foremost, he had to decide where to put ARD's money. There was never a shortage of ideas, but in the Doriot scheme men rank first and ideas second. In his professorial fashion he says that a "grade-A man with a grade-B idea is better than a grade-B man with a grade-A idea."

Few venture capitalists can match Doriot's skill in recognizing "grade-A" men. He seems to have instant insight into people, though he complains that there is seldom enough time to judge a man or his idea. One admirer says he has "a God-given talent" for picking outstanding men, and a scientist observes, "I'm sure it's an art—not a science. I can't tell you what Picasso's secret is either. I don't say Doriot was always right, but there were darn few times when he picked a lemon." Doriot himself says, "If I'm right 50 percent of the time I judge men, I think I'm damn good."

Actually the Doriot approach to people was his usual brew of common sense and intuition. On the wall of his office he had tacked a quotation from the late Dr. Albert Schweitzer to the effect that it's almost impossible for one man to know what another is really like. But Doriot looked for specific attributes in people: a combination of courage and caution, endurance, imagination, and above all resourcefulness. "A man would come in and say he invented the pencil," says Doriot. "Okay. What I wanted to know was whether he could improve the pencil. If the pencil went out of fashion, could he have another idea?"

Doriot concedes that such qualities as courage and caution rarely are found in the same man, especially a young man. But in cases where courage outweighed caution, he tempered the blend by putting a cautious director on the new company's board. Before betting on a man, he wanted to know everything about him—"He is a magnificent questioner," says an aide. But since he is future-oriented, a man's past to him provided only a pale hint of what a man could be capable of achieving. "One shouldn't bet on what a man has done, but on what he can and will do next."

Doriot holds that the lives of men and companies can be divided into four stages: inception, growth, development, and maturity. Accordingly, he tried to place the future industrialist on a

11

"curve of evolution" in this scheme. Always an important question in his mind was whether the man would be able to make the trying transition from stage one to stage two—a turning point where many men and companies fail. "In period one, the man should have an undying creative spirit and some sense. Period one is characterized by hope—a beautiful word. But period two is when results are necessary."

Judging ideas went hand in hand with judging men. Doriot and his aides kept abreast of the latest technological developments, and they met hopeful industrialists with an open mind. "We were good listeners," says Doriot. And when in doubt themselves, they could always call on first-rate scientists for advice.

It is easier, Doriot believes, to find a field of interest than to locate the proper vehicle to exploit it. Since such a vehicle must be manned by "grade-A" men, only a few hopeful industrialists wound up in the ARD starting line. Of the uncounted thousands of proposals ARD has received, it has investigated about ten thousand and invested in slightly more than one hundred. Periodically, ARD gets a proposal to finance the manufacture of a new internal combustion engine. It has been approached with ideas ranging from a new kind of diaper pin to a "rocket automobile." When a proposition is turned down, the judgment can be scathing: "Principals not outstanding, idea not unique." "Very speculative undertaking in the hands of a moderately impressive gentleman." Or, "Competent people doing a routine task."

Most venture capitalists want to see a young company's "track record" before they put money on it. Doriot, however, was willing to gamble on young men with no previous experience in business. One of ARD's investments in the late 1960s was in Memory Technology, Inc., a precocious infant of a company headed by two MIT-trained engineers, John J. Marino and Jonathan J. Sirota, both then in their twenties. The company at first developed a new kind of computer memory unit woven of copper wire by a "logic loom" that Marino and Sirota devised. Later Memory Technology switched to semiconductor memories but couldn't quite make it on its own, and in 1975 the company went out of business. But most other Doriot "children" have survived, even though it took some of them many years to get on their feet.

When it decides to back a brand-new company, ARD may buy voting control, but this doesn't mean it will try to run the company. "ARD directors on my board don't try to enforce a party line," says the president of one small firm. If a company is an already functioning enterprise, ARD usually invests in less than 50 percent of its stock. A favorite way of financing is to give a fledgling firm a loan, repayable in installments, usually with options or warrants to purchase stock.

Sometimes ARD's terms for buying into a company sound pretty harsh. The founders of Digital Equipment, for instance, sold 78 percent of their company for $70,000. But like many other men whom ARD helped get started, they put up only a few hundred dollars of their own money, and they wound up millionaires many times over.

The preliminaries of setting up a new company are the easiest part of the job as far as Doriot is concerned. An avalanche of problems is unleashed when the company finally starts operating. "Starting a company is like getting married," he says. "Most of the problems are discovered after the honeymoon is over." There follows a period "when hopes go up, go down, and often evaporate. Many of our companies have been close to sudden death at least once. In a small company human failures and weaknesses often are magnified in inverse proportion to the size of the company. If General Motors produces one bad car, they have millions of dollars and hundreds of people to fix it. In a small company there is not unlimited money or manpower, so they are very sensitive to accidents.

"Often a man will start a company with a brilliant idea. Then he finds that he has to deal with the Internal Revenue Service, the Securities and Exchange Commission, and people who are stealing his idea. Most want to retrench and go back to the lab. It is a period calling for constant reevaluation, for great resourcefulness, for tactful but strong action."

At this stage, Doriot's role was to "watch, push, worry, and

13

spread hope." What he did to infuse life and strength into a new company is illustrated by the somewhat similar experiences of two ARD offspring, High Voltage Engineering Corporation and Ionics, Inc.

High Voltage was the brainchild of two MIT physicists, Robert J. Van de Graaff and John Trump, and an MIT-trained engineer, Denis M. Robinson. It was built around Dr. Van de Graff's now famous "atom smasher," or particle accelerator. The company was started largely because of Dr. Trump's conviction that the machines should be made available to hospitals to treat deep cancers.

The three scientists looked around Boston for capital, but back in 1946 their ideas seemed to be too far out for investment bankers, even in Boston, where over a period of years a high-technology center was slowly emerging (see Chapter 4). In those days, as Doriot recalls, the bankers invested in General Motors but considered Ford Motor Company as being too much of a risk. And matters weren't made any easier by the fact that the three founders of High Voltage were anxious to keep 51 percent of the stock. "We knew that would be difficult to do since we had no money," recalls Dr. Robinson, now the company's chairman. "You have no idea how little we knew what a financial man would expect in terms of return on investment. We'd never read the *Wall Street Journal*. We were scientists! We went looking for money as you would go looking for electricity and water and all the rest. We had no knowledge at all."

Their quest came to a successful conclusion, however, when MIT's Dr. Compton suggested to ARD that it should back the enterprise. ARD came forth with a $200,000 investment, the Lessing Rosenwald family put in an additional $50,000, and the three scientists agreed to give up 60 percent of the company's stock. By then, according to Robinson, they had become convinced that "it wasn't a question of who has control but getting the right kind of control."

High Voltage began literally as a "garage" operation, in a converted Cambridge parking garage. The shift from campus to corporate life wasn't quite the traumatic experience some people think

14

it is. A lot of scientists make the transition easily. "It's not like picking up bag and baggage and moving to Indonesia," says an executive of one ARD affiliate. "People here use the same language and there are no dramatic differences." Several other scientists who became entrepreneurs in the Boston area add that "the pressures are just as great and security no greater" on the campus and that in today's big technological universities a professor often is at the same time responsible for managing men and money in running a federally sponsored research project. " 'Publish or perish' becomes 'profit or perish,' " says one former professor who founded a company.

Some scientists, however, never quite make the transition or have no desire to do so. An executive of one ARD-supported company not long ago moved up from president to chairman because he had no sustainable interest in the business side of the company. He now devotes his time to writing complex computer programs for his firm. Dr. Van de Graaff was that kind of man, too. "He had no interest in business," recalls Dr. Robinson. "Oh, he *was* extremely interested that his device got the proper price and made money to go into research. But he never looked at a balance sheet and he would have been bored if he had. I didn't feel that way. To me the balance sheet put a label on everything, and I found that helpful."

At High Voltage the problem was not so much management (Robinson gradually evolved into a skilled executive) as the ability of a small company to make very big machines. Besides, the machines were designed for customers that were usually strapped for money—that is, hospitals. As Robinson later remarked, "Though [treatment of cancer with Van de Graaff accelerators] was an outstanding humanitarian achievement, it remained very poor business for our company. Our sales to hospitals were unprofitable, and we nearly went under financially in 1948 and 1949."

Throughout this difficult period Doriot displayed remarkable patience. "General Doriot understood, though he is no scientist, that this would be a slow thing," says Robinson. "He judged us a great deal on the basis of character and not on the basis of our balance

15

sheet. Our balance sheet wasn't very exciting, of course. At the early board meetings, I'd try to give an accurate accounting of the profit and loss. He would sort of look through me and ask what I really thought about when I was shaving. He didn't want me to become a bookkeeper or an accountant." At the time the grateful scientist scribbled in his notebook, "Doriot's outlook inspires and transforms my own, lifting it above the worry plane in which I have been immersed in the last two months."

Doriot, for his part, credits the resourcefulness of the High Voltage executives with saving their company in the end. After hospital sales sagged, they steered the company's thrust toward building atom smashers for basic research in nuclear physics. In ensuing years demand for atom smashers diminished dramatically as government agencies sharply reduced their grants to universities and laboratories. High Voltage executives tried a twofold answer to this critical problem. They attempted to supply high-voltage equipment to electric utilities, but the utilities found themselves in a cash bind during the recession of the 1970s. Much more successfully they pioneered the use of the accelerators to produce a line of shrinkable plastic tubes and insulated wires. The accelerators imparted special properties to those products and created a brand-new market. The effort succeeded so well that it accounted for nearly half of the company's sales and more than half of its profits in recent years.

The general keeps popping in and out throughout the company's early history. He let Robinson run the company, but he was there one day telling Robinson that his sales organization was inadequate. He was there a few months later urging Robinson to take advantage of the Common Market and put up a manufacturing plant in Europe. High Voltage did build a plant in the Netherlands. It was "one of the most outstanding pieces of advice he gave me," says Robinson, because sales to foreign customers became important. Doriot was also there to encourage Robinson to go ahead with construction of a huge new plant that now towers along Route 128 in Burlington, Massachusetts. Later Doriot was walking through the High Voltage plant after what Robinson calls

16

a "black day" in 1964, when High Voltage was forced to let go some of its labor force, and he dressed down one of Robinson's assistants for the plant's untidy appearance. The plant, Doriot said, looked as though it had been abandoned.

High Voltage's success—it registered sales of $41.5 million and netted just over $2 million in 1974—has been something of a surprise to its scientists-founders. Robinson says he remembers John Trump saying that it would be "great" if the company ever reached one million in sales. "We had no conception we would do this well." Furthermore, the company stands on the threshold of still greater expansion into new fields such as radiation treatment of whey, a previously discarded by-product of cheese-making that can be turned into a nutritious food supplement with radiation, and even electron treatment of sewage sludge to sterilize it before it is dumped into rivers, lakes, and oceans.

The story of Ionics until very recently was much less cheerful. The men who started the company expected it to do much better than it did in the beginning. In 1948 Dr. Walter Juda, then a Harvard chemist who served as a technical adviser to ARD, urged that a company be set up to manufacture water-desalting equipment, using a new kind of membrane he had developed with a colleague, Wayne A. McRae. ARD responded enthusiastically with an investment of $50,000 and the result was Ionics. Until a few years ago the going had been rough for the company. In 1967, for instance, nineteen years after the company was founded, sales amounted to only $2.5 million and net to $141,479—not exactly a roaring success. At that time, seated around a large round table in a company conference room, a group of Ionics executives discussed their problems frankly. "We have 95 percent of the world business in electrodialysis [a method of making saline and brackish water potable]," said Wayne McRae, vice president for research. "The business is below our expectations, but after all, we are scientists. We were going to make the deserts bloom. We can still do that—but the world doesn't seem to give a damn."

Thomas Kirkham, another vice president, spoke next: "I don't know if you want to say we were before our time [McRae, inter-

17

rupting, 'Sure we were'] . . . but in 1953 and 1954, if someone had said that fourteen years later we would be where we are now, we just wouldn't have believed we would have had the trouble we have selling this equipment."

The situation gradually improved, illustrating the simple fact that not all high-technology companies are destined for instant stardom. In the late 1960s and early 1970s, Ionics' sales went up to about $8 million a year but growth seemed to stop there. Then in 1972 Ionics received more orders for water-desalting plants than ever before and sales spurted to $15 million. In 1974 sales topped $17 million and net reached $658,000. The company was branching out into energy generation and conservation and applying its membrane technology to high-protein food-processing and medicine. The future looked a lot brighter.

There are critics who insist that one reason for Ionics' anemic growth was Doriot's failure to put in a strong fulltime president from the start. "That headless monster just drifted along," says one man. A lot hinged on the personal relationship between Doriot and Juda, the man who inspired Ionics. Juda now says he had "a father-son relationship" with Doriot, and the fact that he was educated in France, spoke French, and his wife was French didn't hurt. Juda first served as a vice president at Ionics and later as executive vice president, in effect running the company, though Dr. Gilliland of MIT had the title of president.

Doriot would never argue with Juda or Gilliland about technology, but as Juda says, "He will argue with anyone about labor relations and financing." On the Ionics board of directors, "he *was* the board of directors. He has an amusing way of expressing himself. He always says, 'You fellows decide and I'll listen.' " Juda shakes his head and smiles.

Some men close to the situation feel that Juda never successfully made the transition into the industrial world. ARD assisted with management and financial tasks during the company's early years (to save money, Doriot insisted that the advisers go out to the plant by subway) but no attempt was made to replace Juda.

Doriot wanted Juda to concentrate on the scientific side of the operation and not get too involved in business problems. Once, Juda recalls, he asked the general whether he should take some courses at the Harvard Business School. Doriot asked in return, "Why do you want to be a second-rate businessman when you can be a first-rate scientist?" Juda feels Doriot was "dead right."

Juda was primarily interested in scientific research, but he also felt obliged to prove his company could make a profit. "At some point I became tired of going to ARD for money," he recalls. "So we got contracts to do research assignments for a fee so that we could be self-supporting. And I caught hell. General Doriot thought we should concentrate on our own water equipment. When I told him that we had improved financially, I thought he would be pleased, but he said, 'Who told you to do this?' He was not impressed at all by the financial improvement and he was critical that we had neglected our own area. I must say I was very pleased."

In the end, however, the Juda-Doriot relationship deteriorated. Juda wanted Ionics to invest in research and development of fuel cells. Doriot and some of the other Ionics executives felt that the company should not invest its stockholders' money into another new field. In the showdown, Juda quit.

Ordinarily ARD shies away from changing the top management of a company it backs. "How do you tell a man who has put his blood, sweat, and tears into a company that he is no longer wanted?" asks one of Doriot's assistants. On the other hand, ARD often considers it a good idea to put in experienced financial and business managers. In a company run by scientists and engineers, this usually meets with strong resistance. "There's a natural reluctance on the part of technically creative people to accept into their 'family' strangers who are basically nontechnical and to them non-creative," says one venture capitalist. ARD usually tried to handle the problem indirectly. It will tactfully suggest what type of people the company should look for to handle sales or personnel and, if asked to do so, will locate such men. As a last resort, ARD has tried to force management changes, especially in companies where it has voting control. But Doriot didn't relish those occasions: "I

19

had a hell of a time, and I didn't always win. We get too friendly and then the time comes to be a little stronger, and it doesn't work."

ARD's mode of operation hasn't changed greatly since Doriot handed over the reigns to Charles Coulter, a young vice president. Dorothy Rowe, now a senior vice president and long Doriot's right hand, has served without pay as treasurer of many a struggling infant company. A number of vice presidents are always ready to rush into the field when a company requests help. They would never actually try to run a company, but they often serve as on-the-spot expert consultants.

ARD officers perform many other tasks for the offspring. They cope with problems ranging from plant explosions to matrimonial blowups, which aren't unusual in situations where the husband works seventy to eighty hours a week. They help find customers for the fledgling firms. ARD provides exposure for its companies at its big annual meeting, where they can exhibit some of their products. ARD's prestige, as one engineer puts it, "is a door for us into class." Another adds: "Our product is guaranteed for ten years. That's important to us, but if people think we are a fly-by-night outfit, the guarantee is not a selling point. With ARD behind us, they discover that they are in with the savviest people in the business. The general himself will tell you that if you are in Europe and you need help, just get a Rothschild to put an arm around you and walk you across the street."

Finally ARD helps its companies handle the intricacies of going public and thus attaining a measure of financial independence. As a company matures, ARD sometimes will reduce its holdings, selling off at a profit. Sometimes one of these little companies is approached by a big corporation that wants to buy it out. If the approach is welcomed, ARD usually goes along with the idea and winds up owning stock of the larger corporation. It thus acquired holdings in Litton Industries, Textron, and Teledyne, Inc.

What its fledglings most appreciate in ARD is its way of encouraging them even in the dark days when the balance sheet looks disappointing—of "picking us off the floor after we had been dropped," as one president puts it. "This is a lonely job and there aren't many people I can talk to about the problems," says another. "I got plenty of psychic income from Doriot—and that was very important."

Doriot naturally had his critics. There was obviously an element of envy as well as puzzlement as exponents of "scientific" management observed his unorthodox but workable techniques. Because he was never "one of the boys," because he is a nonconformist who doesn't like "the usual men's washroom jokes," as one friend puts it, some people who know him slightly think Doriot is a pompous cold fish. But Doriot can be charming socially and an amusing showman when the occasion demands. At a dinner for business writers once he took off a shoe and waved it over his head to illustrate a point about a new leather product. "People ask why he doesn't slow down a bit and enjoy life," says a former aide. "I think he enjoys life immensely."

In any case, Doriot's drive never abated. His motivation—and he says he doesn't like the word motivation in its modern sense—"is just not to let people down. I am a schoolteacher at heart and I suppose I like to see people do things they didn't know they can do. I think I would have enjoyed being an orchestra leader or a bridge builder, too."

Doriot *has* built bridges that span the Western world. In its first twenty-five years, ARD saw a remarkable evolution in the venture-capital business, which it itself had started. More than anyone else, Doriot and ARD were responsible for the birth of the modern venture-capital industry. Most of the great companies of today were started with venture capital of sorts, of course, but there was nothing organized about the business until Doriot showed the way. Now hundreds of venture capitalists are at work in all corners of the United States, and thanks to Doriot, counterparts of ARD exist in Europe and Canada. He organized these ARD affiliates and also founded a business-management school near Paris patterned after the Harvard Business School and called Institut Européen d'Administration des Affaires.

In the United States ARD not only energized the Boston-area financiers into supporting new companies but also stimulated the creation of a whole new class of government-supported venture-capital firms known as the SBICs (Small Business Investment Companies). Doriot helped write the act for their formation. About eight hundred SBICs have been founded over the years to provide a brand-new source of capital for enterprising innovators, and many of them, patterning themselves after ARD, have concentrated mainly on helping high-technology firms. Doriot also helped many giant companies set up venture-capital operations of their own.

In the end, eager to see ARD continue as a strong company after his retirement, Doriot decided to merge it into Textron, run by his long-time friend and admirer G. William Miller. One serious difficulty ARD had encountered as a publicly held company was a raft of government regulations that hindered its growth. Being a division of Textron, ARD expects an easier life. ARD stockholders benefited handsomely when the merger took place. General Doriot increased their original investment more than a hundredfold. The stockholders received $350 million worth of Digital Equipment stock and another $78 million in Textron stock in exchange for the ARD shares. Ironically, in the early days of ARD Doriot sometimes had difficulty explaining things to stockholders. For the first ten years he was always being forced to say things like "I know you could have gotten more if you had put your money in General Motors—but this isn't General Motors." But he always kept everyone entertained. He would often tell little jokes on himself. Recalling that when he was eleven he had gone to school in England for a year, Doriot remarked: "I am told that when I came back, I had quite an English accent. I don't know what ever happened to it."

"Georges Doriot has enriched a generation of entrepreneurs and managers," says William Miller, the chairman of Textron. "We can never duplicate—or even successfully imitate—his personality, style, wisdom, or genius. But we can, and will, do credit to his ARD concept by building upon it with the same dedication and high principles." Miller adds that ARD now provides Textron with an opportunity to share in new ideas, markets, and technologies. As being equally important he views "ARD's spirit of youth— young ideas and young enterprises." That, of course, is the essence of Doriot and his drive. He expressed it simply but powerfully when he opened the European business school: "Yesterday is gone. Let's work for the world of tomorrow."

CHAPTER TWO

Ned Heizer's Supermarket for Entrepreneurs

Few men have had the good fortune—or the good sense—to prepare themselves for their life tasks as thoroughly and as successfully as did Edgar F. (Ned) Heizer, Jr. One of America's premier venture capitalists and company builders, Heizer is just past his mid-forties, but he already has a remarkable record of success behind him. When he was only thirty-two, he ran a multi-million-dollar venture-capital operation for Allstate Insurance Company. So well did he perform there that on the strength of his reputation Heizer was able to raise an unprecedented $81 million from institutional investors to start a venture-capital firm of his own, Heizer Corporation, which is headquartered on the forty-first floor of a Chicago skyscraper.

Heizer then plunged into an ambitious effort to build up high-technology companies with greater precision and emphasis on managerial skills than anyone had attempted before. General Doriot imposed his unique personal stamp on American Research and Development Corporation; Heizer has tried to institutionalize the process. Although the recession of the early and mid-1970s has interfered to some extent with Heizer's plans, he is, nevertheless, constructing such companies as Amdahl Corporation, which is now challenging IBM and the rest of the computer industry with a supercomputer that experts consider to be about ten years ahead of anything on the market. He is reorganizing Precision Instrument Company, which makes pioneering laser-controlled memories for

25

computers, and he is involved in more than twenty other new firms.

Heizer is singlemindedly dedicated to the idea that creation of new companies is the lifeblood that drives the heart of the free-enterprise system. "Many of our economists, government people, and even many businessmen," he says, "do not seem to appreciate the fact that the industries that made this country were not built by big companies. They were built by small companies which because of their success became big.

"But people do not reflect on that. Our economics professors, in my opinion, do not focus on what it is that built the American economic system. Our economics books do not focus on it. We focus on the established parts of the system but not on how it came about. We use words like 'industrial revolution' or 'new company formation' but people don't really teach what it's all about, at least not in the schools I went to."

Heizer himself was fortunate enough to start learning what the process of company formation is all about at a very early age. He was born in Detroit on September 23, 1929, into a family heavily involved in entrepreneurial activities. In fact, everything he has done in his life, either by accident or design, seems to have been aimed to put him at the apex of business creativity.

One of Heizer's grandfathers invented the electric stove—ahead of his time, it turned out. His patent ran out by the time electric stoves caught on. This grandfather, however, cashed in big on another invention: a side-wall register for better distribution of heat coming up from basement furnaces. The grandfather also was a friend of Henry Ford.

Most of Heizer's relatives were independent men: farmers, inventors, businessmen. "Their psychology was not to go to work on a production line at Ford Motor." Heizer's father, like the fathers of many of his friends in the Chicago suburb of Winnetka, where he grew up, was an entrepreneur. A chemist by training but a businessman and salesman by inclination, he started a chemical company with some friends. It was later merged into American Cyanamid and Heizer's father managed Cyanamid's midwestern territory from Chicago. Heizer recalls hearing his father often remark how much more fun it was creating a new company instead of helping administer a big established one.

All these influences shaped young Heizer's interest toward business, particularly toward the process of company formation. The youngster also leaned heavily toward science and mechanics. "I fussed around with radios, repaired old cars, and conducted chemical experiments," he recalls. "My parents let me have all those things and encouraged me. I had a workshop that had all kinds of things in it—electrical, chemical, mechanical. I also ran a bike repair shop for the other kids in the neighborhood."

In 1947, at eighteen, Heizer enrolled in Northwestern University to study chemical engineering. He was at the top of his class but was unwilling to follow the procedure under which a student had to work for a big company for three months after the first year of college. In Heizer's case, it would have been DuPont. He liked chemical engineering and was doing extremely well in it, but he also wanted to balance his technical education with business and economics. He therefore shifted to the business school after two years in chemical engineering.

All along, the budding entrepreneur kept questioning his family's friends and other men who had helped start and finance new companies. "I was interested in everything," Heizer recalls, "and wanted to know as much as I could about everything."

He was told that engineering would be an excellent background for anyone who wanted to start a technical company. Accounting and management—particularly the appraisal of people and organization—were cited as vital areas. Heizer also received advice that unless he understood legal matters, he would have a difficult time understanding capital and business formation. Many of the men he talked to considered law school more important than business school. "I heard all these things," says Heizer, "and tried to figure out how to educate myself. Flexibility became the key with me."

Figuring that no young man is given real responsibility in business until he reaches the age of thirty, he decided to educate himself as well and as diversely as he could while he was still in his twenties. After graduating in business administration from Northwestern in 1951, he enrolled in the Yale University Law

School and spent three years there, not only studying law but also teaching economics as an instructor. He got his law degree in 1954, but his hunger for knowledge was far from satiated.

He returned to Chicago and went to work for the local branch of Arthur Andersen and Company, a national accounting firm. At the same time he enrolled in the Northwestern Graduate School of Business where he took courses at night.

In both his work and his studies Heizer's approach ran counter to the common pattern. "The parents of most of my friends told them to go to a good school, typically an Ivy League school, then go to the Harvard Business School, then keep your nose clean and work your way up in the executive branch of one of the big companies," recalls Heizer. "Because of my family background, my attitude was that there are many people who can run companies, but somebody has to start them and new companies are very important to the success of free enterprise."

In starting what he calls his "business education," Heizer was following another clever plan. He was determined not to spend more than two years in any job. He wasn't planning to hop from job to job for the reasons most people do, such as to make more money, but for a deeper purpose. "Do not spend five years getting two years' experience" is an admonition he had gotten from older men long ago and he was now following it.

To execute this ambitious plan took sacrifice, of course, for Heizer, his wife, Molly, and their three children. While his contemporaries were out on golf courses or tennis courts on weekends, Heizer was studying. (In his typical competitive fashion, he says, "I love to play golf and tennis and I was a better golfer and tennis player than most of them, but I didn't have the time to play."

But Molly was getting a bit restless with her husband's relentless pursuit of knowledge. He had promised to quit night school and he did after two years, without getting a graduate degree because of a change in requirements but still taking more courses than some graduates did. All told, Heizer spent nine years in college classrooms.

At work Heizer had told his bosses from the start that he didn't want to be a public accountant. The Arthur Andersen executives, however, convinced him that he could gain broad experience in the field and gave him a series of interesting assignments.

Although he liked his work at Arthur Andersen a lot, Heizer continued on his predetermined course. After two years there, to broaden his knowledge he joined the Chicago office of the investment banking firm Kidder Peabody and Company. He was fortunate to work with some of the best men in the business, but he was also eager to get involved in new company formation. Kidder wanted him to work with established corporations.

Knowing that he would have a better chance of gaining experience on how to start new companies, Heizer next went to work for the Chicago branch of the consulting firm Booz, Allen and Hamilton. His former classmates at the time couldn't understand why Heizer would leave one promising job after another, but he knew what he was doing. After about two years with Booz, Allen, he began to think seriously about starting his own venture-capital firm. But the stock market happened to be going through one of its periodic gyrations, and it didn't look like a good time to raise money.

One of Heizer's clients at Booz, Allen was the Allstate Insurance Company. In 1962 it offered him a job that would involve forming and running a venture-capital division for the company. This naturally fitted Heizer's plans and he took the job.

At Allstate, Heizer applied all his previous experience with remarkable success. He started out with about $5 million in "seed money" and within a few years was supervising more than $125 million in investments. He got Allstate in on the initial stages of the formation of a number of companies that soon lit up the Wall Street sky like supernovae: Control Data, Memorex, Scientific Data Systems, Teledyne, Spectra Physics.

What is even more impressive about Heizer's performance is that he got Allstate *out* of some of these investments at the right time, too. Allstate was the largest single stockholder in these glamor high-technology firms whose stocks rocketed into the stratosphere. Typically, Memorex came out of nowhere and soon reached a high of $173 a share.

In that particular case, Heizer disagreed with what Laurence

Spitters, the Memorex president, was trying to do. Spitters, who sometimes slept in his office, so hard and long did he work, was attempting the humanly impossible. He was trying to keep up the sterling performance of his company by branching out into many new areas that demanded substantial and continuous financing. Heizer had invested $200,000 into Memorex on Allstate's behalf. He realized $8 million for Allstate when he sold the Memorex stock. (In ensuing years Memorex went into a steep dive, its stock falling to $3 a share. The company is now being successfully rebuilt, however.)

Heizer's acumen amazed many people. His quick decisions to back entrepreneurs stunned many of them, especially since some had been making the rounds seeking capital without success. Heizer seemed to know exactly what they were proposing even before they fully spelled out their ideas. But he wasn't acting on spur-of-the-moment intuition. All that hard studying and knowledge picked up during his purposeful job-hopping were paying off. From Arthur Andersen he brought the "facts first" philosophy of "knowing what you are doing before you do it." From Kidder Peabody he brought knowledge of finance; from Booz, Allen, a keen insight into promising new high-technology fields. And from his childhood and college study of chemical engineering he brought a quick grasp of science and technology.

Heizer's performance at Allstate, of course, was helped by the soaring stock market of the mid-1960s. But there was more to it than luck. Heizer is one of those rare men whom General Doriot never ceased to seek—one who combines courage and caution. He has definite ideas about values. "I just can't imagine borrowing money to go on vacation or to buy an icebox," says Heizer. "I think an icebox is something a person can save money to buy. My wife and I wouldn't buy a house for a long time because we didn't want a maximum mortgage. That's my attitude toward venture capital, too. I'm very proud that never in my career—never when I had anything to say about it—has a bank lost money after lending it to one of our new companies."

Heizer's great physical stamina has contributed to his success, too. A handsome, tall, fast-moving man with blue eyes and blond hair, he can work nonstop for weeks at a time. "He can wear you out," says an associate. "He has tremendous recuperative power and he doesn't need a lot of sleep. In fact, I think he works when he sleeps, too. He can handle dozens of things all at once, and he hasn't changed in the thirteen years I've known him."

Strange as it may seem, it was Heizer's conservative attitude toward business that led to his departure from Allstate. Heizer had been doing so well that his eleven-man group was soon contributing an inordinately large percentage of Allstate's profits—and Allstate then was a $2.5 billion company. By 1969 Heizer's operation had achieved a consistent annual 40 percent growth rate in invested funds. His budget that year was $40 million.

Heizer's grateful superiors poured more and more funds into the operation. He felt, as he recalls, "like a man under Niagara Falls with an umbrella." The more money he invested, the more they gave him. The Allstate executives further suggested that Heizer should vastly expand his operation by getting more young men like himself to work for him, but Heizer disagreed. His idea was to run a smaller operation than Allstate was proposing but with more experienced people.

In response to the suggestion that he hire more young people like himself, Heizer asked the not unreasonable question where he would find them, since his own background dated all the way back to his family's dinner table. Heizer is an absolutely unpretentious and completely frank man. "I couldn't find Ned Heizers," he says, "not because Ned Heizer is brilliant but because Ned Heizer sacrificed himself and his family to get this background." Even if others had followed a similar course, he suggested that opportunities elsewhere would be so great that there would be no reason for them to work for Heizer at Allstate.

Heizer was convinced, furthermore, that if he had succumbed to the temptation of vastly enlarging the Allstate operation, it would have ended in disaster. By 1967–68 he had begun to feel that high-technology stocks were grossly overvalued and that the time had come to sell many of them and to contract rather than expand the activity.

He left Allstate on amicable terms and in September 1969

31

launched Heizer Corporation. On the face of it, that seemed like the worst of times to start a new venture-capital firm; 1969 proved to be a year of debacle for new issues in the stock market. But Heizer convinced thirty-five institutional investors that he could offer them the long-range opportunity to make large amounts of money. He envisioned a twenty-year program. To finance it, he aimed to raise $100 million but in the end had to settle for the still impressive $81 million from banks, university endowment funds, insurance companies, and such institutions as the American Museum of Natural History in New York City and the Art Institute of Chicago. First National City Bank, Prudential Life Insurance Company, the State of Wisconsin Investment Board, the University of Chicago, and Stanford University are among principal investors. They got convertible notes and common and preferred stock in the Heizer Corporation. Heizer reserved 500,000 shares: 200,000 for himself and 300,000 to be held for sale or option to his key employees—an incentive lacking at Allstate.

Heizer Corporation emerged as the world's largest independent venture-capital firm. In fact, some venture capitalists thought Ned Heizer had raised too much money. But he had a definite plan. He wanted to help start companies that would make a significant impact on the United States economy. He also knew that staying power, the ability to nurse along an infant firm, is one of the secrets of the business.

New companies need a myriad of expensive services. "Our job is first of all to see that every company is organized and staffed properly," says Heizer. "See to it that they have the right auditing firm—and not only the right auditing firm but the right guy from the right auditing firm; that they have the right commercial bank, the right lawyer. See to it that they have all the professionals that they should have. We can do it much better than they can do themselves. We have contacts and know-how. Most entrepreneurs don't have the foggiest notion how to get the best bank or the best auditor—but we do. We can go to the top of Arthur Andersen and say that we need a top-flight guy. The same is true of law firms and banks. We can be very helpful to the companies without in any way interfering with their operations. We can get good operating executives with our contacts—this is an invaluable resource. We can help them go public; we can help with mergers and acquisitions and expansion overseas.

"Once you get them real top professional support, a good outside board of directors, and good management—all the crucial things—then they don't have all those problems new companies usually have. The more independent these companies become, the more valuable they are—the more we are freed of cares about them. So the main part of our game is to put ourselves out of work."

These chores are not always pleasant. Although his basic tenet is noninterference in the affairs of companies he finances, Heizer on occasion hasn't hesitated to change a company's management for the good of the company. "Sometimes the greatest favor you can do an entrepreneur is help him remove his best friend who may have helped him start the company."

When he picked entrepreneurs at Allstate, Heizer always looked for willingness to work hard, and that's the type of men he chooses now. Like Doriot, he believes that often the ability to work with one's hands is important to success. "Much of what's involved in running a company involves mechanics in one way or another," says Heizer. "So you are going to have problems if you literally can't work with your hands." If all an entrepreneur is looking for is easy money, Heizer wants nothing to do with him.

The companies Heizer is interested in supporting have to deal with practical business opportunities. Their products have to be unique—Heizer is convinced that for a new company to become a big success its field must be as exclusive as possible. The harder it is to enter a field, the more difficult it is to stay in it, and the more unique the entrepreneurs must be to make a company succeed, the better he likes it.

Heizer feels that a company's obligation is not only to produce profits for its shareholders but also to provide a valuable service "to their fellow men." "My philosophy of business is that the companies that are doing the best job of providing a valuable service make the most profits."

Concerning a financial backer's relationship with a company,

Heizer has always believed that the backer should "never manage a company but see to it that all of them are properly managed." This involves monitoring a company's progress without becoming a nuisance to its management. Heizer is careful that none of his associates talk to anyone in the companies without getting approval of the company's president first. He also feels that two venture-capital partners are the limit. If there are more, the entrepreneurs will find themselves explaining what they are doing at the expense of doing their jobs.

Heizer shuns the shotgun approach used by some venture capitalists who figure that one big winner in ten is a good payoff ratio. He wants each one of his investments to have a major potential. There is no dice rolling at the Heizer Corporation. Heizer naturally wouldn't have tolerated the Potemkin village approach to bringing out new companies; the field suffered from this false-front method at the height of the high-technology company boom.

Heizer prefers to call his approach "business development" instead of venture-capital activity. Heizer Corporation, he explains, in each of its investments acts as carefully as a big corporation would in setting up a new division or launching a new product. "We are into these operations just like a regular corporation, and if something goes wrong in one of our companies, we'll get as upset as Ford did over the Edsel."

All this Heizer planned to achieve by structuring an ambitious supermarket of services to small companies. He wanted Heizer Corporation itself to be a kind of a revolving conglomerate. It would help new companies grow, get them on their feet, reap the benefits of its investments, and then invest in a new series of companies.

Being a meticulous planner, Heizer was convinced that careful foresight could reduce the risks that new companies have to face. "There is no way for a new company to suddenly leap through space," says Heizer. He knew that the kind of planning entrepreneurs would have to do would have to be very specific. His operating approach, therefore, is markedly different from that of most other venture capitalists. "Instead of starting with an accounting or

34

a financial man," explains Heizer, "you sit down with the management of the company and you ask what they are going to accomplish tomorrow, this month, and next month. And when you talk about accomplishments, you have to talk about very mundane things. In a computer company, for example, you have to say when you're going to complete the interface [interconnections] between your equipment and IBM machines, and then the entrepreneur has to present data on what is involved in completing that interface.

"You can't say, as some people do, that this month we're going to be 25 percent complete on our product, because that doesn't mean anything. But detailing month by month, in almost physical terms, what they are going to accomplish gives you a base for communication."

After spelling out detailed plans and calculating how many people are needed to put them into practice, "the financial statements just fall in line," says Heizer. "So that when the accountants get through with the financial statements there are seldom any surprises."

Into this planning scheme Heizer Corporation ties key milestones that, Heizer says, are helpful to the small company's morale. "It's a very tough period a company goes through during the first two or three years. There's no public market for the stock. The company's sales efforts often haven't even started. That's the period when people get very discouraged and they really don't have much to show for all their hard work. But if you've laid out some milestones, they get a tremendous kick out of reaching them."

Even if the milestones aren't reached, the planning is highly worthwhile. It gives Heizer a chance to judge whether the problems were created by management or were beyond its control. He will stick by a new company's management if it's doing its job. But if the managers fail time after time, "then we get in the recruitment business and replace the management. We have that obligation not only to our own investors, but also to the other employees of the company involved. This may sound like we are managing these companies but actually we aren't. There's a big difference

35

between going through this process of trying to make decisions in general terms and managing companies."

To put these ideas into practice, when he started Heizer Corporation, he brought an innovation to his company. At Allstate he had made all the decisions himself because his staff consisted mainly of young, inexperienced graduates of business schools. At Heizer Corporation he decided to employ more experienced people, giving them much more authority than his young helpers had at Allstate. Specifically, he decided to use "operating" men as his principal contacts with the infant companies he was going to back. The operating men had run companies in the past. Supported by experts in financing, marketing, and other skills at headquarters, the seasoned executives, Heizer thought, would be perfect first-aid men to the emerging companies.

These operating men became "line" vice presidents, meaning that they would work in the field. They had experience in industries where Heizer thought there would be a lot of growth potential. The vice presidents were split into technical and nontechnical groups. The nontechnical men were well versed in merchandising, distribution, new products, and management organization. The technical vice presidents all had engineering backgrounds and had experience in managing technological companies.

From the start, Heizer boldly moved to support companies with big ideas. In 1970 he helped start Amdahl Corporation, in Sunnyvale, California. Gene Amdahl, the company's founder, was one of IBM's principal computer designers. He left to build a supercomputer of his own. "Gene Amdahl didn't have to explain Amdahl Corporation to me," says Heizer. "I had identified the area in my own mind."

The idea of a small new company building supercomputers in competition with IBM and other industry giants may have seemed preposterous to some people. But Amdahl Corporation from the start aimed to outdistance those giants by building a computer of unmatched power.

Heizer Corporation rapidly moved into other areas. In the field of computer accessories, Heizer invested in Data 100, a Minneapolis-based manufacturer of terminals for large-scale computer users. In the medical field it made a sizable investment in Beverly Enterprises of Pasadena, California, which operates medical-care facilities. In all, Heizer Corporation during its first two years invested in eleven companies.

The idea of using operating executives to monitor the new companies looked impressive in theory but it turned out to be a flop in practice. "It took us a couple of years before we saw that this concept wasn't working too well," says Heizer. "This is interesting because the concept makes so much sense."

As it turned out, however, the problem was that the operating men were used to running things. So, inside Heizer Corporation, they tried to run roughshod over financial experts and anyone else they thought was interfering with "their" companies. Heizer's idea of making the operating men invest their own money into companies they monitored, which was intended to add to their zest, backfired because it only made their attachments to the companies even stronger.

While monitoring the companies, the operating men often clashed with the more independent entrepreneurs. "We're dealing with dynamite in this business all the time," says Heizer. "The entrepreneurs are very determined, dedicated guys and you had better not get in their way." At the time these problems were occurring, Heizer told a seminar: "We haven't had any of the entrepreneurs get in a fistfight yet with our line vice presidents, but we've come close. And that's the kind of entrepreneur we like to back."

Aside from striving for independence, men who run small companies are usually tempted to do too much. To begin with, entrepreneurs commonly underestimate the difficulties of starting a company. "I have never seen a lousy projection yet," says Charles Deary, Jr., vice president for administration and treasurer of Heizer Corporation. Once a company is in business, the entrepreneurs, or at least many of them, tend to engage in overambitious expansion. In some cases, Heizer's own vice presidents were egging them on. Heizer says he likes to put his shoes on one at a time, while some of his subordinates were forcing new companies "to put all their clothes on in one continuous motion."

Heizer was discovering that the best planning is subject to all kinds of uncertainties—human, economic, even natural. Manufacturing plants can and do burn down, disrupting operations. This happened at Material Sciences Corporation, a manufacturer of advanced materials in Torrance, California, in which Heizer invested more than $6 million.

The worsening economic conditions of the 1970s made the job doubly difficult. As a result, some companies supported by Heizer nearly went out of business. At one time, five of the infant firms were on the verge of bankruptcy—including Amdahl Corporation, where, Heizer says, "we almost drowned near the middle of the stream."

As it became clear that his experiment with operating men wasn't working too well, those executives were mostly let go or left on their own. "We've always had excellent people," says Heizer, "but we were probably expecting the impossible from them." He tightened the reins and put a new emphasis on hiring financial specialists, since Heizer Corporation for a while was forced to become a venture-management instead of a venture-capital firm. Heizer complains that "it has been very difficult to find people who can relate to this industry. It's very hard to find people capable to doing our work who are willing to lower their egos. There is no training ground for this industry. There is no place to get people who have been exposed to pressures this industry has. Maybe that's why there are so few good venture-capital firms." He adds: "If I had all these problems in good times, I'd really be upset."

If Heizer rode to the crest of the wave at Allstate atop a surging economy, along with everyone else he was now riding downward as the economy entered the doldrums. At the end of 1973 Heizer decided not to finance any new companies for a while but to try to save the ones he had. He sold some investments at a big gain, some others at a big loss, but managed to rescue companies that he really wanted to keep. Amdahl, of course, held promise of becoming his biggest star. Accordingly, Heizer wound up pouring a total of $12 million into Amdahl; even for Heizer Corporation, with its ambitious plans, this was a big investment. But Amdahl sales projections are "mind-boggling," says Deary. Heizer is striving to build Amdahl Corporation into a worldwide computer company, capturing perhaps as much as one-third of the market for big computers. Toward that end, Fujitsu, the Japanese electronics concern, and Nixdorf, a West German computer manufacturer, were brought in early as big investors in Amdahl Corporation, contributing about $10 million each.

The big investments began to bear fruit in June 1975 when Amdahl Corporation delivered its first supercomputer. It was installed at a research facility of the National Aeronautics and Space Administration in New York City and the machine was widely praised by experts.

Heizer also managed to pull from the brink of bankruptcy a number of other companies, including Photomat Corporation, a La Jolla, California, retailer of photo-processing service and film, and Precision Instrument Company, the Santa Clara, California, maker of laser-generated memories for computers. Heizer had known about Precision Instrument when he was at Allstate but didn't think the time was right then to invest. He was convinced that the company was developing a solid new technology, however, and when the occasion presented itself to buy a controlling interest in Precision Instrument, Heizer did so in late 1973. (To get a controlling interest in a company is not Heizer's standard aim, however. Heizer Corporation's investments in companies range from as little as 0.6 percent to 99 percent of potential ownership.)

Like Doriot, Heizer believes that capable men are the key to success in new companies. Eager to enter the semiconductor industry, Heizer and his associates kept an eye on promising managers in the industry. When a chance arose to invest in Nortec Electronics Corporation, of Santa Clara, California, Heizer asked Eugene Blanchette, a former Fairchild Semiconductor executive, to run it. This was easier than starting a semiconductor company from scratch, of course—especially in view of the fact that start-up

39

costs for a semiconductor company may run from $15 million to $20 million today.

Heizer's heavy concentration on California companies, particularly those in that busy nursery of high technology around Palo Alto (see Chapter 3), may raise the question why Heizer Corporation is located in Chicago, where entrepreneurial activity is minimal. Heizer himself says that the difference in attitudes in Chicago and California is striking. When he started Heizer Corporation, some people in Chicago could not understand why Heizer would leave a good job at Allstate to jump into the unknown. But in San Francisco, his fellow venture capitalists and entrepreneurs threw a party to welcome him into their ranks. "One gal who had a few drinks asked me to talk to her husband because she thought something was psychologically wrong with him—he didn't want to start a company of his own. The contrast between the West Coast and Chicago is unbelievable. And the East Coast is even worse."

But the Chicago location has served Heizer well. "If we were in San Francisco," he says, "we would be a competitor with everybody, but being here we are a logical partner to California venture capitalists. We're probably more involved in the exciting San Francisco area companies than anyone in San Francisco." Nine of Heizer's twenty-three current companies are in California.

He is open, however, to investments anywhere, and he sees parts of Florida and Texas, as well as Atlanta, Georgia, and Cincinnati, Ohio, emerging as nascent centers of new high-technology companies.

Heizer Corporation, furthermore, does not confine itself strictly to high-technology companies. Heizer remembers well that a $1 million investment in International Industries—pancake houses— yielded $20 million at Allstate. The bulk of Heizer's investments is in technology companies, however. Automation, information processing, communications, advanced materials, agribusiness, convenience foods, health-care products and services, recreational housing, leisure-time products, and environmental improvement are all areas of interest. Says Heizer, "I'll listen to anything."

His staff has continued all along to sift through proposals from entrepreneurs that have kept coming in at the rate of about a thousand a year. "If a business opportunity is promising," says Heizer, "we don't care how small it is, how old it is, or how many people say it can't be done. We don't care where it is. All we insist on is that the business opportunity has substantial potential and that its management is dedicated to success, not just money. We can make $100,000 commitments or multi-million-dollar commitments."

Toward the end of 1975 Heizer was straightening out his problems and preparing "to play offensive football again," as he put it. "We're following the same advice we've been giving to others," says Heizer about his company's reorganization.

But Heizer Corporation has performed well, considering the shaky state of the nation's economy in the early and mid-1970s. At least six, and perhaps as many as sixteen, of Heizer's companies appeared to have the potential of reaching sales of $100 million a year that would allow them to be listed on the New York Stock Exchange.

To be prepared for future expansion, Heizer Corporation, in April 1974, formed Heizer Capital Corporation, a subsidiary that operates under the Small Business Investment Act. This type of government-supported investment banking for small companies gives Heizer the ability to borrow $20 million from the federal government.

Heizer is concerned that there is less venture capital available in the United States than there are opportunities to finance deserving ideas. He would like to see this country set up organizations similar to savings and loan associations to help new businesses. They would offer, among other things, better tax rates to long-term investors in new enterprises. Heizer also thinks that women and blacks are an untapped reservoir of entrepreneurs that he would like to help develop. There have been notably few female or black entrepreneurs in high technology, but not for lack of ability, to be sure.

"This country was founded by entrepreneurs, but Congress is killing this process," says Heizer. "For most people, free enterprise is probably synonymous with U.S. Steel, IBM, and General Motors. But historically that's not what free enterprise has meant in this country. General Motors is a monument to the success of the system. But instead of making sure that our laws foster the continuation of the programs that created General Motors and IBM, congressmen spend most of their time trying to figure out how to regulate them. What they don't seem to realize is that if we could assure a flow of capital to young companies, then if General Motors in time didn't do a good job, new companies could compete against it."

Once such problems are explained, Heizer says, most congressmen he has talked with agree that a new small-business development act is needed. "They want me to quit Heizer Corporation, come down to Washington, and write the act."

Heizer is unlikely to quit, though. He has become president of the recently formed National Venture Capital Association in order to push these ideas. If more capital were available, he says, venture capitalists would be far more creative than they are. Most now tend to sit back and select proposals that come to them instead of engaging in the more active deliberate structuring of new companies in areas where there are opportunities for innovation. "We are all lazy in a sense and we tend to react to what's there," says Heizer. "I call this a noncompetitive industry because there is an endless number of projects that could be undertaken very successfully."

Great advances that could be translated into spectacular new products sometimes remain buried for years in university laboratories, even in this age of the blossoming of science and technology. Carroll Williams, a brilliant Harvard University biologist, for instance, proposed as far back as 1956 that the key developmental hormones of insects could be imitated synthetically and employed as powerful insecticides that would be safe to man and other life. It was not until 1968, however, that Zoecon Corporation was organized to cash in on this remarkable scientific discovery (see Chapter 8).

This gap between discovery and application has always bothered the best and the most intelligent venture capitalists. General Doriot always kept pushing his associates to visit research laboratories. Heizer, of course, has the advantage of having had a technical education himself and he tries to spot the needs early and structure companies to fill them.

To potential entrepreneurs Heizer offers this advice: "Ask yourself why you want to found a company. Match your source of financing to your objectives, and your objectives to the realism of what you're doing."

"What makes an entrepreneur successful?" he asks. "Motivation and incentive. Money, yes, but more than that. There isn't enough money in the world to compensate a man for what he goes through to get a little company off the ground. The score card is in terms of profits, but his greatest satisfaction, and ours, is making a company successful."

Part II

INVESTMENT GEOGRAPHY

CHAPTER THREE

California's Great
Breeding Ground for Industry

The world's largest and most successful hothouse of high technology, where new companies and millionaires are mass-produced, is Santa Clara County, California. Once a tranquil sea of apricot, cherry, and prune orchards thirty miles south of San Francisco, Santa Clara County has become the place where American industry is thrusting out its newest branches and roots. Nearly one thousand pioneering technology companies, along with numerous service and supplier firms, are clustered in the area, forming the densest concentration of innovative industry that exists anywhere in the world.

The county boasts companies that lead in such fast-expanding fields as semiconductors, lasers, medical instrumentation, magnetic recording, and educational and consumer electronics. Some of them are branches or subsidiaries of big corporations headquartered elsewhere that now feel obliged to establish research facilities in the area. But most of the new industry is home grown.

Almost all of this exciting activity is taking place in a triangular wedge of territory twenty-five miles long and ten miles wide, along the southwestern shore of San Francisco Bay. It is centered in such towns as Palo Alto, Mountain View, Sunnyvale, Cupertino, and the city of San Jose. Some of the action spills over into Menlo Park, Redwood City, and San Carlos in the southeastern corner of adjacent San Mateo County.

The dense concentration of so many scientific companies has

47

created an innovative ferment on a scale without precedent in industrial history. Utilizing components and entire technologies that didn't exist only a few years ago, they are fashioning the telephones and thermometers of tomorrow, electronic games, computerized process-control devices for a wide range of industries, and many other fabulous products.

It is remarkably easy to start companies in Santa Clara County. The place offers all the ingredients venturesome entrepreneurs need to succeed. Thousands of people skilled in the newest technologies already live and work there, as does a small army of knowledgeable venture capitalists who are ready to provide funds for promising new ideas.

The success rate for company founders is so high that there are at least one hundred millionaires—and possibly as many as five hundred—in Santa Clara County. Many of them are in their early thirties. One New York venture capitalist calls the county *"the* success area of investment geography."

No other center of advanced technology in the United States can match Santa Clara County's performance. The famous Boston-Cambridge complex has gone into something of a decline, partly because of its excessive dependence on federal contracts, which stopped coming, and partly because some of the technologies the Boston companies bet on failed to catch on. There's still lots of growth left in centers such as Los Angeles; Phoenix; Fort Lauderdale–Melbourne, Florida; Boulder, Colorado; and Ann Arbor, Michigan, but none even remotely approaches the Santa Clara complex in importance or size.

Why did the elite among industrial shapers of the future pick this spot? For one thing, it's a particularly pleasant place to live and work—a beautiful landscape of hills and plains, a bounteous garden of nature where fruit trees and wildflowers bloom even in February. No sooty smokestacks or shabby old factories mar the scenery. The science companies for the most part operate in sleek modern buildings in fifty-one verdant industrial parks that provide a campuslike setting for research and manufacturing.

Few places on earth so agreeably mix hedonistic delights with

the excitement of urbanity. Although the whole Bay area is celebrated for its equable climate, the technology triangle of Santa
Clara County, sheltered from the Pacific Ocean by the Santa Cruz
Mountains, is especially blessed with good weather. It enjoys mild
winters, fog-free summers, and a balmy spring and fall. Outdoor
sports and recreation are year-round attractions, and even corporate magnates have adopted the casual life-style coveted by the
young. The area boasts four thousand Ph.D.'s—one out of every
six in the state. There are also at least twelve thousand horses,
some kept by those Ph.D.'s right on their home acreages, which
are often within minutes of work. And within an hour's drive are
the shops, restaurants, and cultural offerings of that jewel of cities,
San Francisco.

The builders of this complex have created a kind of a twenty-
first-century community, an industrial and social laboratory that
allows a glimpse into the future. For centuries new industries were
usually started by putting together capital and labor. In a uniquely
American innovation, especially since World War II, however,
capital began to be joined with brains instead of brawn, giving rise
to such pioneering communities of the new industrial age and offering thousands of Americans a real choice about where and how
they would live and work.

In the past new industries also tended to cluster at the intersec-
tions of trade and transport routes. But high-technology industries
depend on brains, not transportation, raw materials, or nearness to
markets, so they can be located where life is most satisfying.

Along with freedom from geographical constraints, the Santa
Clara companies have also found a freer management style. Comparing the area with his native Boston, Paul Cook, the president of
Raychem Corporation of Menlo Park, says, "I'm continually
struck by the fact that things are so informal here, dedicated to accomplishment without the encumbrances of status symbols and
hierarchies. Those things still exist, unfortunately, back East, even
in the technology area."

Many Santa Clara executives work in sports shirts, and they
often eat lunch on an outdoor patio with rank-and-file employees.

Even the receptionist is apt to call the boss by his first name. "Management people here really do what they want to do, not what they think others want them to do," says Cook. "Our values are different."

Part of that spirit, to be sure, is the happy consequence of an influx of highly educated and talented young men and women—"a high-voltage population," as one company president puts it. Since 1950 the county's population has quadrupled to 1.2 million, more than half of whom are newcomers. The population of San Jose has soared from 95,000 to 535,000, making it the world's fastest-growing major city. Today more people live in San Jose than in Pittsburgh, Atlanta, Minneapolis, or Kansas City.

Over the same span of years the number of workers in high-technology companies has increased from less than 3,000 to more than 150,000. As technology has become the major element of the local economy, farm jobs have declined sharply. There are only 6,000 farm workers in the county today, compared with 16,200 in 1950.

The builders of the Santa Clara complex have also created what may turn out to be a forerunner of future communities. For one thing, although the county ranks as the nation's thirtieth-largest metropolitan area, San Jose has almost no downtown shopping district. The whole industrial triangle is one vast suburb. But it is a sophisticated suburb, notable for its cultural and educational amenities—and for the absence of class distinctions. One former Easterner, comparing the area with such places as Fairfield County, Connecticut; Brookline, Massachusetts; and Westchester County, New York, finds "a real sociological freshness" throughout Santa Clara County.

Fittingly enough, the technological community owes its start to scientific discovery. The electronic age really began in Palo Alto, where the vacuum tube was perfected as a sound amplifier and generator of electromagnetic waves. One day in 1912, Lee de-Forest and his associates leaned over a table watching a housefly walk across a sheet of drawing paper and heard the fly's footsteps amplified to make them sound like those of a marching soldier.

Today the white clapboard house at 913 Emerson Street where deForest heard the tramp of the fly is appropriately marked with a plaque as the "birthplace of electronics."

The vacuum tube allowed the development of all those electronic miracles: radio, television, radar, long-distance telephones, electronic computers, tape recorders, and electronic eyes that open doors in stores and office buildings.

DeForest and his associates were then working for the Federal Telegraph Company, of Palo Alto, the oldest American corporate name in radio. The company had been established in 1909 by a Stanford graduate with the assistance of Stanford's first president, David Starr Jordan, who invested $500 himself. Other faculty members and local businessmen contributed funds, too, setting an example for the area's subsequent collaboration between business and education and between money and science.

Federal Telegraph also turned out to be a training ground for men who later succeeded in technical companies of their own and thus set a pattern that has become the special hallmark of the area. Two Federal Telegraph employees left to form a firm in Napa, at the northern end of the San Francisco Bay region. There, in 1913, they invented the loudspeaker. Later their company evolved into the Magnavox Company. The late Charles Litton, the maverick engineer with a touch of genius, was another celebrated alumnus of Federal Telegraph. His Redwood City vacuum-tube enterprise, which he sold, eventually became Litton Industries. Litton had started his company in a garage in San Carlos.

During the twenties and thirties, a number of other Bay area companies also contributed to the advance of technology. The first successful all-electronic transmission of televised pictures was achieved in 1927 in San Francisco. Heintz and Kaufman, Ltd., devised and built advanced shortwave radio transmitters, including those used by Rear Admiral Richard E. Byrd in his South Pole explorations.

Still, it took years before the area acquired enough scientists, companies, and capital to form a critical mass that started a chain reaction of new-company formation. The buildup was almost wholly the handiwork of Frederick Terman, an enthusiastic and inspiring teacher at Stanford.

The son of the developer of the famous Stanford-Binet intelligence quotient (IQ) test, Terman studied at Stanford as an undergraduate and took a doctorate in electrical engineering from MIT. In 1925 he began teaching a course in radio engineering at Stanford and soon started the university's radio-communications laboratory. It was originally housed in the obscurity of an attic in an engineering building, but Terman, an audacious organizer and proselytizer, attracted gifted students, and the frame of the laboratory grew. For years, however, it bothered him that his graduates had to go into "exile in the East" because there were hardly any jobs for them locally.

To end the brain drain, Terman began to encourage some of his students to start companies near the university. In 1937 he made his first significant move. Among his students were two bright young men, William R. Hewlett and David Packard. With Terman's counsel, Hewlett as a graduate student designed and built an audio-oscillator, a device that generates signals of varying frequencies and one that Terman felt had great commercial possibilities. Terman prevailed upon Packard to return to Palo Alto from Schenectady, where he had gone to work for General Electric, and join Hewlett.

On a part-time basis the two started a company in the one-car garage of the house where Packard and his wife lived. Hewlett moved into a backyard bungalow at the same address. Terman could always tell when the fledgling firm had received an order. "If the car was in the garage, there was no backlog," he says. "But if the car was parked in the driveway, business was good."

That modest garage shop gave birth to the Hewlett-Packard Company, which is today one of the world's largest producers of electronic measuring devices and equipment. It now employs more than 28,000 people worldwide (11,000 in Santa Clara County), and its sales are near $1 billion a year.

Stanford's physics department gave Terman's efforts an important assist. In 1937 Professor William W. Hansen teamed up with

Sigurd and Russell Varian, young brothers who also had been backyard inventors in Palo Alto, to develop the klystron tube. This variant of the vacuum tube generates strong, stable microwave radiation that can be focused like a searchlight. The microwave beam penetrates clouds and fog but bounces back like a boomerang from a solid object such as an airplane. The klystron tube became a foundation of radar and microwave communications.

Stanford University helped the Varians in the final stages of their research by giving them $100 for supplies and free use of the physics laboratories. In return Stanford was to share in any profits. That $100 became one of Stanford's best investments. Over the next thirty years the university received almost $2 million in royalties, and the money continues to flow in.

In the late thirties, the only source of financial support the Varians could find for developing the klystron was Sperry Gyroscope Company on Long Island. When World War II broke out, development of the klystron was moved to Long Island. There the Varians and their associates perfected the klystron as the heart of United States antiaircraft and antisubmarine radar. It was 1948 before the brothers could start their own company, Varian Associates.

During World War II Terman headed a big defense research project at Harvard, developing radar countermeasures. The experience put him in the mainstream of wartime electronic research and suggested to him that a lot of money would go into it after the war, too. Realizing this better than most educators, he set out to expand Stanford's engineering school after he returned to the university in 1946 as dean of engineering.

His wartime contacts helped him to attract federal contracts. He encouraged faculty members to get acquainted with engineers in industry to learn of opportunities there. As a board member of fledgling companies and a frequent speaker at industry meetings, he prodded local industrial scientists to learn what the school was doing and how its research might help their business.

Later Terman not only opened regular graduate courses to industry engineers but also used television to bring regular courses

53

into company classrooms. Microphones enable corporate students to ask questions and participate in classroom discussions.

Another successful collaboration between the university and the technical companies on its doorstep led to the successful establishment of Stanford Industrial Park. The university had plenty of land—8,100 acres—much of it pasture. The original bequest of his farm by Leland Stanford prohibited the sale of this land. Struggling for more income in the early 1950s to finance the university's rapid growth, Stanford had no choice but to develop the "farm" itself.

Again Terman helped. To spread the word in the right places, he enlisted the help of his former student David Packard. "He and I began playing a little game," Terman recalls. "People would come to see me about locating a business in the park, and I would suggest they also talk to Packard to find out what it meant to be close to a cooperative university. When people came to him first, he would reciprocate. Our goal was to create a center of high technology."

A novel venture for its time, Stanford's industrial park caught on fast, partly because it lies so close to the campus that it is an easy walk from the classrooms to the plants. Varian Associates and Hewlett-Packard led the parade onto its campuslike grounds, where companies lease land for fifty-one years at a time. As more and more creative companies moved in, the park's fame spread. Charles de Gaulle, on a visit to this country while he was president of France, made a point of visiting it. The French later imitated the idea in suburban areas.

"A steady stream of visitors come here to study the unique situation we have built up," says Terman. "Their hope is to learn enough so they can go home and do likewise, at least to a limited extent."

The 660-acre park now has fifty-five tenants who employ 17,000 people. The university has received $18 million in prepaid leases, which produces $1 million a year of investment income. (Stanford's illustrious neighbor, the University of California at Berkeley, has developed no such industrial complex around its campus, partly for lack of land but mainly for lack of a Terman.)

Another phenomenon of Santa Clara County—the tendency of young scientists to become entrepreneurs—now started to shape the map of high technology. As the older companies—Hewlett-Packard, Ampex, Varian Associates, Lenkurt Industries, and others—prospered and expanded, breakaway offshoots began to appear in large numbers.

In high-technology fields at least, small companies seem to be the best incubators of the skills and nerve that men need to go into business for themselves. People working for tiny enterprises often assume large and broadly varied responsibilities early in their careers. As they master the myriad problems of managing small businesses, some come to feel that they can do a segment of the work better than the company that employs them. And the hope of getting rich as scientific entrepreneurs provides a powerful goad, as do the striking examples of success all around them.

For an engineer in Kokomo, Indiana, or any place else where there aren't such examples, the idea of starting a company "appears to be a step into the unknown," says Arnold C. Cooper, a Purdue professor of management. When he asked engineers at Delco division of General Motors in Kokomo if they knew names of successful founders of high-technology firms, they drew an almost complete blank. This was in sharp contrast with the Palo Alto area, of course, where almost every entrepreneur had friends who had already done it. "All the factors for success are built in here," says a young president of a Santa Clara high-technology company. "We live in an area that enhances our capabilities. My home is five minutes from the office. You have time to think out here. I honestly believe that whatever you can do well you can do better here because you don't have to expend energy overcoming environmental factors." So it is easy in Santa Clara County for friends and associates to form teams to strike out on their own.

Steven Brandt, who has started five new companies since 1965, found the experience extraordinarily exhilarating. He says, "If you are a capitalist—and I am—you graduate to the Olympics of capitalism by starting new businesses."

The phenomenon of company proliferation resulted from an accumulation of forces. "Once you get enough activity, enough creative people in one area, this generates its own head of pressure," says Terman. In this dynamic environment the ranks of entrepreneurs swelled rapidly. By 1955 the Western Electronics Manufacturers Association listed fifty-three member firms in the area, compared with twenty in 1951.

Of those fifty-three, only six had 500 or more employees (Ampex, Dalmo-Victor, Eitel-McCullough, Lenkurt, Litton Industries, and Varian Associates). But it is precisely the companies of that size—usually employing fewer than 500 people—that are the best generators of still other new companies. Cooper, who studied the Santa Clara companies a few years ago, found that such enterprises produce about eight times as many offshoots as larger firms do.

Although the founders of Santa Clara companies usually came from other small companies, even academicians were caught up in the fever. Often Terman helped his faculty members to become businessmen. For instance, when Dean A. Watkins, an engineering professor, founded Watkins-Johnson Company, Terman let him stay on the university payroll part time while his venture struggled to get on its feet. (It employs more than 1,900 people today.) As the number of companies grew, other young executives left established companies to form machine shops and scientific supply firms, providing resources that made it easier for subsequent entrepreneurs to succeed. "It's a beautiful, almost biological process," marvels one professor.

The early technology companies in Santa Clara County had thrived by creativity, and the newcomers continued the tradition. Ampex pioneered magnetic-tape recording. Paul Cook's Raychem Corporation introduced novel ways of processing wire and cable sheathing with nuclear radiation; the company now has 3,600 employees and expects sales of more than $150 million in the 1975–76 fiscal year. Cashing in on those earlier developments in vacuum tubes, microwave technology, and radar, assorted entrepreneurs began to create a whole industry around Palo Alto specializing in novel reconnaissance instrumentation.

Even when they concentrated at first on defense-related work, most of these companies rapidly diversified into consumer products. They had to. The distance from Washington, D.C., often put the Santa Clara companies at a disadvantage vis-à-vis Boston-area firms, for instance, in dealing with federal officials. But in the end their consumer orientation gave Santa Clara County companies much of the strength they needed to survive the vagaries of defense and aerospace spending.

Attracted by the increasing activity, big national firms by the mid-1950s began to set up facilities in the area, further enriching it. Lockheed came at that time, along with Sylvania, Admiral, Kaiser, and General Precision. General Electric centered its nuclear-power research in San Jose. IBM had established a punch-card plant in San Jose back in 1943, but in 1952 the company set up a research center there. It turned out to be one of the area's great spawning grounds for new companies.

It was at IBM's San Jose facility that the magnetic data-storage disk was invented in the 1950s. Compared with magnetic tape, the disk made possible a spectacular advance in the density of data recorded per square inch. It also greatly boosted the speed of data retrieval and made possible random access to information stored in computers. The disk vastly increased the market for computers. Seizing that opportunity, numerous IBM men quit and formed a whole string of independent small firms making disks of their own. Among those companies are Information Storage Systems of Cupertino (it now employs 1,200), Gaelus Memories of San Jose, Iomec and Shugart Associates of Santa Clara, and others.

Mergers and acquisitions brought still other prominent technology companies into the area. Itek came by buying Applied Technology; Teledyne, by purchasing Microwave Electronics.

From these big companies little companies soon began to spring up. The Monsanto Company had moved its electronics special products division from St. Louis to Palo Alto in 1968. It came to the area after considering Los Angeles, Boston, and Denver because management had concluded that Santa Clara County had the best combination of reasons for Monsanto to move there.

With Monsanto came Bruce Blakkan, an ambitious young engi-

57

neer who served as the division's product manager. He decided to start his own business because he thought there was more opportunity in the electronics area than Monsanto planned to capitalize on. Then only thirty-two, Blakkan started with an original capital of $10,000 that came partly from his own savings, relatives, and a bank loan. He did most of his original design work on his dining room table in his Cupertino home. His company, Litronix, Inc., makes light-emitting diodes that yield light when a small current is passed through them. The diodes are used as numeric displays in calculators which Litronix mass-produces by the million. The company recorded sales of more than $50 million in 1974. Blakkan has parlayed his initial investment into a tidy fortune.

Enterprising individuals from everywhere also started coming into the area in large numbers—a process that had begun earlier and continues today. In fact, the diversity of national origins of the Santa Clara entrepreneurs is remarkable. Alexander M. Poniatoff, founder of Ampex Corporation, is a Russian émigré engineer. Konrad W. Schoebel, founder of Precision Instrument Company, once flew fighter missions for the Luftwaffe. Narinder S. Kapany, who established Optics Technology, is a turbaned Sikh who did graduate work at Stanford.

The San Francisco Bay area has, of course, always attracted enterprising people. A magician of company building, Robert L. Chambers, now in his late fifties, is the founder, chairman, and chief executive of Envirotech Corporation, of Menlo Park. The company is only seven years old, but its sales leaped to nearly $300 million in 1975, making it the world's largest pollution-control firm. A native of Salt Lake City, Chambers came to San Francisco without a job in 1942. Later he started Magna Power Tool Company, which introduced the Shopsmith, a multi-purpose tool for home woodworkers. After selling Magna, Chambers launched Envirotech.

More recently, the area has begun to attract entrepreneurs because they know their chances of success are better where the right climate for innovation exists.

David A. Bossen, now in his late forties, and his wife, Doris, are president and vice president–personnel of Measurex Corporation, in Cupertino. She has a doctorate in counseling psychology. They came from Columbus, Ohio, and founded the company in 1968 to make computer-guided controls for paper mills and other manufacturers. "Paper mills are in the woods because that's where their raw materials are." says David. "We are here because our raw materials are brains." The Bossens built Measurex by hiring specialists locally. Even before David left his job with a firm in Columbus, the Bossens knew they wanted to start their company in Santa Clara County—and not only because Doris is a Californian. They knew that the type of diverse specialists they needed were right in the area.

A supplier of robot brains, Robert H. F. Lloyd, who is in his early forties, for many years served as chairman and chief executive of Advanced Memory Systems, Inc., of Sunnyvale. He started his company in Santa Clara County for similar reasons. He came to Santa Clara County with IBM and was a star in its electronics division. He was later transferred to New York but raised funds from institutional investors and returned to start his semiconductor company in 1968. He chose Santa Clara County as his locale because of the availability of professionals and skilled labor. The company's sales have topped $30 million.

The Palo Alto area also boasts a number of "incubator" organizations other than big companies. Stanford Research Institute, in many ways the most successful of such not-for-profit organizations, has given birth to at least a dozen companies formed by its former employees. Its offspring have been technological companies, with one intriguing exception: Ridge Vineyard, founded in Cupertino by a senior research engineer.

Terman kept pouring fuel into this fire. In electronics he had trained a whole generation of scientists-entrepreneurs and had built up Stanford's engineering department to a level where it attracted outstanding graduate students from around the country and began to award more Ph.D.'s in electronics than any other school, including MIT. That helped the region's growth, of course, for many of these newcomers stayed after graduation and went to work for the local firms or founded their own companies.

D. James Guzy was attracted by the Stanford mathematics department where he got a master's degree. A native of Minneapolis, Guzy liked the area and stayed on. He went to work for Ampex and later helped found Memorex Corporation. More recently, after leaving Memorex, Guzy has founded another new company, Arbor Electronics Laboratories.

Nolan K. Bushnell worked his way through the University of Utah by managing an arcade in an amusement park. He came to Santa Clara County because of its high concentration of electronics firms. After working for Ampex for a while, Bushnell struck out on his own. He started Atari, Inc., which has successfully pioneered in electronics games.

In 1955 Terman became provost and in 1958 vice president of Stanford. Thereafter he transformed the university's once mediocre chemistry department into one of the best in the country. He recruited two outstanding chemists: William Johnson from the University of Wisconsin and Carl Djerassi, a Wisconsin graduate who had become vice president for research at Mexico-based Syntex Corporation. Djerassi had acquired worldwide fame in 1951 for synthesizing, with his associates at Syntex, the first oral contraceptive. The university put up a big new building for Johnson and Djerassi. They, in turn, hired other outstanding chemists.

By bringing Djerassi to Stanford, Terman set in motion a whole new chain of company formation in biology and medicine. Largely at Djerassi's urging, Syntex established a United States subsidiary and research arm in the Stanford Industrial Park. With Syntex from Mexico City came Alejandro Zaffaroni, an imaginative biochemist who was Syntex's executive vice president.

Zaffaroni and Djerassi have been responsible for the formation of five pioneering companies, all in Palo Alto. While still at Syntex, they originated Syva Corporation, a joint venture with Varian Associates in medical instrumentation, and Zoecon Corporation, which makes hormonal insecticides (see Chapter 8). Zoecon is now an independent business with Djerassi at its head. After leaving Syntex, Zaffaroni in 1968 started Alza Corporation (see Chapter 6). Another Zaffaroni venture, Dynapol Corporation, is developing food additives that can pass through the digestive system without entering the blood.

60

A large segment of Santa Clara County's technological activity owes its existence to another, somewhat similar chain of circumstances. William B. Shockley, co-inventor of the transistor, returned to Palo Alto, his boyhood town, in 1956 and set up Shockley Transistor Corp. The transistor was the successor to the vacuum tube, perfected in Palo Alto fifty years earlier, and Santa Clara County was becoming the logical place for electronic manufacturing.

In the fifties, Shockley gathered around him a large group of gifted young electronics specialists whom he picked from big companies and universities around the country. In 1957, however, his operation ran into trouble when eight of those bright young men, including twenty-nine-year-old Robert N. Noyce, left and, with the backing of Fairchild Camera and Instrument Corporation, founded Fairchild Semiconductor in Palo Alto. (Shockley subsequently went on to other things, becoming a center of controversy because of his view that intelligence is inherited and that genetics, more than environment, accounts for low scores by blacks on IQ tests.)

Fairchild became one of those amazing corporate seedbeds. No fewer than thirty-eight companies, including Noyce's enormously successful Intel Corporation, have been started by former Fairchild employees (see Chapter 7). They have turned Santa Clara County into "Silicon Valley," the world capital of semiconductor technology. With sales of about $2.5 billion, the valley accounts for about 8 percent of total United States sales in electronics and some 40 percent of the nation's semiconductor output.

Just as oilmen go where the oil is, companies eager to get into the semiconductor business come to Santa Clara County. Baldwin Piano and Electronic Engineering, a southern California company, set up Siliconix, whose sign towers over a fruit orchard just off the busy Bayshore Freeway in Santa Clara. Two successful Boston-area computer firms, Digital Equipment Corporation and Data General Corporation, have set up research facilities in Mountain View and Sunnyvale, respectively, joining the four hundred or so electronics companies already in Silicon Valley.

The semiconductor industry never made much headway in the

Boston area. The land around Boston is littered with the skeletons of semiconductor operations that flopped. Many big companies tried but all failed to make a go of it. It seems that the old-fashioned and rigid management approach of some of those firms proved unsuited to the fast-moving new industry. Others failed to innovate. "Risk-taking is much more prevalent here," says Noyce. "As a result, technology advanced much faster."

Almost at the same time as the semiconductor industry emerged, Santa Clara also became the world center of laser production. Spectra-Physics, of Mountain View, whose founders came from Varian, is now the world's largest laser company, with sales approaching $50 million. Coherent Radiation, of Palo Alto, which ranks second, was formed in turn by two young executives from Spectra-Physics. There are nine other laser firms in the area, as well as Optical Data Systems, of Mountain View, the first company to bring holography into commercial use for check verification and for the storage and rapid retrieval of credit information. The hologram, a three-dimensional image on film, is made with a laser and allows data to be stored in great density.

As the diversity of the area's companies increased, interesting interactions began to occur among them. Semiconductor specialists joined with experts in office machines to produce computerized typewriters, cordless telephones, and other new devices. "I can't imagine any other place in the world," says one company official, "where you could round up thirty-five people who are experts in so many unusual specialties."

The area boasts individuals who are remarkable in other respects. Elliot Levinthal is an example. A New Yorker by birth and a physicist by training, he worked with the Varian brothers during World War II on Long Island and came to Palo Alto with them in 1947 to help start Varian Associates. Later he left Varian and founded a company of his own, Levinthal Electronic Products. He sold the company and joined Stanford University, where he is now associate dean of the medical school. His activities are strikingly diverse. He helped design instruments for NASA's Viking spacecraft, which are slated to land on Mars during the Bicentennial celebration in 1976. He is a director of Zoecon Corporation. In fact, Levinthal, as a director of Syntex Corporation, came up with an imaginative scheme to finance the beginnings of Zoecon. Under this plan Syntex stockholders were given a chance to buy shares in the new company. Levinthal is also a venture capitalist, as a limited partner in Arthur Rock and Associates.

Levinthal is part of a unique intellectual network that spans the county, extending across the San Francisco Bay to the University of California at Berkeley. World-famous scientists such as Joshua Lederberg, a Nobel Prize winner and a founder of modern genetics, and Donald Glaser, Nobel Prize–winning physicist at Berkeley, are part of this network. Lederberg heads the department of genetics at the Stanford University Medical School and is the fount of many imaginative ideas about possible improvement of microorganisms for the benefit of man. Glaser, who when he was only thirty-four received the Nobel Prize for inventing the bubble chamber, a device that records tracks of elementary particles, has since come up with still another remarkable invention.

This is a huge apparatus deceptively dubbed "the Dumbwaiter" that is designed to process 100 million microbial cultures at once, subjecting them to automatic surveillance and screening in accordance with instructions programmed in a computer. The automatic scanning is designed to remove much of the tedium involved in microbiological investigations. Rapid processing of microorganisms is important, moreover, because mutations of interest to science or industry occur quite infrequently. The faster researchers can process large numbers of microorganisms, therefore, the better the chances of discovering mutants with scientific or commercial value.

Out of the Lederberg-Glaser collaboration has come a company with a science-fiction flavor, Cetus Corporation, of Berkeley. Using automated techniques, Cetus is upgrading the production qualities of antibiotic-making microbes that belong to major drug companies. The "bugs," worth millions to their proprietors, are kept in deep-freeze vaults under heavy electronic guard. Cetus is working on recombining genetic material in such microorganisms, and its ability to process large numbers of microbe colonies rapidly will undoubtedly be of great help. The company also expects to be able to develop new microorganisms tailored to do highly specific jobs such as consuming oil spilled at sea or to turn out brand-new commercial products such as insecticides. As one possible strategy, Cetus may sell the superbugs it develops to the highest bidder.

So sophisticated is Glaser's Dumbwaiter that it even has a set of four hundred elegantly slender quartz "fingers" that can pounce on command on the cultures to pick out microbes from a specific colony. When the makers of the Hollywood science-fiction film *The Andromeda Strain* heard about Glaser's machine, they rushed up to Berkeley to film it so that they could build a mock-up of a similar device for the motion picture. Interestingly, Cetus Corporation is named after a galaxy that adjoins the Andromeda star system.

Another part of the same intellectual network are men such as Djerassi and Zaffaroni, who are not only imaginative scientists but also have money of their own to back such frontier enterprises as Cetus Corporation. In fact, one of the first things a successful Santa Clara technologist does is back other promising ventures. Quite a few millionaire technologists have moved into new careers as financial backers of other scientific businesses. In all there are now about 150 venture capitalists who live and work in the Santa Clara area. Their presence gives the field of venture capital a look all its own in Santa Clara County. "In New York, the money is generally managed by professional or financial promoter types," says Robert R. Augsburger, vice president for business and finance at Stanford and former executive vice president of the Wall Street firm of Donaldson, Lufkin and Jenrette. "Out here the venture capitalists tend to be entrepreneurs who created and built a company and then sold out. When problems occur with any of their investments, they can step into the business and help. All in all, venture capital here is more oriented to fundamentals than in the East. That's a significant factor in getting things started and moving along."

Investment Geography

In recent years fledgling firms have often found it easier to find funds at home than anywhere else. "We raised money from all over the country," says Martin Gerstel, financial vice president of Alza Corporation. "But we found more willingness to consider high-risk situations here. In the East and Midwest, people kept asking us how we expected to compete against big companies. Around here it's accepted that a small company with good ideas and good people can do it. Local financial men know the vulnerabilities of big companies because so many people have made it competing with them."

Among the local venture capitalists is perhaps the champion investor of the post–World War II technology era: Arthur Rock, who is now in his late forties. He is reputedly worth at least $20 million. Spotting an opportunity for Santa Clara ventures while working for Hayden, Stone, in Manhattan, Rock moved to San Francisco in 1961. He arranged the original financing for such successful firms as Teledyne, Intel Corporation, and Xynetics. His major *coup* was arranging to sell Scientific Data Systems, which he had helped start on $1 million, to Xerox for $900 million worth of stock. Rock makes it a point not to master the intricate technologies of the companies he backs. He feels that would interfere with his judgment of men as managers.

More typical of the high-technology venture capitalists in the area is Robert Sackman, now in his late fifties. An electrical engineer by training and a native of Brooklyn, he was a radio ham as a youth and once worked in radio-assembly shops for twenty-five cents an hour. Sackman joined Ampex Corporation in 1953 and in seven years helped lift its sales from $3 million annually to $70 million, becoming executive vice president in the process. Sackman became a venture capitalist in 1962, mainly to help friends form new companies. His technical and management background comes in handy in aiding young company presidents. For example, he helped to finance and build up Vidar Corporation, a maker of advanced instruments and telephone equipment, which was later sold for $27 million to Continental Telephone. Sackman is currently president of Rodal Corporation, which has investments

65

in half-a-dozen technology companies. His Palo Alto office over-looks Stanford Industrial Park.

Sackman's right hand is David Berliner, a personable Mexican-trained physician who until recently was a vice president of Alza Corporation. At Alza, Dr. Berliner investigated new areas the company should get into. He finally succumbed to the venture-capital fever. It's not hard to see why when one tours new compa-nies in the county and its environs. Among Rodal's investments is Parker Research of nearby Livermore, which is pioneering the liquid-crystal technology. It makes novel thermometers literally by the mile—the numbers containing the tiny liquid crystals are de-posited on long rolls of plastic slowly moving along. In nearby Milpitas, another interesting company partly bankrolled by Rodal is Sierra Chemicals, which has pioneered encapsulation of fertil-izer into long-lasting tablets.

Seeing a good thing, venture capitalists from the outside have also become active in the area. Texas oil money has come in. Ned Heizer, the Chicago venture capitalist, Nixdorf, a West German computer company, and Fujitsu, a Japanese electronics firm, have invested $30 million in Amdahl Corporation, of Santa Clara, which builds supercomputers. "Rarely do you find the opportu-nities we've found in Santa Clara County," says Stewart H. Greenfield, director of the DL&J Capital Group, an arm of Don-aldson, Lufkin and Jenrette, of New York City, that has major in-vestments in the area. Among the attractions: a "substantial" number of companies whose sales are more than doubling each year and many with profits growing even faster than that.

The venture capitalists have benefited handsomely from such performances, and so have the entrepreneurs. "We've even got a few millionaires on the Stanford faculty as a result of their involve-ment in companies," says Terman. Yet the personal lives of most of the new millionaires have hardly changed. They often move to bigger houses on impressively landscaped grounds in such plush communities as Atherton or Los Altos Hills. But, as one banker says, "You don't see any castles being built here. There are no $2 million homes, although some people could afford them."

The dominant life-style, in the words of one resident, is "exuberant egalitarianism." It's typical of the entrepreneurs to spend their free time with their families, often in outdoor activities. Most of them avoid costly hobbies, though a few do own airplanes. As a group they don't engage in extensive social or club life. For example, Packard rides a tractor in the eighty-acre apricot orchard that surrounds his house in Los Altos Hills, or works in his vegetable garden.

A surprising degree of cooperation among companies, almost Japanese in its closeness, has added further impetus to Santa Clara's ascendancy. It begins on a personal level. Transplanted Easterners are sometimes startled by the openness and lack of abrasiveness in relationships among people in the Far West. "The friendliness and cooperation of the people here are by orders of magnitude higher than, say, in the New York City area," says Thomas Furia, a recently arrived executive at Dynapol. The president of the electronics manufacturers' association adds, "Easterners tell me that people there don't talk to their competitors. Here they will not only sit down with you, but they will share the problems and experiences they have had." Many of the executives in the area got to know one another as students at Stanford or as participants in local business and political affairs. The relatively close proximity of companies makes associations easier; Santa Clara County is a technological community partly because of its geography. The area is mostly flat and easily traversed on superior roads. That kind of a close-knit community where a meeting affecting, say, the semiconductor industry brings out company presidents by the dozens was unlikely to arise in sprawling Los Angeles or in the Boston area, where companies are widely scattered.

Many of the area's entrepreneurs have tried to pattern their companies after Hewlett-Packard, which is widely admired because it has been hugely successful and also because of its benevolent attitude toward employees. Long before profit-sharing became a practice, Hewlett-Packard divided its profits with employees. When the company went public, it gave shares to all its workers. Many blue-collar workers have retired with tidy sums as a result.

Early on, Hewlett-Packard decided not to take on contracts that it couldn't handle without first hiring and then firing a lot of people at the end of the contract. The company held instead that the jobs it offered would be permanent. The result has been great loyalty and an extremely low turnover.

Hewlett-Packard appears to have handled its scientists and engineers with great success, too. Once the company advertised, "If you want to be in business for yourself, come to work for Hewlett-Packard." This policy of giving people a lot of freedom—the company now has flexible work hours so that a worker chooses when he comes to work and leaves—has turned out so well that there have been only three offshoots from Hewlett-Packard.

Moreover, William Hewlett and David Packard are widely praised because of their modest personal life-styles. Although each is worth more than $500 million, they drive to work themselves. At work they have been known to stand in line, waiting for their turn at the Xerox machine. They still barbecue the steaks at the annual company picnic.

They apply this informality to business, too. At Hewlett-Packard, top managers sit out on the floor with the other office workers, with only low glass partitions occasionally breaking up the space. For many years only Hewlett and Packard had private offices; the vice presidents sat out in the open, too. The purpose is to improve communications and cut down on memo writing.

So far the technology bonanza in Santa Clara County has not been marred by any major corporate flops, although some small firms have folded through the years. Technically oriented enterprises have been generally far more successful in staying in business than other types of firms. Only about one out of five new technology firms fails after five years, according to an MIT study, whereas among new companies in nontechnical fields *four out of five* collapse. It may be that technological entrepreneurs have a better idea of what they want to do when they start companies.

To be sure, some companies have suffered setbacks. On his office wall Alan F. Shugart, until recently president of Shugart Associates, kept a memento of his days as a vice president of Memorex, which makes computer auxiliary equipment. It was a pair of Memorex stock certificates for 4,400 shares. Tacked below was a handwritten note: "FOR SALE: worth $750,000 when issued. Worth today $4,400."

Founded in 1961, Memorex experienced a meteoric rise in sales a few years ago, and its common stock hit a peak of $173 a share. Then Memorex began to flounder. But the company has grown to $177 million a year in sales and new management is putting the firm on a sound footing again.

There are flaws in this paradise, to be sure—occasional smog and traffic jams on the Bayshore Freeway—but nothing resembling the eye-stinging, suffocating stuff in Los Angeles or the pervasive congestion of the New York metropolitan area. Public schools are so good that even the children of the rich generally attend them.

The area's explosive growth has aroused belated concern about preserving its beauty. In the beginning the boom was intoxicating. In 1964 Joseph Ridder, publisher of the *San Jose Mercury and News*, dismissed complaints about the disappearance of the orchards with the remark, "Trees don't read newspapers." And A. P. "Dutch" Hamann, city manager of San Jose, had a dubious dream of creating "a Los Angeles of the North."

But as the sprawl spread, some of the scars became highly visible. Subdivisions of boxy houses sprouted almost overnight, without adequate access roads, schools, or supply of electricity.

The area has so far been spared from turning into another Los Angeles (its population per square mile is only about one-eighth as great), partly because of the limiting presence of mountains along the ocean side of the county and partly because many citizens at last awoke to the destructive impact of helter-skelter development. Today city and county officials are trying to guide the growth.

The area is even trying some fairly new ways to cope with its social problems. In San Jose, for instance, halfway houses for alcoholics and counseling of both youthful offenders and their families have partly replaced courts and jails. Menlo Park police have attracted national notice by getting out of uniform (officers wear informal slacks and blazers) and by emphasizing crime prevention rather than arrests.

The county is fortunate to have no pockets of extreme poverty. There are blighted areas but no real slums. Only a few blacks live in the county, and many of them work at skilled jobs. The bottom of the ladder is occupied by Mexican Americans, who compose about 20 percent of the county's population.

Originally drawn to the area as farm laborers, the Chicanos still hold mainly low-paying factory, service, or farm jobs. Most of them live in the older neighborhoods of San Jose. In a study in 1973 the Rand Corporation warned that the persistent disparity between Anglos and Chicanos had become the number-one problem of the area. "Although racial and ethnic tension is nowhere near as strong as in Eastern cities or even the barrios of Southern California, there is tension and there has been violence," said the report.

Whatever difficulties may lie ahead, the racial unrest has up to now had no effect on the high-technology companies. Indeed, the technologists seem to have few worries of any kind about their future. Many local companies now build their manufacturing plants elsewhere because land prices in the county have skyrocketed and skilled labor is in short supply. But Santa Clara County began as a cradle of technology, not as a manufacturing center, and a cradle of technology it intends to remain.

Even the process of starting a firm in a garage has been given a contemporary twist. In some industrial parks, hopeful entrepreneurs can actually rent a garage, complete with a roll-up door, and two or three offices adjoining it. More mature companies, makers of such remarkable products as Intel's computer-on-a-chip, supply components that infant companies need to build imaginative new products. Through such arrangements, the entrepreneurs have created a company-making machine that is unique.

When Terman set out to create "a community of technical scholars," he says, "there wasn't much here and the rest of the world looked awfully big. Now a lot of the rest of the world is here." Spry and vigorous at seventy-six, Terman still goes daily to his office at Stanford, where he is a consultant to the president. It is now nearly half a century since he began teaching, but Terman remains as ebullient as ever about the technology empire he built. He concludes, "As long as we maintain the practices that have made us what we are today, there is no limit to the longevity of this situation."

CHAPTER FOUR

Boston, Cradle of Innovation

Boston, the cradle of our liberty, has also served as the incubator of many of our innovative industries. The pursuit of freedom and the pursuit of free enterprise have intertwined in Boston to a remarkable degree. Paul Revere not only rode to rouse a new nation but he also founded the silverware and copper industry in Boston. A subsidiary of a descendant firm, Revere Copper and Brass Company, of New Bedford, today appropriately makes electronic devices. The great expansion in trade that came with freedom and with the conquest of the world's trade routes by Yankee clippers created capital that enterprising Bostonians put to pioneering uses. A century ago the president of Western Union dismissed the telephone as a toy. His advisers had convinced him that about the only useful function it could perform would be in shipboard (bridge to engine room) communications. But John Murray Forbes, a Bostonian who had made his fortune in shipping, saw beyond that limited use and steadfastly stood by Alexander Graham Bell with financial and moral support. Bell System was the result.

Many other important innovations were born or perfected in Massachusetts. There was a rich base to grow on, of course; the inventive and manufacturing heritage dates back to the workshops of the earliest colonists in the 1660s. But Massachusetts is much more than the birthplace of the textile, shoe, and leather industries. The modern rubber industry had its beginnings there. Charles Goodyear, a native of Connecticut, discovered the vul-

73

canizing process in 1839 while living in Woburn, Massachusetts. Around the turn of the twentieth century the Boston area blossomed as this country's primary automobile-manufacturing center; there were no fewer than one hundred such manufacturers there. From Boston-region companies have come such important products as submarine cables for the first transatlantic telephone lines and for the telephone service that links California and Hawaii. And refined instruments for navigation, weather forecasting, and industrial controls were being produced in Massachusetts even in the nineteenth century.

Much of the early development of electricity took place in the Boston area. The General Electric Company owes its origins to the merger of the Edison General Electric Company with the Thomson-Houston Electric Company of Lynn, a Boston suburb. The Thomson-Houston Company had been bought earlier by a syndicate of farsighted Lynn shoe manufacturers. In fact, it wasn't Thomas Alva Edison, the developer of the incandescent lamp, who became General Electric's first president, but Charles A. Coffin, a former Lynn shoe manufacturer who had become fascinated by the electric business. Edison stepped aside because of his stubborn belief that the future lay in direct current, not the alternating variety.

Electricity made possible the development of radio, and again the Boston area pioneered with inventions and companies. General Radio of Cambridge was the oldest electronics manufacturer in the United States. RCA traces its origins in part to the wireless company operated by United Fruit.

Even the Stanford–Palo Alto high-technology nursery owes its start in good part to the Boston-Cambridge area. It was there, at the Massachusetts Institute of Technology, that Dr. Frederick Terman picked up some of his ideas on how to build up a center of new technology that he later so successfully put into practice at Stanford University. At MIT, as a doctoral student in the 1920s, Terman learned at the side of Vannevar Bush, the famous electronics wizard and science statesman. Bush took an active part in industrial activities. Among other things, he was one of the founders of Raytheon Corporation, now a $2 billion-a-year electronics conglomerate headquartered in nearby Lexington.

Investment Geography

As a result of that early foundation building, the Boston area today is one of the nation's premier centers of science laboratories and innovative companies. More than one thousand firms line Boston's famous Route 128, which brackets the city's western suburbs. In the city itself, in old shoe factories, thrive electronics concerns. A former woolen mill in nearby Maynard was the birthplace and still remains the headquarters of one of the most successful innovative companies in America: the computer-manufacturing Digital Equipment Corporation, which has grown into a $500 million-a-year giant.

Basic science underlies the ongoing industrial development. At MIT's Lincoln Laboratory, in the outskirts of Boston, astronomers have probed the surface of Venus with pencil-thin radar beams, detecting mountain ranges and huge craterlike depressions on the surface of the cloud-shrouded planet. Lincoln Lab is also the place where the founders of Digital Equipment worked. From the Woods Hole Oceanographic Institute at Cape Cod, research vessels strike out to explore ocean depths. The area is also rich in medical-research resources. The heart pacemaker, for instance, was developed by a Boston doctor, Paul M. Zoll, in association with a Boston-area company, Electrodyne Company, Inc., of Westfield.

Being so much older than the Palo Alto area—Boston was a thriving, vibrant city of 100,000 at the time when San Francisco was a settlement of a mere 900 people just before the gold rush began in 1849—the Boston area, of course, has a much more diverse history. Instead of one principal catalyzer of innovative industry, as Terman was in Santa Clara County, it had dozens.

But a single institution—MIT—stands out as the flywheel of high-technology company development in the Boston area. The famous Harvard Graduate School of Business Administration has spawned a few high-technology companies, and Polaroid Corporation was started by Harvard's most famous dropout, Edwin Land. But MIT is the undisputed fountainhead of high-technology firms in the area.

Harvard may boast of its famous scholars. "Where else in the world would you meet all these people within one block?" asked a Harvard professor recently as he strolled with a visitor from the

Faculty Club toward his laboratory, greeting in rapid sequence the economist John Kenneth Galbraith, Edwin Reischauer, a former ambassador to Japan, and a number of other Harvard luminaries. But Harvard has historically kept industry at arm's length. The professor so proud of his famous colleagues, Carroll Williams, is a typical case. He has contributed major findings to the field of insect control with hormone analogues, chemical copies of the insects' own regulatory substances. Williams's work has been instrumental in the organization of a California company to cash in on this remarkable research (see Chapter 8), and he serves as a consultant to the company. But that is about the extent of Harvard professors' involvement in industrial research. Harvard and MIT are only a mile apart in Cambridge, across the Charles River from Boston, but they might as well be located on different continents where their philosophies on dealings with industry are concerned. Their mottos tell part of the story. Harvard's is *Veritas*, or "Truth"; MIT's is *Mens et manus*, or "Mind and hand." Harvard has historically downplayed practical gain in its search for truth, while MIT has emphasized it. When he founded MIT (as Boston Tech) in 1865, William Barton Rogers wrote, "A school of practical science completely organized should, I conceive, embrace full courses of instruction in all the principles of physical truth having direct relation to the art of constructing machinery, the application of motive power, manufacturers, mechanicals and chemical, the art of engraving with electrotype and photography, mineral exploration and mining, chemical analysis, engineering, locomotion, and agriculture."

In keeping with that pragmatic plan, MIT has become the prototype technical university whose delving into theory in order to translate it into practice was bound to generate the hundreds of technical companies to which the school has given birth. "MIT," says Edward Roberts, David Sarnoff Professor of Management at the MIT Sloan School of Management, "takes an activist role of presuming that it's appropriate not just to teach technology but to spawn technology and to move it toward the marketplace and toward utilization." Being a typical MIT professor, in that he serves on the boards of nearly a dozen high-technology companies, Roberts adds, "I find this fascinating."

Putting the ideas of the institute's founder into practice, MIT graduates began to form companies shortly after the school was founded. Arthur D. Little, Inc., for instance, the Cambridge research and management consulting firm, was founded by an MIT-educated chemist back in 1886. This company has grown into a big international organization employing more than 2,000 people. MIT professors, furthermore, seem always to have been active as consultants to companies. As early as the 1920s, the institute established a division of industrial cooperation to handle institute-wide contracts with industrial companies. In addition, MIT professors have always moonlighted for industry with the school's blessing and encouragement. Terman recalls from his student days at MIT in the 1920s: "There was always an industry around Cambridge and Boston and MIT was right in the middle of it. It was easy for a professor to find things to do in industry where his specialized knowledge was of value to them, and it would be kind of fun for him to apply some of his knowledge to real world activities. Every place you looked, you would find guys doing something with some company. Edwin Gilliland, head of the chemical engineering department, for instance, alone started four chemical companies." Even then an MIT professor could devote a day a week to outside activities. But the professors did not neglect their students, Terman recalls. His department head, although an active consultant, was always available.

A sprinkling of companies emanated from MIT in the 1920s and 1930s. Many were located close to both MIT and Harvard. General Radio Company, founded in 1915, was originally only a few blocks from the MIT campus. Harold E. Edgerton, an MIT professor, with two friends from the school started Edgerton, Germeshausen and Grier, Inc. (EG&G), a scientific instrumentation firm in Cambridge. Edwin Land left Harvard in 1937 to found Polaroid. By the time World War II broke out, the Boston-Cambridge area could boast a substantial background in electronics and related technologies. Even then the area companies were engaged in diverse technical activities.

Combined with the MIT-Harvard educational and research prowess, this made the area the undisputed center of science and technology in the country. It was an area destined and pro-

77

grammed for growth—the roots were all in place. The massive infusion of federal funds in World War II made it blossom. From the many wartime laboratories operated under MIT and Harvard auspices emerged some of the fantastic electronic devices that helped win the war: improved radar and jamming techniques against enemy radar, novel gunsights, and many other innovations. MIT's Radiation Laboratory was the most important single wartime research activity, but there were many other enterprises that brought together thousands of outstanding scientists and engineers from colleges and universities around the country. Among them was Dr. Terman, who returned to Cambridge to run the radio laboratory at Harvard. Under his guidance the lab developed the aluminum chaff that Allied bombers dropped over Germany to jam enemy radar receivers. Signals reflected from the falling chaff showed up on radar screens and confused German gunners who thought they were detecting airplanes.

Boston was so far ahead of California during World War II that Terman remembers his lab business manager storming in one day to complain about some Terman associates placing a contract with "a little fly-by-night outfit in Los Angeles called Hughes." The business manager, a New Englander, suggested that the Terman associates, who happened to be Californians, were simply looking for an excuse "to get back to the West Coast a couple of times a year." (That tiny company later grew into the giant electronics concern known as Hughes Aircraft Company.)

The companies that were in the Boston area contributed mightily and grew big in the process. EG&G, for example, spurred on by Dr. Edgerton's invention of the strobe light, conducted much of the developmental testing of nuclear weapons and became the instrument supplier to the Manhattan Project. Raytheon made the vacuum tubes for radar. Some new companies were formed during the war, too. But the really explosive push did not come until after the end of World War II, as the newly emerged technologies spurred on formation of new companies.

Instrumental in stimulating the high-technology boom was General Doriot and his American Research and Development Corporation (see Chapter 1). In a major way, ARD, too, was an

MIT offspring, and the first companies it financed were MIT creations. ARD was established in 1946 as a publicly held venture-capital company, listed on the New York Stock Exchange from the start. There had been no such companies before, and ARD's appearance was greeted with skepticism by some Boston bankers and even some innovators. "Charles Kettering—the great inventor Kettering," recalls General Doriot, "said that in five years ARD would be dead, busted, and forgotten."

Although it is easy to assume that venture capital was always available in a big financial center such as Boston, that wasn't entirely true where new untried industries were concerned. The inclination of most rich Bostonians was to conserve their capital by investing in "safe" industries and enterprises. Whatever venture capital was on hand before the creation of ARD had been quietly provided by the Rockefellers and other wealthy families. ARD brought the whole promising business into the public spotlight and opened the door for others.

Far from succumbing, ARD and Doriot instead spread the gospel of high-technology backing. Now a student could hardly go through MIT or Harvard without knowing that ARD supported technical projects that had merit. As Doriot's technique of betting on people instead of on the balance sheet began to pay off, more and more banks, insurance companies, and independent small firms began to brave the unknowns of high-technology backing. As entrepreneurs became wealthy, they also began to support still other new companies. Today Boston is one of the nation's major centers of venture capital; ARD itself has spawned a number of offspring.

The postwar excitement saw not only MIT professors but even graduate students start companies of their own. Many of them grew out of the continued pressures of the cold war and later the Korean War and the space race. Boston companies that had once pioneered the manufacture of eyeglasses now were making huge airborne spy cameras, and after Sputnik's dramatic beeps signaled the start of the space race, they began to build huge spy satellite cameras, too.

Starting in the late forties, these companies acquired a fitting

79

new setting as Route 128 neared completion. This scenic highway, which runs through the countryside of Thoreau, Emerson, and Hawthorne, starts near Braintree in the south and describes a great seventy-mile arc to Gloucester in the northeast—passing along the way through such historic towns as Waltham, site of the first factory in America (it converted raw cotton into cloth), Lexington, Burlington, and Beverly, as well as near Saugus, where the first ironworks in America was in operation a century before the Revolutionary War. Sleek buildings of companies with science-fiction-tinged names such as Thermo Electron, Raytheon, Trans-Sonics, and many others line much of the length of Route 128. In all there are now more than one thousand companies and other industrial establishments employing 85,000 people along this high road of high technology. At least half of those companies are in science and technology, and more than three hundred of them emanated from MIT, with other Boston institutions such as Boston University also contributing company founders.

Route 128's fame has spread far and wide. For example, it inspired the Soviet Union in its establishment of a science city in Siberia that doubles as a link to local industries. The origins of Route 128 have been studied by the French government and many local governments in the United States eager to try to imitate its remarkable success. It takes, of course, much more than a road to get a high-technology community started. But of all the ingredients it appears that the presence of innovative companies is the most important one. Most great universities have never generated enterprises at the rate MIT and Stanford have; they have lacked either the proper policies or the proper people to do it. When innovators have examples of success before their eyes, however, the innovative process has a better chance to get started.

Ironically, Route 128 was not at all intended as the "Golden Horseshoe," as it later became known, but merely as a bypass to get well-heeled New Yorkers to Maine faster, without getting lost in Boston's crooked streets and crowded traffic circles. A common complaint of local residents about Route 128 was "But it doesn't go anywhere." What's more, in the often blundering fashion of planners everywhere, the Massachusetts road builders had miscalculated. They had originally built a narrow highway without overpasses and bridges and later had to widen the road at a great expense. Cabot, Cabot and Forbes Company, a national real-estate development firm headquartered in Boston, has been Route 128's principal developer. It has built sixteen industrial parks along the road and is constructing new ones along Interstate 495, twenty miles to the west.

There are science companies in other places in the Boston area. Some can be found in Boston proper in old buildings that once housed shoe and textile factories. The scattering of locations fits the independent nature of Boston's high-technology innovators, but it has worked against creating the type of a community and co-operative spirit that marks Santa Clara County.

It was continuing conflict on the world scene that spurred the growth of the Boston–Cambridge–Route 128 complex. The cold war, the Korean War, and the start of the space age all led to expanded activity by MIT laboratories and the creation of new independent entities that the institute operates for the government. The laboratories employ thousands of scientists and engineers and have served as fountainheads of new companies. Taking a census of such companies in 1966, Professor Roberts of the MIT Sloan School found that the Lincoln Laboratory, which had been established in 1951 to develop an air-defense system for the continental United States, had spawned fifty companies; the Instrumentation Lab, thirty companies; the Research Laboratory for Electronics, fourteen; and so on down the list. MIT departments contributed heavily to company formation, too, as did such big, established companies as Sylvania's electronics division, with its thirty-nine "spinoffs." By 1967 Massachusetts electronics and allied companies, concentrated mainly in the Boston area, employed 70,000 people and produced $1.5 billion worth of equipment a year.

Among the many outstanding MIT scientists who have often served as midwives at the birth of the new companies were such men as Jay W. Forrester and C. Stark Draper. Forrester, now professor of management at the Sloan School, invented the magnetic core memory, the principal computer memory, while lead-

81

ing digital computer development at the Lincoln Lab. IBM later paid nearly $20 million for the rights to the memories. Draper is, among other things, inventor of the gyroscopes that enabled American astronauts to navigate to the lunar surface and back to earth.

One former Lincoln Lab engineer, Harlan Anderson, who was co-founder of Digital Equipment Corporation and now is a venture capitalist, recalls that the lab was "in many ways like a corporation but freed from the normal restraints of a corporation because MIT had negotiated a very special relationship with the government, where they didn't have to go through budget justification in a normal way. And Forrester trained a lot of managers to go out and become entrepreneurs."

Since the MIT labs and big companies such as Raytheon and Sylvania were overwhelmingly defense and space oriented, it was only natural that most of the companies they spawned followed in their parents' footsteps. There were important exceptions, of course. Although Anderson and Kenneth Olsen, founders of Digital Equipment, had both worked at the Lincoln Lab, Digital Equipment did not rely on defense contracts but smartly served a wide spectrum of customers from the start and was able to prosper. A few companies along Route 128, such as Thermo Electron (see Chapter 9), successfully resisted the temptation of relying solely on government contracts. But generally the Route 128 firms started in the 1940s and 1950s depended on defense and space business to an extent unknown in Santa Clara County.

This excessive reliance on Uncle Sam bore the seeds of trouble. It was exciting and profitable to make spacesuits for the astronauts, fuel cells to power their spacecraft, gyroscopes to steer them, and antennas to track them, as Boston area companies did, but when the big crunch of government cutbacks hit in the late 1960s, and on top of that the big recession of the 1970s, many Route 128 companies were severely affected. Raytheon alone laid off 10,000 workers and engineers. Smaller companies, some tiny shops making a single electronic component for a single customer such as Raytheon, saw their business evaporate. Ph.D.'s and specialized engineers were forced to drive cabs and tend bars. All told, Massachusetts lost 30,000 defense-related jobs during 1970–72. The

Boston Globe complained of "management myopia" in blaming some small—and big—company presidents for failure to look ahead.

"The process that got many of the Route 128 companies started," says Gerald Bush, director of Boston's economic development, "also predicted their failure. It was MIT's policy to encourage their graduates with an idea to go into the marketplace and the marketplace was space/defense. A guy working on an aerospace contract in one of the university or company labs did something better and developed it in his garage. He'd go down to his buddy in the defense department, who either was a former classmate or friend from work, and could get a defense contract for a prototype product. The entrepreneur would rent loft space and hire six or eight people and the government picked up all the expenses—the contracts were cost-plus. If the thing panned out, he might put up $15,000 and maybe get a partner who would do the same and then get a $1 million contract under which the government paid the rent, paid for the equipment, and every other expense. The contracts involved very little risk—you could write off everything and with equity you had long-term capital growth. With stock options, you could bring in talent for practically nothing. The rate of return was phenomenal—the entrepreneur would make 10 percent profit—which is a $100,000 return on a $30,000 investment.

"The direct support enterprises were here—movers, secretarial help, computer services, and so on—so the area ripened and flourished. If you read the prospectuses of the companies that went public, it was like reading comedy. All of those companies were tied to the military and NASA, and they would mention this and then talk about practical applications to the civilian market.

"Then the market disappeared. Not one of those companies made it. No company of that type ever really spun off a consumer product. Those cats were really funny. You'd ask them what would happen to the business if the market went away and they'd shrug. They were professional scientists; they responded to scientific values. They weren't businessmen; they didn't measure things by the businessman's standards.

"The companies that are successful on Route 128 today grew by intelligent acquisition of other markets. The retrenchment manager is a different breed of cat than the growth manager. Slovenly habits developed under the defense contracts where there was no concern about productivity. If you are passing your costs on to the government, you hire four people, and two work out and two don't. You can't afford this when you have to carry your own costs. When the cutback came, a different kind of selling was needed. You were no longer selling to your buddies in the defense department.

"In the last four or five years we've seen the replacement of the innovators—many of whom became extremely wealthy—with the different type of corporation manager. Now we have a more healthy economy than we did when the companies were dependent on the defense department. On a scale of 0 to 100, I'd say Route 128 went from 100 to 50 and is probably back to 75 in terms of general activity. The companies that came through the crunch healthy went into acquisitions to move to 60 percent consumer and 40 percent government, from 95 percent government. The companies that moved that way did very well, but relatively few did. The ones that were strong enough finally did diversify, but first the bankers had to get rid of the 'George Washingtons.' Running a company was not what gave the inventors their kicks."

The biggest flop on Route 128 in the late 1960s, however, involved not a defense-oriented company but a firm that tried to become "the General Motors of electronics," as its president had put it. This was Viatron Computer Systems Corporation, which began operations in January 1968 with a radical concept of mass-producing computer terminals with TV-like screens and selling them at ten times below the lowest rates then prevailing. Viatron hoped to achieve this by employing the emerging semiconductor devices. Unfortunately, those devices could not be reliably manufactured then and the whole Viatron concept collapsed.

When conversion to consumer products became the battle cry among Route 128 companies, the ones that succeeded best were big corporations because they had greater resources. A few small companies radically shifted their product lines. In one of the most surprising turnarounds, Lance Corporation, a tiny firm in Hudson, a Boston suburb, switched from being a supplier of microwave components to Sylvania to making pewter sculpture.

Of the big companies, Raytheon made the transition most successfully. In 1965, 85 percent of its business came from the defense department. In 1975, 55 percent of its business came from the commercial sector. Raytheon still makes vacuum tubes for radar, but now it also makes such mundane but profitable items as refrigerators, air conditioners, and dishwashers.

The older companies sometimes had a difficult time making a transition to brand-new technologies such as manufacture of semiconductors. The old vacuum-tube men couldn't quite make the mental and managerial shift to the fast-moving newer technology that is now overwhelmingly consumer oriented. The Boston area is littered with carcasses of semiconductor operations of big companies that didn't make it. The smarter companies, like Raytheon, located their semiconductor facilities in Santa Clara County, the California mecca for semiconductor industry. It takes a special, intimate interplay among the innovators to make such a complex technology develop and move forward. The semiconductor innovators had all flocked to northern California.

But Boston has had its big success stories, too. The area has emerged as the country's primary center for design and manufacture of medium-sized and small computers. This whole development was started by young researchers without vested interests in older technologies, and it has succeeded spectacularly. The famous breeding effect that took place in the semiconductor industry in the Palo Alto area occurred in the Boston area in computers. Digital Equipment has not only grown to a $500 million-a-year giant but has also spawned a number of other computer companies, including its principal competitor, Data General Corporation, of Southboro, whose sales in 1975 reached $108 million and net income a healthy $12.8 million. In the tradition of many high-technology enterprises, Data General started in a bankrupt beauty salon in what one man calls "a one-horse shopping center" in nearby Hudson. Its founders were mostly in their twenties, led by Edson DeCastro, a Digital Equipment engineer. They are all millionaires now, many times over. Another major computer operation that is a local product is Honeywell's computer division. It was the result of a joint enterprise between Raytheon and Honeywell.

A large number of other companies in the area have pushed forward such complex and important uses of computers as graphic displays of computations for bridge and automobile design, architectural planning, and even pilot training. The computer in some of these applications becomes an extremely powerful tool. In designing a bridge, for instance, the computer becomes, in a very real sense, an electronic wind tunnel. A model of the bridge can be displayed on a TV-like screen and subjected to simulated stresses and strains—such as high wind, for instance—to see if it can withstand the stresses.

Aside from becoming a center for production of computers, the Boston area had developed a sufficient diversity in company activities to absorb the shock of the defense-spending decline. Damon Corporation, of Needham Heights, for instance, successfully shifted from heavy reliance on government work to medical instrumentation. It is now the country's largest operator of medical laboratories and produces a variety of medical electronic equipment. Its sales topped $140 million in 1974 and net income $8 million. Advent Corporation, of Cambridge, never participated in defense work but has instead successfully concentrated on producing television sets with screens as large as four by six feet. Another Cambridge concern, American Science and Engineering Company, has developed not only X-ray telescopes for NASA's Orbiting Astronomical Observatory but also an X-ray inspection system that detects weapons and contraband in packages and baggage. Bose Company, originated by an MIT professor, has successfully applied a very fanciful technology—computer-aided design—to the making of high-fidelity speakers. Wang Laboratories, Inc., of Tewksbury, is one of the nation's largest producers of calculators, while International Equipment Corporation, of Needham Heights, is the world's largest producer of centrifuges.

All in all, there are more similarities than differences between Santa Clara County and the Boston area. Both are pleasant places to live, with rich educational, entertainment, and recreational facilities. "We've had two polar models on opposite coasts acting as intriguing technological magnets, and a guy who was comfortable in Cambridge could be comfortable in Palo Alto because there will be very similar guys, with similar classes of education, types of attitudes, and I think you can find a lot of migration between the two areas," says Professor Roberts of MIT, who has studied the high-technology business in the Boston area.

An intellectual bridge does link Boston with Palo Alto. Jerome Wiesner, the MIT president, Jay Forrester, and many other prominent MIT and Harvard men serve on boards of Palo Alto–area science companies, while MIT graduates such as Paul Cook, founder and president of Raychem Corporation, of Menlo Park, California, serve on the board of MIT overseers. There are many other MIT graduates who head companies in Santa Clara County.

Some entrepreneurs who have moved to the Palo Alto area from Boston miss "the cold wintery nights discussing politics," as Alan Michaels puts it. "But day-to-day life is much more pleasant here," adds Michaels, a former MIT professor of chemical engineering who founded a Route 128 company, Amicon, and is now executive vice president of Alza Corporation in Palo Alto. Unlike Palo Alto, the Boston area, of course, offers four distinct seasons, although summers can be scorching and winters severe. "Unfortunately," says Dr. Roberts, "Cambridge doesn't have Palo Alto's climate. There are a lot of people who like that climate and that style of living. Similarly, we do have a life-style here that a lot of people find more attractive than the California life-style."

Physically, many of the low-slung, sleek, high-technology buildings located along Route 128 could be transplanted to Santa Clara County's Bayshore Freeway, and they would fit in there perfectly, their science-fiction-tinged names and all. The problems new companies have to go through are identical in both places. "We spent two months planning this company and making forecasts—with a specific product in mind," says Nicholas DeWolf, chairman of Terradyne, which makes test equipment for semiconductor manufacturers. But after a new company gets under way, he adds, "the facts begin to come in. Sam is an alcoholic; your wife has left you. . . ." But Terradyne, which the ebullient De-

Wolf calls "the biggest electronic company in the shoe-leather district of Boston," has done well. It reported sales of more than $56 million and a net of $4.3 million in 1974.

One of the striking differences between the two areas is that large outside companies fostered a lot of the growth in the Santa Clara complex by locating advanced laboratories there. This happened to a much lesser degree in the Boston region, and then mainly in the early years of Route 128. "Much of our growth has been indigenous," says Professor Roberts. "For a period of time, it was great—we were self-sufficient. But after some time you can't run onto yourself. California has had the benefit of others seeing it as a desirable place, and I think there has been some further positive feedback acceleration in California which Massachusetts hasn't had."

The slowdown in the Boston area has become a subject of concern to a lot of people, and they are trying to do something about it. The concern is sharpened by the continuing erosion of manufacturing jobs in old industries such as textiles and leather. Therefore, both MIT and the state of Massachusetts are investigating new ways of generating high-technology enterprises. The state recently entered the high-technology venture-capital business. Among other things, it provides loans to new companies through the Massachusetts Science and Technology Foundation, a quasi-public agency. MIT in 1972 organized the MIT Development Foundation, Inc., an experimental launching pad for new companies that will exploit MIT-developed technologies. The foundation is supported by a number of large corporations, banks, and insurance companies. It has already started a number of small companies. Richard Morse, a senior professor at the MIT Sloan School, is the foundation's president. Appropriately, he teaches a course entitled "New Enterprises"; it covers organization, financing, and management. Morse is an entrepreneur of note himself. In 1940 he started National Research Corporation, which pioneered in vacuum technology, and after World War II applied this technology to the dehydration of orange juice. Minute Maid was the result. Morse has also served as the army's director of research and development and more recently has been involved in an effort to devise a steam engine for automobiles.

Another MIT-generated development has been Technology Square, a kind of a compact, in-town Route 128 within shouting distance of MIT. It occupies fourteen acres and consists of four large buildings housing science companies. Construction of Technology Square signified the first time an academic institution joined with a private real-estate developer (Cabot, Cabot and Forbes) in a partnership to pursue a project of that type.

MIT executives and other public-spirited citizens are working to improve the general attitude toward business in Massachusetts. Strange as it may seem for an area that has been losing manufacturing jobs, Massachusetts has extremely high taxes on business. One result has been striking. As Route 3 enters New Hampshire, only thirty miles north of Boston, the motorist is confronted with the gleaming buildings of Sanders Associates, a high-technology firm that chose to escape Massachusetts taxes by locating right across the state line in Nashua, New Hampshire. And Sanders hasn't been the only loss.

In the last few years the Boston-area technology business has recovered. New companies are being started again, although money is somewhat more difficult to raise. Still, money is available. Says William Congleton, "I've yet to see a good project turned down." Congleton, who once was a vice president of ARD and now is a partner in the Palmer Organization, a Boston venture-capital firm, recalls with obvious poetic license, "Venture capitalists would hang around the gates of MIT and Harvard in the 1960s trying to catch a professor and find out what ideas he might have." Another venture capitalist agrees: "The days of two guys with a soldering iron finding financial backing are gone, at least temporarily. But good ideas still get funded."

There are so many good technical people in the Boston area with bright ideas that they are continuing to seize opportunities opening up in new fields. A century ago Oliver Wendell Holmes called Boston "the hub of the solar system." Today it is turning into the hub of solar-energy systems research. A number of small

89

companies have sprung up in the field in recent years. Professor Roberts, who serves on the board of one of these companies, Solar Power Corporation, predicts that "with present state of the art, and some improvements in technology, I think it should be possible to create a $100 million company—certainly a $10 million company. And breakthroughs would improve the outlook even more." Being an electrical engineer as well as an economist by training, Dr. Roberts has firsthand knowledge of the field.

Other opportunities continue to attract enterprising men and women. Even physical handicaps don't seem to hinder determined innovators. Kenneth Ingham was seriously injured in a chemistry laboratory explosion in high school. He lost an arm, part of a leg, and was blinded. But having "the heart of a lion and the intelligence of a genius," as a friend puts it, he got a doctorate in electronics at MIT, married a blind girl, and went to England, where his wife studied on a Fulbright fellowship. Returning to the Boston area, Dr. Ingham worked in advanced electronics at MIT. Richard Morse of MIT and some other friends provided the seed money to allow Ingham to start a small company in Watertown that makes a voice response system being used to teach blind children foreign languages. The company is now being backed and helped by the Palmer Organization.

Some experienced entrepreneurs think that the time of an economic downturn is the best time to start a new high-technology company. Olsen of Digital Equipment says, "The time to start a company is when the times are hard. Salesmen are very helpful, space is available, you can get people to work for you easily."

Good times or bad, the most effective builders in the Boston area, just as in Santa Clara County, are imaginative individuals. Harlan Anderson is one of them. Once a $10,000-a-year engineer in the Lincoln Lab, he left Digital Equipment, which he helped found, with millions of dollars and set up an office as a venture capitalist in Darien, Connecticut. His investments are mainly in the Boston area.

Anderson's interest in venturing arose when the value of his Digital Equipment stock mushroomed. "Suddenly I had some significant financial resources—I felt like I could have an interesting life-style at a relatively young age," he says. "Now I could invest and maybe provide some helpful advice to companies and also it wouldn't tie me down day to day. I have been doing it for six years now, and it has worked out that way."

Anderson has invested in ten companies so far, including Modicon Corporation, an Andover, Massachusetts, manufacturer of computerized process control devices for industry; Computer Displays, a graphics firm that was later merged into Adage, a Boston company; and others. One of the more creative venture capitalists, Anderson has helped start companies from scratch. A consulting company in Boston owned rights to an idea for a hand-held computer printer; Anderson and a group of fellow young venture capitalists bought the rights and started a company called Thermoflex to manufacture the device. Anderson sees promising opportunities for entrepreneurs in applying microcomputers—computers on a chip—in a whole range of new products.

Like many other young innovation millionaires, Anderson has been able to indulge in new hobbies. He keeps a two-engine Cessna Citation jet in Westfield, Massachusetts. He uses the plane for both business and pleasure, such as flying his family to Vail, Colorado, to ski.

Today, thinks Anderson, it's still possible to succeed in the Boston area the way he succeeded with Digital Equipment Corporation. The region, as one Harvard professor notes, has "a sympathetic alignment of institutions pointing in the same direction, or charged with the same brand of electricity." This includes sources of venture capital that are at home with technological innovators, the great educational institutions, and hundreds of examples of success for entrepreneurs to emulate. The area still has a lot of vitality. "And the process of technological innovation," says Harlan Anderson, "is not finished by a long sight."

Part III
THE ENTREPRENEURS

CHAPTER FIVE

Kip Siegel: How a Small Company Showed the AEC the Way to Laser Fusion

In the afternoon of March 13, 1975, Keeve ("Kip") M. Siegel, a pudgy mathematician and businessman, was testifying before the Joint Congressional Committee on Atomic Energy in Washington, D.C. In the past Siegel had often been maligned for what his critics felt were outrageous claims of having come close to lighting, in his company's laboratories on earth, the magic fire of nuclear fusion that powers the stars. In the world of thermonuclear fusion, bigness prevails—immense potentialities for the future, grand-scale efforts to overcome the technical obstacles, huge costs that only governments can afford. Yet here was Kip Siegel, agitating that world with some seemingly audacious claims of success. His company, Siegel kept telling anyone who would listen, had mastered the key mechanism of laser fusion—a feat that had eluded the big and powerful teams of government researchers in both the United States and the Soviet Union, as well as smaller groups in Great Britain, France, Japan, and West Germany.

What's more, Siegel insisted, his brash little company attained its results with exceedingly low laser energy. This raised embarrassing questions about the soundness of American and Soviet plans to build mammoth lasers, which many scientists in both countries think are needed to attain success.

On the face of it, Siegel's insistence in the past that his tiny company, KMS Fusion, of Ann Arbor, Michigan, part of his KMS Industries, Inc., was leading the world in laser-fusion research seemed preposterous. On the other hand, hardly anyone made allowances for the possibility of its being true. The American press may pride itself on its independence, but it often fails badly where accuracy is concerned, especially in complex scientific or technical matters. Few reporters bothered to find out firsthand if Siegel was telling the truth. It's possible that his own highly enthusiastic and optimistic nature misled them. In any case, one news magazine published a highly critical story about KMS Fusion's claims on the basis of a telephone call to Siegel. A trade journal that was not even on the company's press-release list and whose representatives had never talked to KMS Fusion, much less visited it, nevertheless ran a story ridiculing KMS Fusion reports.

Things had started to change in KMS Fusion's favor, however, by the time Siegel started his testimony that March day. Experimental proof that laser fusion could be made to work would strengthen hopes that this new approach would leapfrog the older, more ponderous schemes to achieve fusion through magnetic confinement. In the conventional approach, which American, Soviet, and other scientists had been pursuing for nearly a quarter century, ionized hydrogen gas, or plasma, is confined inside artificial magnetic fields, or "magnetic bottles," in the innards of big and expensive experimental devices. In the interior of the sun and other stars, fusion takes place because of gravitational pressure. Inside the experimental devices on earth, the plasma has to be compressed and heated electrically to ignition. Although encouraging progress has been made lately, none of these machines has yet produced full-fledged plasma burn; among the difficulties are leakages from the magnetic bottles. In the United States alone, expenditures on magnetic confinement have amounted to at least $500 million.

Laser fusion, a glamorous newcomer, would greatly simplify the confinement scheme. Instead of a magnetic field, converging laser beams would hold a tiny ball of fusion fuel for a brilliant moment, compressing it to a density one hundred times that of lead and thus starting ignition. The resultant flux of neutrons would be captured as heat and transformed into electricity or made to do other useful work.

The Entrepreneurs

Large-scale work on laser fusion began in the United States in 1969. The Soviets started earlier and rapidly built up an impressively large effort. The United States has been building up a similar enterprise, with $64 million in federal funds going into laser fusion in fiscal 1975. As part of the expanding federal program, a huge $25 million laser is being built at the Energy Research and Development Administration's (formerly AEC) Lawrence Livermore Laboratory near San Francisco to become operational in 1977. The Soviet Union is building a similar laser. Official American plans do not call for possible commercial use of laser fusion until about the end of this century. This projection was based in part on the fact that the federal laboratories at that time had failed to achieve compression of the tiny hydrogen pellets, much less make them yield neutrons.

Yet here was Kip Siegel, a man of globular girth and an ego to match, insolently proclaiming in his droning monotone that his company had just attained a 1,000-fold compression of hydrogen pellets and "that we probably lead the world in the generation of compression neutrons by a factor of 1,000."

Siegel now faced—as KMS Fusion had faced all along—the big problem of where his next money was going to come from. Siegel had just come to the place in his testimony reading, "We are asking the government to help us," when his words became blurred. He tried to say the sentence again but couldn't. While Siegel reached for a glass of water, a sympathetic congressman tried to smooth over the lapse by talking about a related subject. Siegel sipped water while the congressman talked. Then Siegel suddenly slumped in his chair. A lawyer sitting behind him thought he heard the scientist say "stroke." Siegel was rushed to George Washington University Hospital. He died there at five the next morning.

A few days later the *Washington Post* devoted an editorial to Siegel in which it said that AEC secrecy and resistance to outside ideas, "as well as the AEC's rejection of entrepreneurs like Mr. Siegel, may well have slowed the development of atomic energy. Mr. Siegel's work is a forceful reminder that even in this complex and extremely expensive area of research, there is a place for devoted and gifted scientists who don't fit into the conventional molds of normal government administration."

By this time the critics had no choice but to admit that Kip Siegel's KMS Fusion had indeed left its competitors far behind. *Science*, the journal of the American Association for the Advancement of Science, commented that it had "become clear that KMS has a very large fraction of the world's data on laser fusion." It also quoted a grumbling AEC official as saying, "That's not the way it should be." Soviet scientists, with fewer axes to grind, were more generous in their praise of KMS Fusion. One leader of the Soviet program declared after a visit to Ann Arbor that KMS was ahead of the Soviet effort.

Although Siegel was no longer present to hear the accolades, his company continued in business. In fact, in a dramatic turn-around, the Energy Resources and Development Administration, the successor to the AEC, in July 1975 awarded a $3 million contract to KMS Fusion to help it define the conditions needed to attain significant thermonuclear burn. The amount of the contract was later increased to about $7.5 million.

What KMS Fusion has done so far, to be sure, is a very early step toward eventual construction of laser-fusion reactors. The company's scientists succeeded at the end of 1973 in using laser light to produce a slight compression of tiny glass pellets filled with deuterium and tritium—isotopes of hydrogen. In May 1974 they compressed the pellets further and started getting some energy output in the form of neutrons from the pellets—the first time anyone had obtained compression neutrons. In late October 1974, by turning up the laser power a little, they got much greater compression and a lot more neutrons—the accomplishment that Siegel disclosed in his March 1975 testimony. The company thus appeared to be on the right course toward the next step, ignition inside the barely visible pellet. This would be equivalent to the first successful chain reaction in fission.

There is a great difference, of course, between the tiny sizzle in the microscopic pellet that KMS has achieved so far and the brilliant intensity of the full-fledged fusion burn that must precede net energy production. In the words of one government scientist, who speaks with obvious poetic license, it is "the difference between a firefly one hundred miles away and a giant lightning stroke." KMS Fusion scientists think the gap between the two is much shorter than that. The significant point, however, is that KMS overcame what many scientists in the field considered to be the critical challenge in laser fusion: compressing the fuel pellet symmetrically so as to avoid producing instabilities that would prematurely break it apart. In a reactor, the laser would have to explode dozens of such pellets each second, one after another, much as a spark plug sequentially fires to ignite the fuel in the cylinder of an automobile engine. Before KMS Fusion conducted its pathfinding experiments, there was a question whether a fusion "cylinder" could be made to work. The company's experiments showed that it could. That's why scientists in both American and Soviet government laser-fusion efforts now call the KMS feat "a significant first step" toward attainment of controlled laser fusion.

That a small private company had outdone huge governmental research efforts was no surprise to the energetic Kip Siegel. He believed in the "lesson of the Cavendish Laboratory," the famous British research establishment, "where a few bright people out-invented the world for a long period of time. And they did this literally with wires and chewing gum. There the people motivated each other. In a small company there is that same kind of drive for success. Whether the drive is motivated by the scientific people, as it was at Cavendish, or by the desire to make a buck, I think that's all incidental."

Siegel's own motivation included but also transcended the desire to make money. He was already a millionaire from a previous venture in high technology, so he could afford to indulge in some philosophy, too. With the intensity of a prophet—"the man developed a Jehova complex over laser fusion," says one physicist—Siegel spoke convincingly about this new source of potentially unlimited energy at once freeing this country from its dependence on Arab and other foreign oil and cooling the inflationary fever.

There is little doubt that the mastery of thermonuclear fusion, in which nuclei of hydrogen or its isotopes, deuterium and tritium, are forced to merge to form helium, giving off energy mainly as neutrons, would indeed signal the start of a new era of energy abundance. Of all the proposed technological solutions, fusion appears to be the most promising, surprisingly inexpensive, encouragingly clean, and safe source of energy. The earth's waters could be easily made to yield deuterium as fusion fuel, with an ounce of the isotope producing in an hour's burning the same energy that results from the consumption of three hundred tons of coal.

A boldly innovative aspect of the KMS approach is the idea of utilizing fusion neutrons not to produce electricity, as almost everyone else in fusion research wants to do, but to produce methane, the principal ingredient in natural gas. The others' standard plan is to capture the "hot," fast-flying neutrons and then use the heat they generate to make steam and electricity in a conventional, time-tested way. Such somewhat cumbersome coupling of the newest technology with an old existing one has often blurred the vision of innovators. But it has become the standard approach in almost all fields. The tractor, for instance, was designed to match the width and to imitate the linear plodding of a plowhorse and to pull implements designed for the horse. In keeping with "the tractor must resemble the horse" syndrome, in proposed "hydrogen economy" visions, specialists until now have talked about making nuclear electricity first and then using the electric energy to produce hydrogen. KMS wants to bypass that wasteful intermediate step. Instead of going to fusion electricity, KMS would go directly to hydrogen production with neutrons by breaking down water into its constituent elements, hydrogen and oxygen. The hydrogen would then be converted into methane by conventional techniques, and methane could be put straight into the nation's pipelines.

This clever idea evokes admiration from experts who until now have talked about a "hydrogen economy" in which hydrogen would be substituted for natural gas in a horrendously complex and enormously expensive scheme that would require extensive changeover in distribution lines, storage facilities, pumping stations, household appliances, and other hardware. The "methane economy" that KMS is preaching would in contrast neatly supplement our diminishing supplies of natural gas—which is more than 80 percent methane—while leaving pipelines, pumps, and appliances intact. Interestingly, KMS Fusion is already producing hydrogen "by the thimbleful and bucketful," as Siegel once put it, with neutrons from conventional accelerators, in an effort to prove out the process.

Since fusion can generate more energy per pound of fuel than any other reaction, the use of fusion neutrons to produce hydrogen could be an inexpensive and highly efficient process. The lack of cheap hydrogen has been an impediment to economic coal gasification. With inexpensive fusion-generated hydrogen, it would be possible to produce methane cheaply and abundantly by making hydrogen react with coal or with carbon derived from limestone. "If it works," says the chairman of Texas Gas Transmission Corporation, a pipeline company that supports research at KMS Fusion, "it will be like the invention of the electric light."

Siegel and his associates figured that by taking the shortcut from pellet to pipeline, their company could cut years from the development of economic fusion power. The design of a methane generator would be simpler than that of an electricity-generating fusion plant. Scientists at KMS Fusion talk about having a pilot methane generator operating by about 1980 if the company gets enough financial and technical help from the government and from larger companies. Most researchers at the successor agencies to the AEC and at universities consider such optimism nothing short of reckless. Although they admire the technical achievements at KMS Fusion, these experts, almost to a man, don't see a demonstration power reactor until the mid-1900s.

Crucial tests to settle the issue will be performed in the near future. Ignition will be a critical step. After that must come "scientific break-even," where the flux of energetic neutrons and alpha particles from the fusion process equals the energy in the laser beam applied on the pellet. Another steep height to be scaled will be "total break-even," or "engineering break-even," where the energy produced by the pellet exceeds the energy put into the overall system that powers the laser. After that comes the tough engineering task of developing the fusion reactor.

So far, KMS Fusion has invested $23 million in laser fusion.

Some outsiders doubt the company's ability to survive what they view as a long and arduous race. Siegel, who shortly before his death put the cost of a methane pilot plant at about $75 million, readily conceded the possibility of having to drop out. "You are not talking to a corporation whose future is assured," he said, "and as chief executive I have told that to my shareholders."

The answer to the question of what such a small company is doing in such an expensive and demanding field involves the ambitions and dreams of Kip Siegel. He was energized by a pressing need to be liked, praised, and appreciated. Siegel was born on January 9, 1923, in New York City, the son of a prominent attorney. As a boy, he loved to watch his father perform in a courtroom and he hoped to become a lawyer. When Kip was thirteen, however, Supreme Court Justice Louis Brandeis, a family friend, advised him first to get a degree in mathematics or physics, even if he intended to become a lawyer. That set Siegel on his scientific path. He majored in mathematics at Rensselaer Polytechnic Institute and after graduation in 1948 joined the faculty of the University of Michigan, eventually becoming head of the radiation laboratory. He became a recognized expert in electromagnetics, but he had long cherished the dream of building a major corporation. In November 1960 Siegel wrote letters to a number of companies he thought might want to support him, telling them that he was planning to start a company. He accepted an offer from a technical subsidiary of Paramount Pictures to back him and started a firm he called Conductron that would specialize in radar, optics, and electronics. Siegel put $12,000 of his own money into the enterprise. Siegel's instant grasp of scientific and business problems helped the company prosper; in the end he made at least $4 million from it. But his pleasures were rather simple. When his fellow executives had bought big houses, Kip was still living in a small development home. Later he did move to a bigger house and occasionally indulged in a hobby. Being something of a gambler, he became part owner of a stable of trotters and liked to watch his horses run.

At Conductron he got accustomed to dealing with an unbelieving world. He proposed a technique to make the nose cones of American missiles less vulnerable to enemy radar. Some scientists said it couldn't be done, but Siegel went ahead and proved it could. His company also developed the so-called side-view radar—airborne mapping radar that utilizes an antenna that "looks" down from the side of an airplane at the terrain below. This was another project that some people said would never work.

His laser-fusion venture was, of course, a far bigger gamble, for Siegel had to put his successful company on the block, piece by piece, to support his bet. He managed to attract two high-powered backers: Burmah Oil Company, Ltd., the giant Scottish concern, and Texas Gas Transmission Corporation, a Kentucky-based pipeline company. Burmah Oil has committed $12.5 million to KMS Fusion so far, while Texas Gas supports research into hydrogen production with neutrons to the extent of about $1 million a year. To fill in the huge financial gaps, in addition to selling off divisions of the parent company, Siegel put about $3 million of his own into KMS Fusion, and he naturally stood to lose it all if the company failed.

Siegel had had no intention of getting into laser fusion or presiding over the liquidation of a successful company in order to nourish a dream when he started KMS Industries, KMS Fusion's parent firm, in 1967. He had earlier merged Conductron, a profitable company, into McDonnell Aircraft. After a disagreement with chairman James S. ("Mr. Mac") McDonnell, Siegel had resigned. He thought he had come up with the best merchandising idea of his life. Under a plan he was negotiating with Montgomery Ward, Conductron was to manufacture half of the big retailer's radios, stereo, and television sets for ten years under a known-cost contract with a percentage of the profit. "I was sitting in heaven," recalled Siegel, who had a habit of closing his eyes and reclining in his chair when he spoke at length. "I saw Conductron growing from $50 million to $200 million in sales. I felt I had put together the greatest deal of my life." One of the sidebars was a Siegel proposal for a new kind of advertising. He thought he could create with holography—the laser-generated imagery—three-dimensional pictures of giant-sized soft-drink bottles, automobiles, and other objects hanging in the air on the sidewalks right in front of stores to attract customers. People could walk right through these ghostly images.

Mr. Mac had other pressing business. He was tied up with his long-desired acquisition of Douglas Aircraft. He asked Siegel to postpone his proposed expansion. Feeling that such an opportunity would never again present itself to Conductron—"Life is made up of few opportunities"—Siegel resigned, a shattered man.

Siegel recovered with amazing speed, for it took him only a week to get KMS Industries started. The new company, named after Siegel's initials, deliberately shied away from defense business. Doing it the second time around, Siegel avoided the pitfalls that befall most new high-technology enterprises. He assembled a pool of scientists—many followed him from Conductron—and began inserting them into old, experienced, but technically backward companies that he acquired with KMS stock. His idea was to invigorate these old-line firms with new technological skills and products and have them market their new products through their established sales channels. To help him run Conductron, Siegel had hired a "bunch of professors," as a KMS executive puts it. But when he started KMS Industries, he lured about a dozen presidents and executive vice presidents from various companies to run KMS divisions. He was determined again to build a major corporation.

The idea worked so well that KMS Industries reached sales of $13 million in its first year and leaped to $59 million in its second, partly thanks to acquisitions. During 1967–69, KMS Industries acquired no less than thirty-two companies, ranging from book producers to optics makers. Few opportunities to make money escaped Siegel's attention. Once when he noticed that KMS Industries had some mathematicians with time on their hands, he put them to work designing mathematical games and toys in their spare time. He could see significant growth ahead for his science conglomerate. Then in 1969 he discovered laser fusion.

The concept of harnessing the power that rages in an uncontrolled fashion in a hydrogen bomb (where an atom bomb serves as the fusion trigger) had occurred to a brilliant weapons designer named John Nuckolls in the late 1950s. At the Lawrence Livermore Laboratory, Nuckolls hit upon the idea of microscopic fusion explosions that could propel spaceships as well as power earth-based plants. Beginning early in 1960, Nuckolls made a series of computer calculations. He figured that the deuterium-tritium fuel contained in a microscopic capsule would have to be compressed and imploded to tremendous densities to start the fusion reaction before the fuel flies apart. He sought a computer answer to the question of how small a microexplosion would be feasible and what sort of power source would be needed to implode the capsules.

That same year, 1960, the laser was invented. Nuckolls's work was secret, but scientists in both the United States and the Soviet Union soon began to discuss publicly the idea of blasting hydrogen plasma and pellets of fuel with laser beams. "Anyone with imagination who worried about the laser would give it at least enough thought to put some numbers on the blackboard," said Siegel. Some of his Conductron scientists wrote papers on laser fusion. But all the publicly aired ideas talked about simply heating the fuel; Nuckolls's notion of compressing and imploding it remained classified.

Under Nuckolls's prodding, a small and secret effort on laser fusion got underway at Livermore. It culminated in 1965 in the construction of a ten-beam ruby laser for compressing and imploding pellets of hydrogen. The laser beams were to converge on a tiny pellet inside a firing chamber and compress and heat it to more than 100 million degrees Fahrenheit to start the explosive fusion reaction. But the Livermore scientists encountered serious problems in synchronizing the laser, which wasn't powerful enough for the job anyway, and gave up on the attempt. Secret studies by Nuckolls and other AEC specialists continued, however. But the results remained so tightly classified that even some high AEC officials apparently didn't know about them or didn't believe in them. As late as the summer of 1969 an AEC advisory committee reached the negative conclusion that while laser concepts seemed interesting, they appeared to have no practical significance. Among other things it was believed that lasers of tremendous power would be needed; the fact that Nuckolls had concluded that fusion could be achieved with much less laser energy remained classified.

In what must appear as a comedy of errors, the two major AEC

105

laboratories, Livermore and Los Alamos, were represented at that meeting by men who didn't take the possibility of laser fusion seriously. Livermore's representative was a laser specialist, while Los Alamos had sent a scientist working on magnetic confinement of plasma. Ironically, even as these scientists were drawing negative conclusions, Nuckolls and his associates were refining their calculations and had arrived at an even better implosion scheme. But Nuckolls's work wasn't even partially declassified until 1972, and then only after Soviet scientists started publishing papers about compression of pellets.

It isn't surprising that the AEC consultant who chaired that meeting came away from it perplexed. The consultant, Keith A. Brueckner, an imaginative and gifted nuclear physicist, had earlier served as an adviser to the Livermore Laboratory. He knew Nuckolls and had even discussed the compression-implosion idea as it applies to nuclear weapons with him years earlier. But Brueckner didn't know about Nuckolls's interest in laser fusion or about Nuckolls's set of calculations that revealed the theoretical possibility of laser-driven fusion. Brueckner had tried to prod the AEC into getting an active laser-fusion program under way. After the unproductive meeting he could only conclude that the AEC had no serious interest in laser fusion for commercial applications. The commission by that time had a vested interest in achieving fusion through magnetic confinement of plasma; it had invested hundreds of millions of dollars and years of work into it.

Its lack of excitement about laser fusion was all the more strange since, Brueckner knew, Soviet and other European scientists pursued an active program in the field. In fact, Nikolai Basov, the Soviet Nobelist and co-inventor of the laser, in 1968 had already reported getting some neutrons from heating a pellet of hydrogen. That same year, in his capacity as an AEC consultant, Brueckner had attended a meeting at Novosibirsk where French and Italian scientists gave papers on laser fusion. Starting that year, Brueckner had divided his time between the KMS Technology Center in Irvine, California, a subsidiary of KMS Industries, where he had become a part-time employee, and teaching at the University of California at San Diego. (He spent about eight days a year as an

AEC consultant.) One of the projects Brueckner worked on at KMS was an evaluation for the defense department of the French and Italian laser-fusion calculations to see if a great flux of neutrons could be released to simulate nuclear explosions. Siegel had worked on this contract, too, and the two men quickly established that the French-Italian approach would not lead to a significant neutron production. Siegel suggested to Brueckner not to renew the contract because of the negative findings. Brueckner, intrigued by the possibilities of laser fusion, asked what it would take for KMS to continue to work in the field. "A new idea," said Siegel.

Brueckner went beyond the French-Italian approach of simply heating the pellet. He calculated that if the pellet were made to implode with laser beams converging on it, high compression and neutron production would be the result. He didn't realize that Nuckolls at Livermore had arrived at the same conclusion almost ten years earlier. Just as cognizant as the AEC was about the laser's potential use as a trigger to set off a hydrogen bomb, Soviet scientists had also refrained from mentioning the implosion-compression concept in public print. Basov had obtained fusion neutrons in 1968 not from compression of the pellet but from a hot corona created around the pellet by the laser beams.

Excited by Brueckner's apparent discovery, Siegel and Brueckner approached the AEC. They assumed that Brueckner's results could not be patented because of the possible role of laser fusion as an H-bomb trigger and other weapons applications. To their surprise, the AEC's research director urged them to file patents since it seemed to him that they had arrived at conclusions different from those of the AEC labs. Actually, as Nuckolls says, the research director didn't know what he was getting into. The news of KMS's entry into laser fusion hit the AEC labs like a time bomb; after all, Nuckolls had pioneered the approach almost ten years earlier. What's more, the AEC suddenly realized that Brueckner's ideas touched on its own secret work aimed at a potential use of the laser as an H-bomb trigger. (Even today, that concept remains impractical because a laser costing perhaps $10 million and so big that it would have to be shipped by a freighter would be needed as a bomb trigger. As Brueckner says, "You could do more damage by dropping the laser than by dropping the bomb.")

Brueckner and KMS got caught in the whiplash. At first the AEC tried to talk them out of entering the field. Siegel wouldn't budge. Then the AEC tried a different tack. The commission's assistant security chief tracked down Brueckner at a scientific meeting in Florida. The security man flashed a classified letter directing KMS to stop its laser-fusion research because the work fell into the classified area. The AEC conceded that it couldn't stop Brueckner from thinking, but instructed him to stop discussing the ideas with his co-workers. He was also prohibited from doing any calculations, except in his head.

The AEC hadn't counted on Kip Siegel's determination, however. Siegel seemed to thrive on trouble. "He operated best when the situation got the toughest," says a former colleague. The fact that laser fusion was such a big field didn't faze him at all. He felt that once the country recognized there was an energy crisis, financial backers—both industry and government—would flock to KMS to support its work. Accordingly, Siegel decided to fight the AEC, after checking first with KMS Industries' principal financial backers, John Hancock Mutual Life Insurance Company and White Weld, the Wall Street investment house. He hired some high-powered attorneys and lobbyists, including former AEC secretary Roy Snapp and former air force secretary and AEC commissioner Eugene Zuckert. He also wrote a letter to President Nixon. This enlisted in his cause Lee DuBridge, then the president's science adviser, who asked the AEC to reconsider the matter. Glenn Seaborg, then chairman of the AEC, said he wouldn't stand in the way of research, and the commission voted four to one to allow KMS to proceed with some limited studies without access to government information, without government funds, but under government control. At first the AEC allowed only some paper and pencil studies. Six months later it permitted KMS to use a computer for these studies, but since the field was classified, KMS had to issue a contract to the AEC that would allow the company to use a classified computer facility in New Mexico.

Slowly the AEC eased its restrictions and in February 1971 gave

KMS a no-fee contract that in effect amounted to a license to work in the field, the first such contract ever given to a private company. KMS would get no AEC funds or technical data and would have no access to AEC facilities or equipment. But the AEC could use KMS findings if they applied to weapons work. The company was required to classify documents, materials, or equipment it generated in its work, and all its employees had to have an AEC security clearance. It had to act, in short, as if it were an AEC laboratory. AEC also reserved the right to contest any patent issued to KMS since it claimed that Brueckner got his ideas in the course of being a government consultant.

The toughest provision prohibited KMS from hiring any scientist, technician, or engineer who had ever worked in federal laser-fusion or nuclear-weapons programs. The AEC interpreted this provision literally. Once, KMS officials recall, when they submitted a list of fifteen proposed employees, the agency turned down thirteen; it approved only the two secretaries on the list. This effectively limited KMS Fusion's hiring to new college graduates.

To infuse leadership into this young group, Brueckner took a leave of absence from his teaching post and he and five other scientists from the Technology Center in California moved to Ann Arbor late in 1971. To strengthen further the newly organized KMS Fusion, Inc., Siegel had brought in as its president a veteran nuclear physicist, Henry J. Gomberg. Once head of the University of Michigan Department of Nuclear Engineering, Gomberg had battled atomic bureacrats before. He successfully had led the construction of the largest nuclear reactor built with private funds at the university at the time fission research was largely shrouded in secrecy. Gomberg at that time had also obtained a small private grant for a young physicist, Donald Glaser, who had an idea that the experts at the AEC had turned down. That grant helped Glaser invent the bubble chamber, a nuclear measuring device, for which he received the Nobel Prize.

The employment situation at KMS Fusion eased significantly toward the end of 1971 when Gomberg requested from the AEC a new interpretation of the AEC contract. He found a receptive listener in James Schlesinger, who had just become AEC chairman.

Schlesinger had quickly noticed that KMS seemed to be a permanent item on the AEC agenda. It struck him as ridiculous that the five AEC commissioners had to meet to approve the hiring of a stenographer by a small private company. Schlesinger made a new interpretation of the AEC contract so that KMS could now hire scientists who had left AEC or defense jobs two years earlier.

Delayed in its schedule by the AEC for about two years, KMS could only now begin large-scale work. From Compagnie Générale d'Electricité in France, it bought for $1 million the biggest and most powerful commercially available laser. It could be made to discharge a one-kilojoule pulse of light in three nanoseconds, or billionths of a second. This laser, made of glass tinted with a touch of the rare-earth element neodymium, was so large that it could only be flown from Paris to New York in a Boeing 747. It was then shipped in specially equipped vans to Ann Arbor.

A laser amplifies its emitted radiation and can be made to fire a highly directed beam at a target. But how to ensure the microscopic pellet is bathed in laser light equally from all sides, to compress the pellet symmetrically? The approach chosen by most laser-fusion researchers is to split the initial laser beam into a number of subbeams and have them converge on the target from as many directions as possible. The Soviets are using a nine-beam neodymium-glass laser and are building one with twenty-seven beams. At Livermore, when a huge laser to be housed in a three-story building is completed in 1977, researchers will use ten or twelve beams to blast laser pellets. While this approach increases uniform illumination, it introduces the great difficulty of synchronizing the firing of the beams in the realm of billionths and trillionths of a second to hit a target the size of a grain of dust all at once. Siegel called the multiple-laser beam approach "the Parkinson's law of lasers." Since KMS had to accomplish the most for the least cost, it decided to split its laser beam only once and then illuminate the pellet from all directions using mirrors and lenses. Brueckner directed the design of this apparatus; the leader of a rival laser-fusion team calls it "clearly the nicest two-beam focusing system in the world today." Using this system, KMS scientists were able to compensate through uniform illumination for low laser power.

Another important advance was a pioneering device called a "pulse stacker," which shapes the ultra-short laser pulse so that it can be made to fit the pellet surface perfectly. With this instrument, the ultra-short laser pulse can be stretched accordionlike so that when the pulse hits the pellet the pressure is applied in a graduated way. Without a "pulse stacker," the laser's short blast would hit the pellet like a hammer. The first such device in the world, the pulse stacker has been a key in KMS's success. Its absence in the AEC labs is one reason they have lagged behind. "If a laser doesn't have this control," says Brueckner, "it becomes an extremely inefficient device for laser fusion."

KMS also started developing new types of the microscopic fuel pellets and learning how to mass-produce them. This was no easy task since it involves extremely high tolerances and the use of radioactive tritium gas. The gas is infused into the tiny glass spheres, which are barely visible to the naked eye, by heating them and is trapped inside after the pellets are cooled. KMS has mastered the process to an extent that it can mass-produce the pellets for less than one-hundredth of a cent.

Financially, however, it was about the worst time for KMS Industries to gamble on the tantalizing dream of laser fusion. Shortly after Siegel fell in love with fusion, his company suddenly found itself gazing into a financial abyss. Its major creditor, Commonwealth Bank of Detroit, ran afoul of federal authorities and, trying to recoup its losses, seized on a minor technical violation by KMS to convert its $15 million term loan to a demand loan repayable in about six months. Adding to the trouble, John Hancock, which had purchased a $5 million twenty-year convertible debenture, decided it wanted its money back; the insurance company had at first agreed to support KMS but later got a new chairman who was wary of the fusion venture. On top of that, the 1969 recession began. Conglomerates seemed to be going out of style and some KMS divisions weren't doing too well. KMS stock plummeted from a high of $60 a share to $10.

Getting tied up with Commonwealth was one of Siegel's worst business errors. But he was fast on his feet and he started selling off divisons both to pay off the debts and to start the fusion project going. "I think Kip and his associates did a Herculean job with the gun at their temples in winding down and paying it off in the threat of having the loan called," says a friend. "The bank was paid back in full. Most companies caught in that kind of a pincer move don't get a second lease on life."

Siegel had estimated that it would take $50 million to take laser fusion to practical demonstration. So he now turned some of his considerable sales magic on private companies to enlist them as backers. In Ann Arbor, Siegel had a friend and admirer in A. P. Fontaine, a one-time University of Michigan professor who had originally brought Siegel to the university (Siegel was often addressed as "professor"). Fontaine had by then become chairman of the Bendix Corporation and was prepared to invest $10 million of his company's money into the fusion venture, contingent upon participation of other corporations.

Siegel began talking with other big companies. For one reason or another, the potential investors hesitated. There was the lingering patent controversy with the AEC. It didn't help when a hostile AEC commissioner told the *Wall Street Journal* that KMS "essentially stole our patents." (Years later the man insisted he really didn't mean it.) Actually there were no patents in the area because the AEC had considered weapons-related discoveries not to be patentable. But the accusations put a chill into the investment environment. The enormity of the unknown and the AEC's often expressed feeling that KMS was using a faulty technical approach also helped scare off potential investors. KMS wound up almost without any backers at all. Regulatory approval of Bendix's proposed entry dragged on for almost a year, until November 1971. By that time Fontaine was near retirement and Bendix's new chief executive, A. M. Blumenthal, wasn't too excited about laser fusion. Bendix dropped out.

Income from sales of divisions kept KMS Fusion in business. Siegel also kept pumping his own money into the operation. Out-

112

side scientists admire this commitment. "They are really putting their money where their mouth is," says John Emmett, a young physicist who directs laser research at Livermore. This dedication understandably found less admiration on the part of some of the executives of KMS divisions being sold off. "To keep the morale up while the company is on the block, so to speak," says Robert A. Olsen, president of KMS Industries and its chief financial officer, "is very, very difficult." The divisions were being starved for cash, which was being diverted into fusion. To ease the problems somewhat, Olsen stretched out their payables and sometimes leased equipment for them instead of buying it. "But we kept them pretty tight," he says. "If they criticized me, I'd say I'd go back to the board and ask them to cut back on fusion. They didn't want that done since they had stock in the company."

In most cases Olsen tried to sell the divisions to previous owners and often succeeded. Graphic Services went back to its original owners for $1.7 million. So did the lens division, for $896,000. A few months later, Vail-Ballou, a book-manufacturing company, was sold to Maple Press for $4.8 million. The divisions went fast after that; five were sold in 1970, eight in 1971, and five each in 1972 and 1973. Today KMS Industries has only four divisions left, counting fusion. And it is seeking to dispose of the remaining non-fusion work. With sale of divisions, KMS sales have fallen from a high of $59 million in 1969 to $4.8 million in 1974; its stock declined to an all-time low of 1½ in 1973, then rose slightly in 1974 and 1975. But the company took in $33 million from this "cannibalizing," as Siegel called it, enough to pay off $20 million in debts to its bank and to John Hancock and to have money left over for fusion research. To keep up its pace of spending about $5 million a year for fusion, KMS obviously needed outside help. This finally came in 1972 when Texas Gas Transmission Corporation approached KMS. William E. Elmer, chairman of Texas Gas, and his associates had long been concerned over the dismaying possibility that the company's natural gas pipelines would be only half full in 1980. Texas Gas had settled on coal gasification as a means of producing additional natural gas, but it needed a cheap source of hydrogen to process the coal. Now KMS could see that it could go directly to making hydrogen and methane with fusion neutrons. This would simplify the design of the pilot plant.

Texas Gas so far has invested about $3 million into the experimental generation of hydrogen with neutrons. In this process, which both companies consider proprietary, chemicals are apparently added to water to assure its easier breakdown with neutrons into hydrogen and oxygen. Testing of hydrogen production with neutrons from a conventional source is already taking place at the full temperatures and pressures required in a pilot plant. The pilot plant will cost about $75 million. Texas Gas appears ready to invest the money if the fusion work proceeds as planned. "This could be a hundred times more important than coal gasification," says Elmer. Not only would fusion-produced natural gas be substantially cheaper than gas from coal, but cheap hydrogen and methane furthermore could be used as basic building blocks for the chemical industry. "It would be worth almost anything," adds Elmer. "It disturbs me to see the tremendous amounts of money being talked about for Project Independence and here is a potential solution and the government is not giving much help to make it go," he frets.

In late 1973 Siegel achieved another *coup* when he signed on Burmah Oil, the huge British petroleum concern. In a complex deal, Burmah has so far contributed $12.5 million to KMS Fusion and had an option to buy 20 percent of the company for $20 million, depending on whether KMS reached "total breakeven" in energy production by a set date. Its own and Burmah's money allowed KMS Fusion to construct and equip a "shooting gallery," the only such operational facility in this country, where the riflelike cracks of laser firings resound as the tiny pellets are being blasted in a vacuum chamber at the rate of about ten shots a day.

Brueckner's calculations had looked so good that Siegel had expansively predicted that KMS would achieve scientific break-even by December 31, 1973. But the technical problems turned out to be tougher than expected. By the end of 1973 KMS Fusion was still far from scientific break-even, although it could report some slight compressions of the pellets, without generating "true" fusion neutrons (the neutrons can also be generated by simply heating the corona that forms around the pellet). The Russians were reporting similar results. The climax of KMS Fusion's drive for what Siegel called "the most neutrons for the buck" came at 4:30 P.M. on May 1, 1974. The pop of pellet shot number 1036 had just sounded through the "shooting gallery" when Roy Johnson, a young physicist who supervises the experiments, tore off a Polaroid print from a recording camera and shouted somewhat hysterically, "We've got neutrons!"

Other instruments were also indicating that the pellet had been compressed and imploded. If they were right, KMS scientists were the first in the world to see laser fusion taking place on a tiny scale. Brueckner went out and returned with a case of champagne for the scientific crew. (This team has been so close-knit that only one scientist and one engineer ever left KMS Fusion, and both were fired. The company now employs 120 people, of whom 39 have doctorates.)

Siegel called Robert Hofstadter, a Nobel Prize–winning physicist at Stanford University, whom he had recruited to be KMS Fusion's "test monitor." Hofstadter then directed the big high-energy accelerator laboratory at Stanford. He flew in to observe additional tests. The experiment was successfully repeated four times before KMS reported the facts to the AEC, which reviews KMS's progress and all its public statements. The scientist who directed laser-fusion research for the AEC suggested the company should include in its news release the word "unambiguously" when referring to the origin of the neutrons as being released from the core of the pellet. The news hit other laboratories like a bomb. Scientists generally frown on release of scientific data before its publication in the journals. Accordingly, some accused KMS of creating a ballyhoo to atttact investors. The SEC, of course, requires companies to release such data to the public; this conflicts with the scientific procedure. Some other scientists accused KMS of withholding data, but they did not know that the AEC had withheld it for reasons of "security." For example, the AEC declassified the fact that KMS had been using a new kind of a pellet, a glass sphere filled with hydrogen isotopes, only in September 1974. One newspaper not familiar with the AEC's role in the disclosures even claimed that the AEC had questioned the use of the word "unambiguously" in the KMS news release. There were other ill-informed press reports.

The skepticism generally faded after a large contingent of AEC scientists came to KMS for a briefing and after KMS showed it could repeat the neutron-yielding compressions easily. "These are the best laser implosion experiments so far," says Nuckolls. In those tests, KMS scientists got about 300,000 neutrons in most successful shots and had compressed the pellets one hundred times by volume. This was still trillions of neutrons and hundreds of additional compressions away from break-even. But the feat had been achieved with an average sixty joules of laser power, a remarkably small amount. What pleases Brueckner and other KMS scientists is that predicted plasma instabilities and other problems either didn't show up or were manageable. Such instabilities and other difficulties could have been "devastating," in Brueckner's words. Continuing to scale up compressions and neutron yields, by the end of October 1974 KMS had achieved compressions of 250 and obtained 7 million neutrons per shot, indicating it is going in the right direction. The next big step would be a thermonuclear burn. That would yield 100 billion neutrons but would still be only 1/100 of break-even. But Gomberg adds that if KMS can sustain that drive, "with proper funding we can have a methane pilot plant by 1980."

To get to that exciting peak, Siegel drove himself relentlessly. He often worked night after night and thought nothing of staying up until 3 A.M. at home to finish a paper. Being a good-natured person who saw good in everyone, he remained surprisingly serene through all the trials and the ridicule. He showed no visible scars of the battles. Arriving half an hour late for a speech in Toledo, Ohio, one day in 1974 because he had been given imprecise directions, he remained calm even when he noticed that the meeting's organizer had distributed to those present copies of a nearly three-year-old *Wall Street Journal* story entitled "Nuclear Fantasy?" The story had sneered at Siegel's past activities, implying that he was a fast operator, and suggested that KMS Fusion was little more than a movie set. Siegel later mildly complained to a companion about such an old article being circulated again. Siegel's performance in business actually had been pretty good; Conductron never had a losing year when he was there and KMS registered its first loss year only after it went into fusion.

Some friends suspect that Siegel's unforgiving pace helped bring on the cerebral hemorrhage that felled him at age fifty-two. His colleagues at KMS Fusion were fortunate, however, because, as Dr. Gomberg puts it, "Kip did carry us through the most critical period. Now, if we don't make it, it will be our fault. But we don't expect we'll have to face that." Dr. Gomberg continues as president of KMS Fusion, while Dr. Russell D. O'Neal has taken Siegel's place at the helm of KMS Industries as chairman and chief executive officer.

Siegel was smart enough to have brought in capable men so his companies could continue. O'Neal, Siegel's old friend, was hired originally to direct the eventual methane pilot-plant construction. He brought a rich experience in both research and management to KMS Industries. A nuclear engineer by training, he once ran Bendix Corporation's domestic operations and has also served as an assistant secretary of the army in charge of research and development.

When O'Neal learned of Siegel's death, he and Robert Olsen, now president of KMS Industries, addressed KMS Fusion's staff in the long, low-ceiling laboratory. "Let's continue what Kip has started," said O'Neal, "and let's make it a great success." Some scientists worked until 1 A.M. Saturday morning—a dedication one is unlikely to find in a big company.

Most government scientists by 1975 had acknowledged KMS Fusion's scientific leadership at least temporarily. "It was enough trouble for them to acknowledge our existence." remarks Gomberg. But Nuckolls .and some others still raised questions whether KMS Fusion can keep up the pace; the company hopes to achieve ignition and scientific break-even in the next year or so.

In sunny Livermore they proudly point to a big hole in the ground where a three-story building will rise to house the huge laser. Government scientists there express doubt that KMS can move as fast as it says it can. "KMS," says Nuckolls, "has come out of the starting gate with a quarter horse in a mile race. The race has gone about a quarter of a mile so far and just watch the next quarter. I think they have about run their horse out. Now the longer-running horses can take over."

Nuckolls means that the KMS laser is not powerful enough for KMS to get much further, but he admits that he doesn't really know whether scientific break-even can be achieved with a laser that size. It's a difficult time to be a theoretician in this fast-moving field, and KMS Fusion appears to be rewriting the theory. The AEC badly underestimated KMS when it blandly stated in 1971: "We do not foresee KMS proceeding at a pace in advance of our laboratories. We do not believe it will be possible for such a firm to compete with the vast experience and resources of our laboratories."

So far, KMS Fusion has proved the AEC wrong. Gomberg adds: "And we expect to stay in the lead. We don't see it as a mile race with one horse—we think it's a relay race. We're going to put in four quarter horses. They'll never catch us." Gomberg was talking about a big new laser that KMS was installing in 1975, with five times the power of its original laser. His belief furthermore is bolstered by the big government contract that KMS Fusion finally received in 1975. The new laser should enable the company to scale up neutron yields dramatically, moving closer to those important milestones.

But even if the company soon attains a net energy gain with its present laser, a number of tough engineering barriers stand in the way of a laser-fusion reactor. The laser would have to fire at pellets at a rate of as many as six thousand times a minute. No such laser exists today, although there are prospects under development.

Another difficult task is designing reactor chamber walls that would withstand the constant battering by neutrons and alpha particles and the mechanical strains of millions of consecutive pellet explosions, each amounting to several pounds of TNT. But KMS believes that it has made significant progress in designing reactor walls for hydrogen production. Siegel once dismissed other scientists' doubts with an optimistic "What they think are hard problems aren't." In his view the problems KMS faced were no longer scientific. "I don't think it's science anymore. It's financial breakeven," Siegel said.

Even before it showed that significant energy could be produced by its approach, KMS Fusion began to explore some other money-making possibilities. It has signed a marketing agreement with General Electric under which the two firms will supply companies, universities, and other countries with copies of KMS Fusion's "shooting gallery." Among potential buyers is Saudi Arabia. The Arabs, looking ahead to the time when their oil wells will run dry, appear to exhibit more foresight about the future of energy supplies than Uncle Sam does. Another possibility is to build medical units for cancer treatment with fast neutrons as a kind of a new, much more efficient surgeon's scalpel. Still another possible use of fusion neutrons is to impart new properties to electronic and other materials. Of course, attainment of full-fledged fusion power remains the company's primary goal. Scientists around the world see the prospects for achieving it as being much brighter today because of Kip Siegel's dedication to a dream.

CHAPTER SIX

Alejandro Zaffaroni:
Visionary on a Golden Shoestring

Among the thousands of post–World War II high-technology entrepreneurs, Alejandro Zaffaroni towers like a giant because of his
dazzling accomplishments in *both* science and finance. Some
spectacular performers have streaked across the economic skies in
recent years only to fade into obscurity. Perhaps the most famous,
James Ling, a Dallas-based manipulator of companies and financial structures, parlayed a $2,000 stake into LTV Corporation, at
one time the fourteenth-largest company in America. But Ling
and others like him were building on sand. Their abilities, no
matter how great, were limited to one sphere, and they thrived,
and wilted, with the stock market.

Far less known, Zaffaroni, like the other innovators in this
book, is a genuine builder of solid new companies that not only
are revolutionizing their industries but also are improving our
lives. He has chosen as his area of innovation one of the most difficult of fields: the drug industry, where giant companies dominate
the markets by compounding powerful new medicines and tightly
holding on to them with patents. It would seem to be the least
promising place to start a new company. For one thing, the costs
of medical research can be astronomical. But that hasn't deterred
Zaffaroni, a Uruguayan-born biochemist and businessman, from
building an extraordinary company in Palo Alto, California. Other
men may dream of castles in the sky, but Alex Zaffaroni, as he is
known to friends and associates, builds his particular castles and

sells portions of them to investors for millions of dollars. With a mind that soars where few others venture, the articulate, distinguished-looking Zaffaroni operates in the hazardous, uncharted terrain where new companies and technologies are born as if it were the most familiar ground. He does it with immense confidence because he has long worked with great success as a mapmaker and explorer of unknown business and technical continents and has been building superhighways and daring bridges in those virgin lands.

Even before his Alza Corporation marketed a single product, Zaffaroni raised the phenomenal sum of $52 million, with a large portion coming from institutional investors and wealthy men eager to finance his ideas. Attracting bright young researchers from many parts of the world, he has assembled as unlikely a team of scientists and engineers as any drug company has ever seen—polymer chemists, mechanical engineers, physicists, and other professionals strange to the drug businsess. And he is trying to introduce an entirely new scientific approach to the ancient art of administering drugs—an approach so radical that he counts for his success on revolutionizing medical practice itself.

Zaffaroni's idea is to seize an opening left by a strange anomaly in the development of medicine. Over the years, especially since the discovery of the so-called wonder drugs, the pharmaceutical companies have developed increasingly powerful potions to fight disease. Yet the methods used to deliver these drugs to affected organs in the body have not kept pace. We still depend predominantly on pills, which the Egyptians were popping in their mouths in the days of the Pharaohs—as long ago as the fifteenth century B.C.

The gap has become dangerous. A pill must contain thousands, even tens of thousands, times more medication than is needed at the target organ. The drug contained in a pill must survive the attack of the digestive enzymes, penetrate the stomach and intestinal walls, and pass through that efficient filtering plant, the liver. It flows through 60,000 miles of arteries, capillaries, and other tubing, reaching all sorts of organs to which it is *not* directed and often causing undesirable side effects. The approach is about as sensible as flooding a skyscraper to put out a fire in a wastebasket in a tiny office cubicle. Small wonder that ailments induced by drugs intended as cures are responsible for an increasing number of hospital admissions. And the problem is intensifying as more and more people depend on long-term, even life-long, administration of potent medications, to control blood pressure, a diabetic condition, or to assure contraception.

Zaffaroni believes what society needs is not more powerful drugs but better ways of delivering those already in existence, particularly better utilization of the body's own healing substances. He has set his mind to developing novel devices as complex and as fascinating as microminiaturized spaceships, designed to release in minute amounts a finely controlled flow of medication as directly as possible to the affected organ, cutting down on dangers of side effects and greatly increasing the efficacy and convenience of therapy. Now, after nearly a decade of work, Zaffaroni has brought Alza to a point where it has won regulatory approval to begin selling its first products abroad and in the United States.

The first of these products, appropriately invented by Zaffaroni himself,* is a tiny oval reservoir called an Ocusert, which contains an antiglaucoma drug; a patient can wear it under his lower eyelid. A single Ocusert lasts a week, and it controls glaucoma by administering, in a steady flow, about one-tenth the amount of pilocarpine, a drug normally taken as eyedrops four times a day. The quantity is tailored to a patient's need. Another product is a birth-control device, a kind of successor to the pill. It is inserted into the uterus, where for an entire year it steadily releases amounts of progesterone so minute that they equal the medication contained in just three of the daily birth-control pills. Since the progesterone is not circulating in the body, the side effects associated with the pill appear to be eliminated.

Born a banker's son in Montevideo on February 27, 1923, Alex Zaffaroni in his childhood and adolescence was mainly interested,

---

* Zaffaroni had invented the device but after checking the literature found that an ophthalmologist in Minnesota had patented a similar idea. Alza then acquired the patent.

123

as he recalls, in enjoying "life at large." He exhibited no liking of
finance, despite his father's occupation. A cousin who was a doctor interested Alex in medicine and he became a medical student
at the University of Montevideo. But it was only in the third year
of medical school that he discovered something that really captured his full attention—chemistry. As so often happens, an imaginative teacher kindled his interest in the subject. He laid bare to
Alex Zaffaroni the central nature of the carbon molecule—its
amazing malleability and its ability to combine with so many other
molecules.

Zaffaroni next went to the University of Rochester, where he
earned his doctorate in biochemistry. As a graduate student he already displayed flashes of brilliance. He developed what has been
entered into chemistry textbooks as the Zaffaroni System, a
method for separating steroid compounds by paper chromatography, which served as a stepping stone toward large-scale production of steroids by big companies such as Upjohn.

Zaffaroni's talented investigations attracted the attention of Syntex, then a tiny firm in Mexico City that was pioneering the
production of synthetic steroid hormones that became the basis of
oral contraceptives and other drugs. He joined Syntex in 1951 as
associate director of biological research and eventually rose to executive vice president, supervising both research and marketing.
Over the years he underwent a remarkable metamorphosis. He discovered that he enjoyed business as much as science. He emerged
not only as an exceptional organizer of basic research but also as
an innovative marketing strategist and clever arranger of unusual
financial deals. An ardent adherent of the concept of leverage ("It's
always a key word in my mind"), he applied it in surprising ways.
For example, he worked out a formula whereby European drug
companies shared their profits with Syntex after buying active drug
ingredients from Syntex. It was Syntex's success, in the end, that
led to Zaffaroni's departure. By the late 1960s he had helped transform the company into a pharmaceutical house with sales approaching $75 million; he had created a marketing structure and
had established research facilities in Palo Alto, where he had
moved from Mexico City. "When all this work was done," he
recalls, "I didn't see any other major new task."

The Entrepreneurs

When he started Alza in 1968, Zaffaroni brought the leverage principle to medicine. Ever since his days as a medical student, the soft-spoken, persuasive Dr. Zaffaroni had been interested in coupling physical principles to medical therapy. He later became especially impressed with nature's own exceedingly effective use of leverage in the release of tiny amounts of hormones to perform prodigious jobs in the body.

At Syntex he could see that even close synthetic imitators of the body's own hormones still caused side effects just as severe as those of any other medication when administered in old-fashioned ways in massive doses. Zaffaroni felt certain that the classical approach to drug development that emphasizes all new chemical structures was wrong. He felt it would never achieve that dream of ideal drugs propounded at the turn of the century by the German bacteriologist Paul Ehrlich—"magic bullets" so specific that they would have no side effects. That dream had a much better chance of becoming real, Zaffaroni thought, not by developing and administering ever more potent new drugs but by finding new ways of giving existing drugs. Ideally, he would use the most harmless drugs of all, the body's own hormones. They would be administered in minute amounts by novel devices designed to replay the body's own program for the release of these chemicals, either to replenish them or to cure ills.

Zaffaroni also knew that he could hardly expect to try to put his ideas into practice in the framework of an established drug company. Such companies, and Syntex was no exception, religiously follow the well-worn chemical route—searching for new compounds to be used as drugs—because the only way they can have a product is to have a chemical structure they can protect with patents. The drug companies would like to be doing something new, but they can't change the course of their research dramatically without destroying the whole enterprise. A certain logic forces them to continue to do what they have been doing. If they tried to shift research directions all the time, they would have no products. But the conventional approach catches them in a quandary where innovation is concerned.

As usually happens with new technology, about the only way to introduce it is to start a new company, and Alex Zaffaroni was ready. At Syntex he had from time to time expounded his ideas to his associates, but they thought that he was ahead of his time. Besides, Zaffaroni didn't really expect Syntex to commit $30 million or so to back his ideas, which he admits were at first vague, although his conviction was strong.

Zaffaroni had always been convinced, in any case, that the best crucible of new technology is a new company being created under pressure. He helped start two satellite firms for Syntex shortly before he left there: Syva, a joint venture between Syntex and Varian Associates in medical instrumentation, and Zoecon Corporation, which is developing novel biological weapons against insects (see Chapter 8). To Zaffaroni, the most efficient way for business enterprises to grow is to imitate nature's most efficient way of growing: by reproduction rather than "by enlargement of the cell that finally bursts. I believe that there is no limit to growth by reproduction while there is a limit to pyramidal growth within one single structure."

New companies, more often than not, suffer from financial anemia. First they often have trouble raising the funds they need and then they usually underestimate the costs of staying alive before those sales dollars and profits start rolling in. Zaffaroni carefully avoided the pitfalls. He is at least ten years ahead of everyone in science, but where realistic knowledge of financial needs of a new company is concerned, his feet are firmly planted on the ground. From his long experience in managing research, Zaffaroni knows how naïve is the notion of many scientists wanting to start a new company that all they need is to conceive a brilliant new idea. "It doesn't take too long to get a group of gifted individuals together and invent and invent—and you can go on inventing forever," says Zaffaroni in his softly accented English. "There's always an opportunity to make a better switch or something. Now, to go from the idea to prototype in some cases is a major hurdle. But to go from the prototype to the product—that is the mountain. That always comes the hardest."

To make mountain climbing easier for Alza, Zaffaroni paved the road with gold. He had left Syntex a millionaire many times over. Thus he was able to get Alza going with $2 million of his own money—an ideal way to start a new company since those "gestation juices" are usually the hardest to get from venture capitalists, most of whom prefer to bet on a company with a proven "track record." In 1968 Zaffaroni resigned from Syntex and rented an elegant suite of offices in Palo Alto. He called the company after himself, taking the first two letters of his first and last names, not because of megalomania, he says, but "because I wanted to have my head on the platter. I was prepared to live and die for it, so to speak."

Zaffaroni sold 575,000 Alza shares to Syntex for $325,000 and other considerations; Syntex distributed these shares to its own stockholders in January 1970, thus creating a public market for Alza. Meanwhile, Zaffaroni was attracting to his board of directors men whose experience would be helpful and whose presence wouldn't hurt when the time come to raise quite a bit more money. He had learned at Syntex the importance of dealing with and hiring the best people in any field. Zaffaroni with seeming gall dispatched a paper outlining his ideas to some prominent men he had never met: Jerome B. Wiesner, former science adviser to President Kennedy and now president of the Massachusetts Institute of Technology; Lloyd N. Cutler, a prominent Washington lawyer and expert in food and drug laws; Jay W. Forrester, professor of management at MIT; Rudolph A. Peterson, then chairman of the executive committee of the Bank of America; and Joseph Wilson, then chairman of Xerox. All but Wilson agreed to become Alza directors, and Wilson suggested an illustrious substitute: Max Palevsky, the entrepreneur who built Scientific Data Systems and sold it to Xerox for about $900 million in stock.

At the same time Zaffaroni rounded up a remarkable cast of scientific advisers. Although he hadn't done any of his own research for years, his ideas and accomplishments led first-rate working scientists to accept him as an equal. "I resonate with him easily," typically says Dr. Wiesner, the president of MIT. Among the advisers he attracted, Zaffaroni personally knew Arthur Kornberg, a Nobel Prize–winning biochemist at Stanford; Robert Woodward, a Harvard Nobelist in molecular synthesis; Nevin S. Scrimshaw, director of the department of nutrition at MIT; Paul J. Flory, a

Nobelist and chairman of Stanford's department of chemistry; and Hans Selye, the famous student of stress at the University of Montreal. "I admire not only his extraordinary genius as a chemist," says Selye, "but also his unbelievable talent for organization. I developed a particularly warm feeling of friendship for this man because of his irresistible personal charm and great general culture." The others whom Zaffaroni recruited as advisers knew him by reputation: Judah Folkman, a noted young surgeon at Harvard who was experimenting on drug-delivery techniques, and Harry Eagle, a renowned cell biologist at the Albert Einstein College of Medicine.

A computerized projection of the company's financial needs from start-up to the development of the first marketable products produced the figure of $30 million, double what most Alza executives had thought they would require. Zaffaroni and his associates raised even more than that. They began by approaching institutions and some of Zaffaroni's well-to-do friends, including Ewing Kauffman, president of Marion Laboratories, and Laurence Spitters, then president of Memorex. Before any public offering they raised $21.5 million by selling common stock and warrants. A rights offering later brought in $11.4 million, and $4.1 million has come in from the exercise of warrants and options.

Some of the early investors have recouped their bets on Alza many times over by selling part of their stock. In December 1969 Alza shares, traded on a when-issued basis, soared to a high of $54, more than five times what private investors paid for a share in the first private placement. In 1973 investors put a market value of more than $100 million on the company before it had sold a single product. By 1975, this had gone up to $160 million. Zaffaroni is the largest shareholder, with 25 percent. Having raised $52 million to start with and a total of $55 million by the middle of 1975, with the promise of more to come, Alza began life on a golden shoestring.

Zaffaroni assembled his executive team with equal care. While at Syntex, he became convinced that a company president, or any other manager for that matter, can make his biggest contributions, or his biggest mistakes, in selecting the kind of people he will work with. "It may take six months to find a guy," he says, "but you're six months ahead if you've got the right guy." In 1968 Zaffaroni asked friends for the names of the three most gifted graduates of the Stanford University Graduate School of Business for the preceding five years. Topping their lists was Martin S. Gerstel, now in his early thirties, who had worked at Cummings Engine and then went off to study at Stanford, where he graduated at the top of his class. Tall and articulate, Gerstel became financial vice president and played a major role in Alza's financing. Another young executive, Steven D. Goldby, with degrees in both chemistry and law, came to Alza as a patent attorney, but Zaffaroni soon spotted in him a talent for marketing and named him president of an Alza subsidiary. Zaffaroni believes success in one field leads to success in another—just as his own experience at Syntex demonstrated—and he is quick to move young people into new areas.

Two other principal executives at Alza were physicians and old friends. Virgil A. Place sold his consulting business to Alza and joined the company as vice president for medical affairs to guide clinical testing. From the University of Utah came David L. Berliner, a Mexican-born endocrinologist whom Zaffaroni hired to lead a program aimed at administering medicines through the skin. Soon Dr. Berliner gravitated toward the "business side" of Alza and became a vice president and adviser to Zaffaroni on a wide range of management matters. He also looked for non-medical applications for Alza's technology and, though Alza itself is a new company, for new ventures the company could start up and spin off. (Berliner later left to become a venture capitalist in Palo Alto.)

It took Zaffaroni much longer and it proved much more difficult to find a man of broad vision who could assemble and lead Alza's team of researchers in diverse scientific and engineering disciplines. Zaffaroni needed, after all, a team that could construct miniature drug-delivery machines. He saw precedents for such machines outside the drug industry—for example, in the Polaroid Land process, in which chemicals separated by thin membranes are programmed for timed release to produce a photographic print. But in classically constructed pharmaceutical companies there

129

were few scientists and engineers capable of developing such technologies.

After searching for nearly two years, Zaffaroni finally found Alan S. Michaels, a former professor of chemical engineering at MIT who was then president of Amicon Corporation in Lexington, Massachusetts. A no-nonsense but friendly man, Michaels, in his early fifties now, had founded Amicon in 1962 to develop advanced membrane technology for pollution control and other nonpharmaceutical applications. On his own he had become interested in applying polymer-membrane technology to medicine, and by the time Zaffaroni approached him, he was ready for a new challenge.

To make the job financially attractive to Michaels, Zaffaroni set up a new company called Pharmetrics to perform research on contract exclusively for Alza, which had an option to buy it. Meanwhile, Pharmetrics sold stock to Michaels and issued options to many of the scientists he hired. (The company was not public at this point, but the optionees expected Alza to acquire it eventually and thus they would end up with options on Alza shares. In 1972 Alza did buy Pharmetrics. Michaels became second in command at Alza, with nearly $1 million in Alza stock, and his scientists got options to buy an average of 778 Alza shares each, at $5 a share.)

The research staff now includes 200 full-time scientists and engineers (backed up by 63 outside consultants) who have widely varying specialties and perform unusual tasks. Some came from the photographic industry, others from plastics processing, still others from water desalination. "One of the greatest challenges," says Michaels, "was to weld together a group of people with these disparate backgrounds." One scientist did his doctoral thesis on the freeze-drying of orange juice. Michaels himself has drawn on his expertise in secondary oil recovery and other nonmedical fields to design drug reservoirs. A space scientist trying to build a better contraceptive device took up the study of fluid dynamics of the uterus.

These creative people have a lot of freedom. As one of them puts it, "There isn't any company outside the Metropolitan Opera that functions this way." Another scientist describes Alza employees as "the biggest group of individualists who ever worked together." A third compares the company to a university, with this big difference: "When the chips are down, there's one person to say this is the way we'll do things."

The avalanche of money that Zaffaroni collected was put to work to give Alza the instant look of a going concern. Its facilities are spread around nine buildings near its impressive $2 million steel-and-brick headquarters structure. No starting in a garage for Zaffaroni. He likes to live and work in style, so expensive black leather furniture decorates the headquarters building. Outside, sculptures from his personal collection tower over acres of carpet-smooth grass. "To make the environment attractive, nice, and tasteful, I think, is a plus," says Zaffaroni. Alza executives are driven to and from the airport in a chauffeured car equipped with radio telephone, which for a new company may be another first. Michaels says it's been "a blessing" not to watch pennies or work in marginal facilities, as he had had to do at the beginning of his own company, Amicon.

Applying his rich experience in managing research, Zaffaroni places scientific project leaders above vice presidents when it comes to creating a new product. Operating within an agreed budget, the project leader oversees the design of the product, its preparation for regulatory approval, and its marketing. Everyone whose skills he needs reports to him. The system reflects Zaffaroni's belief that a strong entrepreneurial organization comes first, then technology, and then—from the two—come products.

Proving itself in the marketplace with a brand-new technology will be the test of Alza, of course. But even here Alza seems to have a few things going for it. Unlike most consumer products, new drugs and new drug-delivery devices, at least those sold by prescription, must be sold first not to the public but to a fairly small group of specialists. If they accept the products, their patients will, too. Here Zaffaroni applies the concept of safety engineering. In a refreshing counterpoint to Naderism, he believes that American technology owes its huge success to safety-engineering concepts—the careful design of such new airplanes as the Boeing 747, for instance. Zaffaroni applies safety engineering every place

131

he can. In the Ocusert program, for instance, the company recruited some of the world's top ophthalmologists to test the little disks and the response was highly favorable. Alza distributed about a thousand console film cassette viewers to physicians with a film that shows doctors and patients how to use the Ocusert. It's much easier to get used to the Ocusert unit than to contact lenses; the tiny disk comes in contact with the white of the eye, which is much less sensitive than the cornea where contact lenses fit. The revolutionary device was approved by the FDA in August 1974, and Alza started selling it soon thereafter.

The Ocusert is placed in the conjunctival cul-de-sac where it floats in the tear film, releasing pilocarpine at a uniform rate for a week. It replaces the need for taking eyedrops four times a day. When pilocarpine is taken as eyedrops—the usual form of administration—most patients' vision becomes blurred for one to two hours because of the relatively high dose of the drug. Some become temporarily blinded. Ocusert avoids this serious inconvenience; minor blurring of vision occurs only when the device is first inserted. The Alza eye disk avoids most of the side effects by using only one-tenth of the amount of pilocarpine that a patient normally administers. Glaucoma is a serious disease that affects more than one million Americans and is the leading cause of preventable blindness in the United States. On a worldwide basis it is estimated that this condition affects approximately 2 percent of the population over the age of forty. One woman with glaucoma wrote to Alza in a tribute to the Ocusert: "The invention of the Ocusert should be placed among the miracles of our time. Imagine having an incurable disease that one only has to think about once a week! I am so terribly grateful once again to be able to enjoy a totally healthy life. I no longer have to spend countless unproductive hours each week when my drops used to plunge me into darkness or a blurring world."

The number of ophthalmologists is fairly small, about ten thousand in the United States, and Alza covers most of them with about thirty salesmen. Even though the market is small for anti-glaucoma drugs—it amounts to only about $10 million a year in the United States and another $10 million abroad at the wholesale level—Alza's strategists feel that they have a good chance of snaring a major share of it quickly. They also hope to balloon the dollar volume by selling their drug disk at higher prices than the eyedrops it is intended to replace; the disk is expensive to make. The cost to the patient is high, about $1 a day, but the therapeutic effect justifies it, many users believe.

Alza hopes to tap a much bigger market with its uterine contraceptive device, Progestasert, for which it received preliminary FDA approval in June 1975. Unlike the pill, the Alza device appears to produce no side effects such as blood clotting and weight gain. Progestasert is a small and flexible drug reservoir shaped like a T that delivers the natural female hormone progesterone to the lining of the uterus. Because the hormone is released directly to the target organ continuously, an extremely low dosage of progesterone is capable of preventing conception.

Zaffaroni argues that oral contraceptives will never be used by more than a small fraction of the world's women. "If polio vaccine had to be taken as a daily oral dose, it would not have covered more than 10 to 15 percent of the population effectively." He thinks that a major company could be built on Alza's uterine contraceptive alone. He sees particularly good sales opportunities in Japan, where an oral contraceptive has never been approved, in Red China, and in many underdeveloped countries. Alza will have certain obstacles to overcome, of course. The United States, where the wholesale market for oral contraceptives amounts to about $160 million a year, or half the world total, is a pill-oriented society. All told, however, less than 10 percent of the estimated 750 million women of child-bearing age in the world today are using any form of contraception. Progestasert, therefore, could help meet an urgent worldwide need for a safe, effective, and easy-to-use new contraceptive method.

Other products under development at Alza include:

·Devices that pass medications through the skin. Patches made of a new multi-layer polymer adhesive impregnated with drug molecules are pressed onto the skin. Unlike a pill, the patch transmits the drug through the blood directly to the target organ, and unlike an injection, it releases the drug slowly over a period of

133

hours or days. Important drugs can be administered this way: vaso-dilators for heart disease, analgesics, and antinausea compounds. To control motion and seasickness, Alza scientists are testing the administration of scopolamine, a well-known and highly effective compound for the relief of motion-induced sickness. The drug is not widely used, however, because the traditional dosage produces serious side effects. In the Alza approach, smaller doses of scopolamine will be administered through a drug-impregnated patch placed behind a person's ear, where the skin is easily permeable. "Potentially we can administer any type of compound that doesn't cause problems to the skin," says an Alza scientist.

·An aerosol can to dispense antiasthma and other pulmonary drugs without the use of Freon propellant, which is suspected of having caused deaths when it was inhaled with medicines. This dispenser (which is nonexplosive) could also find use in non-medical products, from hair sprays to shaving cream.

·Polymer drug reservoirs that harmlessly dissolve after they have served their purpose. Implanted in the body, they could be used in cancer therapy and for improved treatment of drug addiction. Both injectable and oral vaccines could be put inside these miniature reservoirs for timed release in the body.

·A powdered blood substitute, not yet tested on humans, that could eliminate the need for whole blood in transfusions and do away with problems of blood typing and hepatitis.

·A portable small, flat plastic container and accessories for the intravenous delivery of drugs. Unlike the present cumbersome systems that employ big glass bottles turned upside down to force medication into the patient's veins by the force of gravity, the Alza device incorporates pressure right into the plastic bottle. This makes the Alza I.V. (intravenous) bottle portable—a patient can walk about or even use it in his home. The rate of drug release is set automatically. Alza has put the device in clinical trials, before applying for FDA approval. The American Cancer Society is interested in the Alza I.V. device for possible delivery of chemicals to cancer patients without hospitalizing them.

·A preprogrammed pill that works by osmosis, the process that cashes in on the tendency of a fluid to move from higher concentration to a lower one in the adjoining fluid. When swallowed, this device can deliver a drug, including antiulcer medications, at a constant rate for hours. In 1975 Alza licensed A. H. Robins, a major drug company, to manufacture and sell such a pill.

Looking at Alza's research, Michaels says, "There's easily five to ten years of product development visible today. My problem is not trying to think of new ideas, but trying to keep the kids [his young scientists] out of the candy store."

In 1974, Michaels moved up to become senior vice president for technological resources development for Alza, concentrating on longer-range planning. John Urquhart, a young Harvard-trained physician, became president of Alza's research division. Before he came to Alza, Urquhart was a professor of biomedical engineering at the University of Southern California. Zaffaroni had spotted his imaginative research reports on the dynamics of the adrenal gland and attracted him to Alza. Urquhart's appointment coincided with a significant change at Alza. Until 1974 major emphasis at the company was on development of prototypes, but today the emphasis is on applications since Zaffaroni and his associates feel that their technology is fully developed for short-term use.

The ultimate goal of Alza researchers is to do nothing less than replicate the functions of living organs, such as the pancreas. An ideal drug-delivery device would measure and respond to changes in the body's biochemical milieu, just as many organs do. The body's own indicators of disease would trigger the release of drugs from reservoirs floating in the blood or anchored in the stomach. "Take a patient who has bad circulation in his legs," says Richard Buckles, a senior engineer at Alza. "He puts out lactic acid. If you had a delivery system that could respond to the level of lactic acid in the blood, you would have a beautiful system."

Zaffaroni himself plays an important part in Alza technology. His fertile brain seems constantly whirring. For a biochemist he reads "some crazy things," as he puts it—journals in electronic, aeronautical, and mechanical engineering, for instance—as sources of ideas for drug-delivery mechanisms. He often reads in the garden of his big house in Atherton on weekends. Sometimes he disappears for days into an office he rents near Alza to think without interruption. He may awaken at 5:00 A.M. on Sunday and jot down an idea. Later in the day, excited, he will call Michaels or another colleague.

That intellectual horizon scanning has already given birth to an idea for another pioneering company, which Alza spun off in 1972. Having read about how hormones act on the surface of a cell, Zaffaroni asked himself why one couldn't manipulate molecules of sugar or artificial sweeteners so that they would do their job at their target organ—the tongue—and then pass harmlessly through the stomach without entering the bloodstream and causing weight gain or possibly severe side effects, including even cancer.

It wasn't just the cyclamate scare that set Zaffaroni on that particular path. He had long been concerned about the possible deleterious effects of sugar, too. Unlike carbohydrates, which are broken down and employed in building up components of the body's cells, sugar—a relatively new food in the history of man—brings out the release of insulin and that in turn produces fatty acids, which may lead to diabetes, obesity, and heart disease.

A recent discovery showed that certain sites on the tongue respond to particular molecular structures that impart the sensation of sweetness; it is the structure of the material that gives the sensation. If the molecules of sugar or an artificial sweetener were tied to the molecules of a bulky, inert substance—"molecules on a leash," Zaffaroni calls them—the new structure would impart the sensation of sweetness but would not be broken down in the stomach. Zaffaroni asked an Alza scientist to test the theory in the lab, and it looked promising.

"I went out of town one day," recalls Michaels, "and when I came back there was Dynapol." To get this dream within a dream going, Zaffaroni raised $6 million from such well-heeled friends as Carl Djerassi, a long-time associate of his at Syntex who now runs Zoecon Corporation, with which Alza shares a backyard. Alza retained a two-thirds ownership in Dynapol, which has a good chance of growing into a major company as concern intensifies about the possible harmful effects of artificial sweeteners, food additives, and preservatives. An average American already consumes about three pounds of such chemicals a year, and their use is bound to rise as the population increases without a matching rise in the sources of protein.

After two years of intensive work, the research effort at Dynapol began to bear fruit. Its scientists have been successful in developing three kinds of improved food additives: food colors, antioxidants (preservatives), and nonnutritive sweeteners. In the food-color program, Dynapol has prepared polymeric equivalents of the three largest-selling food colors: sunset yellow (orange), tartrazine (yellow), and amaranth (red). The polymeric dyes are identical in color and solubility to those products but possess superior light stability, have higher tinctorial strength, and are almost totally nonabsorbable in the body. Toxicity testing of the dyes began in 1975. Dynapol has also started toxicity testing of antioxidants. This product is expected to be essentially nonabsorbable, to be more effective in retarding rancidity than the most widely used food antioxidants, and not to be lost from food in cooking, as are the present preservatives. Dynapol's nonnutritive sweetener program is at an earlier stage of development. Although its scientists have produced new molecules with five hundred to a thousand times the sweetness of sugar, they have not yet succeeded in leashing a sweet molecule to a polymer without losing the sweet taste. Late in 1975, Dynapol's research on novel sweeteners got a big boost when the Coca Cola Company agreed to underwrite it.

Before they can be marketed, food additives must be subjected to rigorous biological testing and be approved by the FDA, as well as by corresponding health authorities in other countries in which the additives are to be sold. Establishing the safety of the food additives developed by Dynapol is expected to require several years of testing, after which applications will be filed with the FDA. Therefore, it will be several years before Dynapol can market any of its new food additives if FDA approval is ultimately obtained.

The commercial rewards for Dynapol could be substantial. Millions of pounds of colors, antioxidants, and sweeteners are annually added to foods, and the volume is growing at 6 to 7 percent. With the increasing demand for processed food, this trend is expected to continue.

Alza executives are particularly encouraged with Dynapol's

progress since food companies, much like drug companies in their search for drugs, ploddingly keep looking for new compounds to be used as sweeteners, while Dynapol is approaching the problem from an entirely new direction. "I think this represents part of the uniqueness of this environment," says Buckles. "Alex has this beautiful gift to translate exciting technology into exciting reality."

In Zaffaroni's ambitious scheme, Alza and Dynapol are just the beginning. Utilizing the treasure trove of technology being developed by those brainy Alza researchers, Zaffaroni plans to mass-produce new subsidiary companies at the rate of about one every two years—companies specializing in novel ways of applying pesticides and fertilizers, dealing with water pollution, processing chemicals, and innovating in many other fields.

Zaffaroni feels that man has been just as thoughtless about polluting the world with pesticides as he has been about flooding his body with drugs. Indiscriminate use of pesticides has introduced them into the oceans, with the currents carrying residues of such chemicals as DDT as far away as Antarctica, where they have been found in penguins. Here again, precise targeting and timed release of such substances might be the answer, Zaffaroni thinks.

If there is a unifying concept to what he does, says Zaffaroni, it is his tremendous confidence and belief in the biological strategy. He applies it to designing new products and new companies. "It would be hard to arrive at better processes than biological processes which have been proven out over such long periods," he says. "Biology has taught us that if an organism goes beyond a certain point in its growth, it can perform fewer functions." So he wants his new companies to grow "like insects, growing out of a new shell, getting rid of one shell to grow again, whereas the process of growth of the corporations we're familiar with is just to grow fat."

He wants to create a whole universe of interconnecting companies—a kind of benevolent corporate society whose members would contribute new technology to solve ever more complex problems. "My motivation is creating new technologies as a more and more powerful concept and unifying the commonality of resources—it's a kind of religious feeling. I would like to see Alza not necessarily be the heart of the operation but the heart of creations. I think there is no better way to achieve success than to detach yourself from success to start a new cycle of growth."

In creating new companies, Zaffaroni is unlike venture capitalists because they usually wait for people to come to them with ideas. "The best chance for an entrepreneurial company to succeed," says Zaffaroni, "is to emerge from another entrepreneurial company."

Zaffaroni has other motivations, like making money, although that is not a prime concern for him. But he wants Alza not only to make an important impact on medicine but to make a lot of money, too—as part of the "leverage effect" that he likes to see.

If Alza's current and subsequent products catch on—a new product should be emerging about once every nine months—Alza could earn impressive amounts. It's not unusual for a drug company to collect a whopping 50 percent before taxes on a high-volume product, and if all goes well, sales of $50 million a year or more would seem reasonable within the next few years. Some of the more advanced thinkers in the drug industry believe Alza's technology will dominate drug delivery in the years to come.

Zaffaroni feels that Alza's area of "blue sky," or unknown, is smaller than that of the established drug companies with their concentration on new chemical structures. Only an estimated eight out of every thousand new chemicals synthesized ever reach the marketplace; a drug company pursuing this traditional approach may spend a decade and a quarter of a billion dollars with nothing much to show for it. "In fact," says Zaffaroni, "pharmaceutical industry managements have expressed their doubts as to the future opportunities in the ethical drug field sector by engaging in a frantic race to diversify. A broad program of mergers and acquisitions has brought the industry into fields as diverse from pharmaceuticals as consumer products, cosmetics, and food processing." Besides, with all the regulatory restrictions now imposed on the introduction of new drugs and a subsequent dramatic decline in recent years in the number of new drugs brought to the market, Alza's concentration on a field of medical therapy largely overlooked for many years may be about the only route toward fast growth in the pharmaceutical industry.

All in all, in his ambitious way Zaffaroni sees Alza growing into a giant in his lifetime. In the end, Alza's success depends on how well Zaffaroni and his associates can communicate their ideas and enthusiasms to the medical profession, a conservative lot, and on timely approval of the products by regulatory authorities. Alza has enough money not to worry about the near future, and the Food and Drug Administration appears highly receptive to the idea of applying drugs at one-thousandth, or even one-millionth, the "normal" rate.

Other companies, of course, will fast wake up to the money-making potential in the new drug-delivery systems if Alza proves it, but Alza is far ahead of them now. "I see a great prospect of accomplishment for those who follow this path," says Zaffaroni, "but it will require a major reversal of the present research direction and will demand a much deeper commitment to therapeutics by the pharmaceutical industry. This approach will open up a new era for medicine and for the pharmaceutical industry. It will be the era of controlled therapeutics."

Zaffaroni's great vision of the future of medicine includes widespread use of the body's own agents as medications. This is, of course, what Hippocrates, the father of medicine, believed in: that the body tends to heal itself by natural processes and the role of the physician should be ancillary to that of nature. "Only when we fail to find the right compound within the body," says Zaffaroni, "we ought to go to the one that's man-made."

This is where Alza holds a significant advantage over other drug companies. Conventional drug research deals with a paradox in the search for biologically active agents of mammalian origin. First, long years of arduous effort must be invested to isolate and chemically characterize the important active agents. But as soon as the structure of such an agent is defined, most of the previous work must then be undone. The natural agent's molecules must be modified to increase its biological half-life, which is usually very short: the agents can't be administered, furthermore, in conventional dosage forms. "This forces us to abandon the values built through evolutionary processes in which the natural molecules evolved as those best able to elicit biological effects, but do so in harmony with the body," says Zaffaroni. "By modifying the molecular structure of the natural molecules, their intrinsic safety is jeopardized or lost. The synthetic analogues or derivatives are new drugs and their therapeutic potential and toxicity need to be assessed anew."

As a result, Zaffaroni sees a major challenge for pharmaceutical research in the development of therapeutic systems able to deliver effectively the natural active agents which thus opens to use in therapy the treasure trove of healing substances made by the human body itself. Alza's development of the Progestasert system is the first example of this exciting new approach to the use of drugs in harmony with the body, since the active agent delivered by the "plastic pill" is the natural female hormone progesterone. Controlled delivery of drugs from timed-release reservoirs such as the Ocusert or the Progestasert, furthermore, sharply reduces another problem that plagues medicine: failure of patients—through absentmindedness or for other reasons—to comply with the prescribed dosage regimen. Since the drugs in Alza devices are delivered over extended periods of time, faulty patient compliance is reduced, if not eliminated.

Zaffaroni also sees a great promise for controlled drug-delivery systems in tackling effectively chronic and infectious diseases in the underdeveloped world. The Ocusert already is being tested as a means of delivering antitrachoma drugs. Trachoma is the leading cause of blindness in the world. Cashing in on its clever drug "launch platforms," Alza appears well on its way toward becoming a Polaroid or Xerox of its industry. Even if it doesn't, there's always Dynapol and half a dozen other ideas hatching in the Zaffaroni incubator.

CHAPTER SEVEN

How Intel Won the Memory Race

Individuals who start technological companies are seldom endowed with great abilities as both business managers and production experts. Even more rarely have they learned through personal experience just what it takes to organize and run a small company and make it grow quickly into a big one. Lacking such insights and skills, technical men—no matter how brilliant—often let their enthusiasms run wild, only to trip over mundane production and management hurdles.

Robert N. Noyce and Gordon E. Moore are two bright exceptions. They avoided the technology-is-everything trap. Instead, they relied on their production, management, and marketing skills at least as much as they did on their technical expertise—with striking results. In 1968 they started Intel Corporation, of Santa Clara, California, to make tiny semiconductor memory components for computers and their supporting equipment. In so doing, they bet that they could outdo competitors many times Intel's size in opening up a new segment of the semiconductor industry. When Intel went into business, no market existed for its principal product. Today, thanks to the company's trailblazing, no big computer is designed without semiconductor memory components.

It helped tremendously, of course, that Noyce and Moore had struggled through the company-building process once before. They had been among the eight founders of Fairchild Semiconductor. Moreover, they actually ran that operation, Noyce as general manager and Moore as director of research. In eleven years

143

they built Fairchild Semiconductor into a $150 million enterprise, one of the big three in its field, along with Texas Instruments and Motorola.

At Intel (a contraction of "integrated electronics"), Noyce and Moore overcame both technical and production obstacles that had prevented the semiconductor industry from realizing the potential of "large-scale integration." This is the technique that now makes it possible to jam thousands of transistors onto a sliver of silicon scarcely bigger than any two letters in this sentence. Their success has made possible a big leap forward in the electronic technology that is changing life in our factories, offices, and homes.

As memory chips and related semiconductor devices become more reliable, ever more miniaturized, and steadily less expensive, they are increasingly replacing electromechanical relays, switches, and timers that control a wide range of industrial and consumer products, from typesetters to elevators. In computers, the major new market, the semiconductor memory chips are supplanting the much older and now technologically obsolete ferrite ringlets known as "cores." A single core can store one "bit," or one "yes" or "no" of binary computer language. A single chip, not much bigger than an average core, can hold thousands of such coded instructions in the microminiaturized maze of its circuits. Chips lend themselves to mass production, while cores must often be strung on their connecting hair-thin wires by hand. Because of their structure, the chips function faster than cores, allowing better computer design and faster operation. And chips now compete with cores in price.

Thanks to these advantages, the market for memory chips has roughly doubled every year for the last five years. Sales are expected to reach $400 million in 1976, about a tenth of the semiconductor industry's total volume. Demand is still increasing so fast that makers of memory components envisage sales of $1 billion by 1980.

Among the major computer manufacturers, only IBM makes enough semiconductor memories to meet its own needs. Other manufacturers, such as Honeywell, Univac, and Burroughs, depend on outside suppliers, and Intel is foremost among them. As a result, Intel's growth has been startling. In 1968, with 42 employees, it had sales of $2,672. By 1972 its work force had grown to 1,000, its sales to $23.4 million, and its net profit to a healthy $2 million. In 1975, with 3,200 employees, Intel expected to net about $20 million on projected sales of more than $140 million, nearly $50 million of it from those marvelous memory chips.

In 1971 Noyce and Moore pioneered again by introducing a microcomputer, the long-predicted "computer on a chip." With auxiliary electronics, a $300 microcomputer no larger than a file folder packs into its tiny space the capacity of a refrigerator-sized computer of 1960 vintage, which rented for $30,000 a year. Smaller versions of the microcomputer sell for as little as $20; the largest ones cost about $1,000.

Already these slices of electronic brain power are finding their way into a host of products, among them wristwatches, traffic lights, pinball machines, and cash registers. The full impact of the microcomputer on our lives will not become evident for some years. The penetration of electronics into all sorts of consumer and industrial activity is likely to hold down production and operating costs for manufacturing companies. Microcomputers will free people from drudgery, but on balance they seem likely to create more jobs than they eliminate. Already many innovators are starting new companies to manufacture devices controlled by the "micro-brain."

Noyce likens the arrival of the microcomputer to the development of the fractional-horsepower electric motor, which spread the benefits of the industrial revolution into all corners of our lives. And the normally taciturn Moore says, "We are really the revolutionaries in the world today—not the kids with the long hair and beards who were wrecking the schools a few years ago." Noyce, forty-eight years old in 1976, and Moore, forty-seven, earned distinction as scientific pioneers some time ago. Noyce holds a doctorate in physics from MIT and was the co-inventor of the integrated circuit. Moore, a chemist with a Ph.D. from the California Institute of Technology, made some of the major basic discoveries that led to the integrated circuit and subsequent advances.

Both had been interested in science from early childhood. Bob Noyce was born in Denmark, Iowa, in 1928, third oldest of four sons of an itinerant Congregational minister. Growing up in small Iowa towns where farm machinery is commonplace, he would find an old discarded gasoline engine in a junk yard and start tinkering with it. Noyce recalls that he was always working in a shop of some sort—motorizing bicycles, building mechanical gadgets. When he was twelve, he constructed a glider, starting a life-long love affair with flying and airplanes. "It was really an overgrown box kite. We would run with it along the roof of a barn, then jump off the end of the roof with it and float down to the ground. It didn't work very well but we didn't kill ourselves."

Noyce always had good grades in school. This was expected of him since his two older brothers had gone through school at the top of their classes. His interest in solid-state physics was first aroused while he took general physics courses as an undergraduate at Grinnell College in Iowa. The transistor had just been invented. One of Noyce's professors happened to be a friend of John Bardeen, a co-inventor of the tiny, miraculous new device that promised to start a revolution in electronics by replacing the bulky vacuum tubes. "Professor Grant Gale made quite a big thing out of the transistor," Noyce recalls. "It seemed like quite an interesting area to go into." With that in mind, Noyce applied to MIT and was accepted. When he got there, he found that the famous institution was not yet offering any courses in semiconductors. But he was able to study subjects that had a close bearing on the area. The expansive enthusiastic youngster often startled his fellow students with the quickness of his mind. While his friends would be preparing for a weekend of studies, Bob Noyce, homework completed, would be off for a weekend of skiing.

After getting his Ph.D. in physics from MIT, Noyce worked for two and a half years in Philco's semiconductor division in Philadelphia. One day in 1956 he got a telephone call from William Shockley, another co-inventor of the transistor who had gone back to Palo Alto, his boyhood town, to organize a semiconductor company. "When he called," says Noyce, "I jumped at the opportunity. I had never been to California, but the story I had gotten from my brother Don, who was teaching at Berkeley, was that it was a lovely place to live, and I was eager to move out there. For my own development it was important to find out that I could play in the big leagues and keep up with the pace of the game. Shockley was recognized as the father of the transistor."

Noyce and Moore reported to Shockley on the same day. Moore, a son of an undersheriff, grew up in San Mateo County near San Francisco. When he was ten, he was given a chemistry set as a present and was so impressed by it that he decided to become a chemist. He went on to get a Ph.D. in chemistry from Cal Tech and was working in the Applied Physics Laboratory of Johns Hopkins University when Shockley called him.

The imaginative Shockley had assembled a group of bright young scientists, but the operation fell apart when eight of them left only a year later. Even then they looked upon Noyce as a leader. His enthusiasm—and his approach to everything with the idea that it is going to work—easily infects people.

One of the members of the group wrote to a friend of his family who worked for Hayden, Stone, the New York investment firm. Hayden, Stone soon arranged to finance the company the young entrepreneurs wanted to organize. The start-up money came largely from Fairchild Camera and Instrument Corporation, which had an option to buy the new semiconductor company, known as Fairchild Semiconductor. The eight young founders contributed about $500 apiece, but when Fairchild Camera bought their company in 1969 and made it a division of the parent concern, they each got about $250,000 worth of stock in Fairchild Camera. "For a young guy—the age of the group ran from about twenty-nine to thirty-five—to walk away with a quarter million dollars a year later was not a bad deal," says Noyce. "That was a major turning point in your career, if you will. You had ten or fifteen years' salary in your pocket. You could take a more independent attitude toward life."

A number of Noyce's friends did; they left Fairchild to found companies of their own. But Noyce and Moore stayed on. Noyce didn't start out by running Fairchild Semiconductor; he was director of research and development in the beginning. In fact, the first thing the young scientists did was to hire a boss; none of them felt confident enough to run the operation. They brought in Edward Baldwin from Hughes Aircraft; although Baldwin had a Ph.D. in electronics, he also had managerial experience.

After a year Baldwin left to found a semiconductor company of his own and Noyce became acting general manager. "We looked around for a couple of months," recalls Noyce. "Then I decided, hell, I could do it as well as anyone else. I had the trust and faith of critical people in the organization. I went ahead and took the job and frankly learned what I was doing as I was doing it. I didn't know what a balance sheet was, essentially, at the time I took on the job. But I found it a lot more interesting than I expected it to be. You suddenly become the focus of information, so you know what's going on better than anybody in the organization and you are in a better position to run it than anybody else."

The company that had started in a rented building in Mountain View was growing fast. By the end of 1957 it had 25 employees and next year it sold $100,000 worth of semiconductors. In 1959 its sales went up to $7 million and the company employed close to 500 people. The growth continued by giant leaps so that by 1968 Noyce was supervising nearly 15,000 employees in the United States and abroad. Both he and Moore had achieved major technical advances in semiconductor technology at Fairchild, but both men had begun to find big-company life less and less satisfying. A gregarious man, Noyce began to miss contact with the broad spectrum of his co-workers as the executive organization increasingly asumed the shape of a pyramid. Although he is an ardent pilot in his spare time, he was also growing tired of flying from northern California to New York for frequent consultations with executives of the parent company, Fairchild Camera and Instrument.

Both Noyce and Moore were beginning to feel, too, that a company as big as Fairchild Semiconductor could not easily expand into new areas of semiconductor technology. In the beginning new ventures in such a complex field usually lose money—sometimes a lot of it—and it is often difficult to justify big losses to directors and stockholders.

The manufacture of semiconductor memories looked attractive

because big companies had not exploited the possibility, despite the prospect of a fast-growing market. Noyce and Moore decided that their new company should try to establish itself as a leader in that field—an area that would be narrow in terms of products but wide in terms of usage. As Moore explains, "It's very tempting for a little company to run in all directions. We went the other way."

A new company has the best chance of success in pursuing the strategy Intel did. A hopeful entrepreneur should try to locate an area that is not being exploited by anyone and one that can be expected to grow fast. Says Noyce, "It is our objective to dominate any market in which we participate."

They also knew that they would need quite a bit of money. As Noyce says, one of the traps that endangers young companies is "running out of money right on schedule but not getting the product out right on schedule." Fortunately, Noyce had already had considerable personal exposure to the investment community. Among his acquaintances was Arthur Rock, who had helped to arrange the original financing for Fairchild Semiconductor while he was at Hayden, Stone. Later Rock had become a successful venture capitalist in San Francisco and had helped start Teledyne and Scientific Data Systems. In fact, Rock is probably the premier venture capitalist in high technology today.

"It was a very natural thing to go to Art and say, 'Incidentally, Art, do you have an extra $2.5 million you would like to put on the crap table?' " says Noyce. Rock had long before become convinced of Noyce's abilities as a manager. But he also knew that men who run big companies for others don't necessarily make good entrepreneurs. So Rock, a cautious man, grilled Noyce on his goals and his emotional and financial commitment to the idea. "My way with people who want to start companies is to talk to them until they are exhausted—and then talk to them some more," says Rock. "Finally, I get an impression what their objectives are, whether they have integrity, whether they are interested in running a big company, whether their goals are big enough. One of the things I'm interested in is does the management put a limit on the company they want, and if they do, I get fearful."

He was pleased with Noyce's response and by the fact that both

149

Noyce and Moore were willing to invest substantial amounts of their own money, about $250,000 each. By the time they left Fairchild, each had amassed a fortune of more than $1 million from his original $500 investment.

Intel started in the enviable position of having so many would-be investors that it could choose those it preferred. "People had known Bob and were kind of lined up to invest in the company," says Rock. He purchased $300,000 worth of convertible debentures and brought in other investors who took an additional $2.2 million. Noyce's alma mater, Grinnell College, also became a major investor by acquiring $300,000 worth of the debentures.

Later Intel sold 154,000 shares of common stock in private placements for $2.2 million. The company went public in 1971 at $23.50 a share, thereby raising $6.8 million more. All told, paid-in capital for Intel has amounted to about $17.5 million. Between them, Noyce and Moore still own about 27 percent of Intel's stock, a holding worth more than $100 million at the recent price of $80 a share.

Since the initial debenture issue, Intel has not found it necessary to borrow and has never used its line of bank credit. The company has financed its expansion with its own capital and owns all its facilities except one, which it rents. In order to continue its fast growth, however, the company eventually may find it necessary to take out a loan.

Noyce deliberately organized Intel as a kind of partnership with Moore—a "two-headed monster," as he calls it. He did so because when he was at Fairchild he had felt that he could never turn over the affairs of the company to anyone when he was away. The pressure of that unremitting responsibility bore heavily on him.

At Intel, Noyce at first became president and Moore executive vice president. Rock became chairman, but he takes no active role in managing the company. In 1975 Noyce moved up to chairman, Moore to president, and Rock became vice chairman. Noyce concentrates on external matters, while Moore concerns himself mainly with internal affairs. Noyce is an optimist in terms of what can be accomplished technically, while Moore is a realist. "It makes a good foil," says Noyce. "We can argue the advantages and disadvantages of a project."

The Entrepreneurs

Their co-workers marvel at the smoothness of the relationship. When Noyce and Moore disagree, they unhesitatingly say so to each other, but both are well-controlled men and they do it without rancor. It helps, of course, that they have known each other for twenty years.

While running Fairchild Semiconductor, Noyce felt that wherever he happened to be he should be within reach of a telephone to keep track of what was going on at the company. The constant pressure at times made him jealous of the workers on the assembly lines who could go home after work and sleep without worries. He wanted to be able to take a vacation without constantly being concerned about the company. It wasn't until 1973 that Noyce was able to take his longest vacation since he got out of high school—two weeks at a stretch. But he has found time to ski in the winter and hike in the summer. He has found time to lead a madrigal group and to work with the Audubon Society. Once he flew in one of his planes six puffins from Newfoundland to an island in Maine, part of which he owns, so that the birds could get established there.

Moore, too, finds work at Intel more relaxing. An ardent fisherman and nature lover, he can be found fishing for tiny surf smelt near his beach house north of Santa Cruz or for giant tuna off Prince Edward Island. When fishing far away, he may drop Bob Noyce a postcard to tell him how the fishing is—secure in the knowledge that Intel is being run well.

When Noyce and Moore decided to gamble on semiconductor memories, it was clear to many people in the industry that these devices sooner or later would start displacing cores. But it was not clear just how soon this would occur and whether the time was ripe for a new company to jump into the field. Although large-scale integration had excited the imagination of semiconductor engineers for about five years, it was still largely a laboratory curiosity. It also had a bad reputation because of unsolved technical problems, chief among them contamination during manufacturing. The production of integrated circuits involves one of the most complex manufacturing processes ever devised, with numerous tolerances as fine as a few microns—millionths of a meter. Even a fleck of dust can result in a faulty device.

Moreover, semiconductor memory chips then had only highly specialized and limited applications in computers. IBM employed so-called bipolar chips as small, auxiliary speed-up memories in some models of its computer line. But these chips were too costly to comprise the main memories of computers. Other kinds of semiconductor chips were used in the small, relatively slow-operating memory banks of computer terminals. The terminal chips contained at the most 200 memory bits, or about 1,000 transistors per chip. But their speed was too slow for computer main memories. Noyce and Moore decided to leapfrog those early devices by devising a chip of the same size but much cheaper, faster, and with 4,000 transistors.

This twentieth-century wizardry recalls the medieval fancy that an infinite number of angels could stand on the head of a pin. But making semiconductor memory chips requires extraordinarily complex manufacturing techniques. The process takes Intel four weeks and involves 112 separate steps that must be performed in sequence.

First, draftsmen create a big maplike design of the circuits and bits, usually about five hundred times as large as the actual chip. The drawings are then reduced photographically, and the resulting "photomask" is used to transfer the maze of circuits and transistors onto a piece of silicon roughly one-eighth of an inch square. As if all that were not intricate enough, each chip must undergo repeated etchings and backings at temperatures as high as 2,200 degrees Fahrenheit in electric ovens before it is completed. Noyce and Moore felt that this miraculous technology, if mastered, would drive the cost of a transistor down ten-thousand-fold or more.

Big companies failed to see the full potential of the memory field, were too busy doing other things, or couldn't afford to invest millions in a new area because they had to cope with overcapacity and brutal price wars in existing lines. So Intel became the first small concern to concentrate specifically on memory. It soon had plenty of company—all small fry. Three of Texas Instruments' principal specialists in metal oxide semiconductors (MOS) left to form Dallas-based Mostek Corporation. Two competitors, Advanced Memory Systems, Inc., and Computer Microtechnology,

152

Inc., went into business on Intel's own turf, a sector along the Bayshore Freeway south of San Francisco now known as "Silicon Valley" because of the dense concentration of semiconductor companies. In Phoenix a group of scientists from Motorola started Semiconductor Electronic Memories, Inc. (Semi). In Wappingers Falls, New York, George Cogar, a high-school dropout and one-time television repairman who had become a millionaire by helping found Mohawk Data Sciences, began an ambitious semiconductor operation as part of his Cogar Corporation.

Despite all the competition, Intel emerged within three years as the undisputed champion among suppliers of computer memories. Mostek has thrived by making both calculator and computer memory chips. But Cogar's operation collapsed after burning up about $27 million in those treacherous process furnaces. Semi went bankrupt and was taken over and revived by Electronic Memories and Magnetics. Computer Microtechnology sold its facilities to Advance Memory Systems, which itself has been losing money lately.

In its quest for leadership Intel concentrated more talent on memories than any of its rivals, including such giants as Texas Instruments. In a rented building in Mountain View, Intel engineers began work on novel memory chips that utilized a brand-new concept in making them. This was the so-called silicon-gate approach. Silicon is a highly desirable material for semiconductors, which basically consist of three layers—an insulator, a conductor, and a semiconductor. Silicon gate refers to one of the layers in the structure, an electrode that controls the passage of voltage through the chip.

Before Intel's pioneering, aluminum electrode gates were built into semiconductors. But the use of metal made the manufacturing process so delicate and tricky that only 5 percent of the devices manufactured were usable. So Noyce and Moore decided to substitute polysilicon, a form of silicon, for metal in the gate. Their experience at Fairchild had convinced them that the switch would allow greater component density, higher production yields, and therefore greatly reduced costs. They were vindicated when they got yields of 10 percent on their first memory chip.

But it was their second MOS product that became famous. The

153

1103 memory chip held more than 1,000 bits, or more than 4,000 transistors. Intel wasn't first with its 1,000-bit chip. Advanced Memory Systems had started delivery of a similar chip a few months earlier in 1970. But Intel's 1103 quickly grabbed the major share of the market. The first semiconductor component to challenge cores, it became not only the industry standard but also the largest-selling semiconductor component in the world. Today the 1103 is employed in computer memories by fifteen of the world's eighteen major computer manufacturers.

A crucial element in the acceptance of the 1103 as the industry standard was the cooperation of a Honeywell team in testing the device to get rid of hidden bugs and in devising circuit specifications that suited makers of computers. The 1103 attracted so much attention and looked so promising that Texas Instruments, Fairchild, and almost everyone else in the semiconductor industry sought to become a "second source" for the chip. Even the biggest and best-known companies in the industry are required by customers to provide an alternative source of components, in case the primary supplier encounters production difficulties. To have leaders of the industry clamoring to become its backstop was a major achievement for a new company.

The AMS device was buried in this avalanche. "We had a better design but we blew it in the marketplace," says Robert H. F. Lloyd, former chairman of AMS. "They just bowled us over with their prestige, salesmanship, and the publicity their device got. AMS was just about broke then. We were a sick company and had a very low profile."

Soon Intel drew so far ahead of its competition that most rivals decided it wouldn't be worthwhile to copy the 1103. For this reason Texas Instruments chose not to enter the 1,000-bit memory-device race. It started working, instead, on the even denser chip. Meantime, Intel established its own second source. For a $2 million fee, it licensed a Montreal company, Microsystems International, Ltd. (MIL), and taught its engineers how to make the 1103. Only one other company, American Microsystems, Inc., makes the 1103 in quantity today.

The money from MIL came at a propitious time for Intel. The

market for semiconductors slumped in the spring of 1970, and price competition became intense. Some new companies found themselves in a cash bind. Intel escaped much of the impact because it was not yet in volume production. Even so, it was forced to lay off about one-seventh of its employees. Some directors asked whether construction should not be halted on a $2.3 million headquarters and production building in Santa Clara, but Noyce and Moore convinced the board that such drastic action was unnecessary. Still, the building stood unoccupied for about four months until Intel's orders picked up.

The key to Intel's success has been its ability to live up to its manufacturing promises. It was not easy. Two months after the 1103 was introduced, a complex reliability problem cropped up. An excess electrical charge on the surface tended to erase data stored with the chip. Recognizing that the company's whole future might be at stake, Intel's engineers worked at a panicky pace for two months to identify the cause of the problem, and six more to clear it up. How it was done remains a company secret. "This place was a madhouse," recalls Andrew S. Grove, then vice president and director of operations and now executive vice president. "I literally was having nightmares. I would wake up in the middle of the night, reliving some of the fights that took place during the day between various people working for me.

"The 1103 was a brand-new circuit-design concept, it brought about a brand-new systems-approach to computer memories, and its manufacturing required a brand-new technology," adds Grove. "Yet it became, over the short period of one year, a high-volume production item—high volume by any standards in this industry. Making the 1103 concept work at the technology level, at the device level, and at the systems level and successfully introducing it into high-volume manufacturing required, if I may flirt with immodesty for a moment, a fair measure of orchestrated brilliance. Everybody from technologists to designers to reliability experts had to work to the same schedule toward a different aspect of the same goal, interfacing simultaneously at all levels over quite a long period of time. This is a fairly obvious example why structure and discipline are so necessary in our operations."

To bring order to growth so phenomenal that "it's either a fantasy or a nightmare, depending on one's mood," Grove helped evolve a special operating style. Grove and his colleagues were trying to disprove the contention of the noted management consultant Peter Drucker that "today's growth companies are tomorrow's problems."

"The operating style that has been evolved at Intel is based on the recognition of our own identity," says Grove. "The semiconductor industry consists of companies that typically fall into one of two extremes: technology leaders and manufacturing leaders. Neither of these types of leadership would accomplish what we wanted to do. We wanted to capitalize on new technology and we wanted to sell our technology and our engineering over and over again. This means high volume. We regard ourselves as essentially a manufacturer of *high-technology jelly beans*.

"The first thing that a manufacturer of high-technology jelly beans needs is a different breed of people. The wild-eyed, bushy-haired, boy geniuses that dominate the think tanks and the solely technology-oriented companies will never take that technology to the jelly-bean stage. Likewise, the other stereotype—the straight-laced, crewcut, sideburn- and mustache-free manufacturing operators of conventional industry—will never generate the technology in the first place. Our needs dictated that we fill our senior ranks with a group of highly competent, even brilliant, technical specialists who were willing to adapt to a very structured, highly disciplined environment.

"Acquiring this relatively rare breed of individual is a problem all by itself. The first method we use is a fairly deliberate mixing of both old and young individuals—'old' meaning highly experienced people, 'young' meaning the technical geniuses who, because the industry is young, tend to be young themselves. The mixing itself has to be done carefully. It is not enough to simply mix them into a group. You have to mix them vertically. The second method that we use is an extensive college recruitment program." In addition to the excitement of working for a pioneering company, there's a big financial attraction for a new college graduate in starting with a company like Intel. An engineer fresh out of college gets a stock option on about $10,000 worth of Intel's stock—something he wouldn't get at a big company at all. On top of that he then can participate in a stock-purchase plan that Intel offers all its employees.

Having acquired a large number of skilled people, Intel then organized its engineering activities by orienting them toward market areas, such as computer main-frame memories, microcomputers, and timing circuits.

"Our manufacturing activities are organized along the lines of a totally different concept," adds Grove. "We actually borrowed from a very successful manufacturer of medium-technology jelly beans, i.e., hamburgers. When McDonald's wants to grow, it doesn't increase the size of the outlets, it just adds new franchises. That is exactly the principle we have adopted. We add production capacity in modular increments. Each module is meant to be identical to every other module, in the same way each McDonald's is the same, so that when we want to add capacity, we can ideally reach into the bookshelf and take down 'Specifications for Starting an Assembly Plant' ; let's see, steps 1, 2, 3 . . . and so on, all by the book. We really have gone a fair distance in this direction.

"This approach has some obvious advantages. Starting up a new franchise in a new location doesn't interfere with the hamburgers coming out of the existing facilities. You don't stumble over construction or get confused by the chaos that inevitably accompanies it. By making sure that everything from the process techniques to the personnel files are identical in every franchise, it is easier for us to develop management for the new location. The second echelon in franchise Number 2 will make good candidates for running franchise Number 3. They've faced all the problems before and can walk in and immediately find everything. After all, when you've seen one McDonald's you've seen them all. And, of course, our customers demand that all hamburgers manufactured in each of our franchises should be identical. Since they are made exactly the same way, in the same equipment, with exactly the same process, this is easy for us to achieve. This is an absolute must for us, since in order to utilize our production capacity efficiently, we must be able to shift production of certain items between the different manufacturing areas."

There's also a sociological reason, to be sure. Noyce is convinced that the day of the huge plant is gone, that today's workers perform much better in smaller, more informal facilities. Intel now has small production facilities not only in California but also in Oregon, in the Philippines, and in Malaysia.

To build up a first-rate production organization, Grove, among other things, introduced what may be the toughest process monitoring and quality control in the semiconductor industry. And he devised a system of bonuses for superior performance to reward teams in wafer processing and individuals in other critical jobs.

Even at that early stage Intel began to make a name for itself for keeping its promises. At one point early in its history, Intel convinced Honeywell to give it a contract for a custom memory device. Honeywell had already placed contracts with six semiconductor manufacturers, including Texas Instruments and Fairchild. "We started about six months later than the others," recalls Grove, "and we were the only ones to deliver the device, about a year later." That component is still being made.

Out of its on-time production feats Intel evolved a motto: "Intel delivers." If that sounds boastful, consider the peculiarities of semiconductor manufacturing. "This business lives on the brink of disaster," explains Moore. "As soon as you can make a device with high yield, you calculate that you can decrease costs by trying to make something four times as complex, which brings your yield down again." As a result, a gap between promise and performance has been endemic to the industry. Overeager technologists have often miscalculated future yields and therefore pledged deliveries that they could not meet or set prices that turned out to be below their costs.

"If you take an automobile and melt it down for steel," says Noyce, "the steel is a reasonable fraction of the selling price. But if you look at our stuff and melt it down for silicon, that's a small fraction of it—the rest is mistakes. The cost is highly dependent on how many mistakes you make. But we choose to work on the verge of disaster because that means that the job must be done by finesse rather than brute strength." Finesse to Noyce is "good people," while brute strength is "money and people." As another Intel executive puts it, "Part of the key to this business is knowing where the wheels are going to fall off."

Noyce, Moore, and the others they brought with them from Fairchild knew from experience how to calculate those all-important yields conservatively, and they made no extravagant promises. The second time around, says Noyce, "you get an idea what can go wrong and when it's going to go wrong." Edward L. Gelbach, senior vice president and director of marketing, turns down orders as a matter of course if he suspects that Intel can't deliver when expected. Intel makes more than 90 percent of its shipments on schedule, an extremely good record in its industry.

Lessons learned at Fairchild also helped anticipate the spurts in Intel's growth. In the early days at Fairchild it was difficult for Noyce and Moore to visualize what one could ever use big production space for, the whole industry being so tiny. Moore recalls having that feeling when he once looked at a 40,000-square-foot building offered to Fairchild. But having seen the industry burst at its seams, Noyce and Moore laid out plans for Intel's production facilities to occupy about 500,000 square feet. "You are able to think on an order of magnitude of different scale as a result of having gone through it once before," says Moore.

Intel has an insatiable need for skilled personnel and has tried some imaginative ways of meeting it. The company hired new employees for its wafer-processing facility at Livermore months before that plant went into operation and bused the employees thirty-five miles each way daily to Santa Clara to train them. To hang on to skilled people, Grove uses a technique that he calls "Peter Principle recycling." Instead of firing foremen and other managers who flop when promoted to more demanding jobs, he splits their tasks, giving them smaller responsibilities. Some of these "recycled" men have again advanced to higher positions; only a few have left.

Middle managers at Intel are monitored carefully but have a lot of operational freedom. "Lots of guys starting new companies are interested in keeping their fingers in every part of the pie," says Moore. "I think Bob and I are relatively willing to relinquish day-to-day details." For example, they have streamlined purchasing to the point where the engineer in charge of a project can buy a $250,000 tester, or whatever he needs, by simply signing for it—provided it's in his budget. "We feel very strongly that one of the ridiculous things a big company has is one of those deals where you need seven different signatures on a piece of paper to spend any money," says Moore. "That puts them in a situation where anyone can turn it down. All seven guys have to agree before it happens—anybody can say no but everybody has to say yes." Partly because of such decentralized decision making, Intel operates today with five vice presidents, only two more than it had at the start.

Despite the company's explosive growth, Noyce and Moore are trying to keep operations as informal as they can. Spaces in the huge Intel parking lot are not marked with officials' names as they are at big companies. "If Bob gets to work late," says Moore, "he parks way out in the corner of the lot. I think this will continue. Sometimes it's a pain in the neck. But the other problem is, once you start marking parking spaces, where do you stop? Once you start putting names on parking places, eventually you come to the level where you put one fellow's name on and not another's. That's a much tougher line to draw than in not doing it for anybody."

Noyce and Moore's approach to management is collaborative rather than hierarchical. They both practice persuasion rather than command. Noyce, in particular, would rather spend a couple of hours convincing a colleague how something should be done rather than forcing him to do it. Noyce may be deliberate in his dealings with people but his mind is razor sharp. "He has an incredible ability to have a quick understanding of almost any topic," says a former executive. "He can join in a debate on life-insurance actuarial rates—why it should cost three dollars and not four dollars. If you have a trading problem in Japan, you will find out that Bob not only speaks a little Japanese but also understands the Japanese temperament and the Japanese mode of doing business."

Noyce and Moore now spend far more of their time on management and business matters than they do on developing new technology. "Maybe you can do good technical work for ten years, if you work hard at it," Noyce explains, "but after that the younger guys are better prepared. It's a question of technical obsolescence, if you will."

The breakneck pace of innovation in electronics makes products—no matter how good they are—grow obsolete even faster than people. The 1103 was only three years old, just achieving its production peak, in 1973, but the trade press had already dubbed it a "DC-3." The supersonic transport that is about to zoom past the 1103 is the 4,000-bit memory chip, which squeezes some 14,000 transistors into its tiny confines. It isn't clear yet whether Intel will win this new race or whether there will be a clear-cut winner. Competitors, especially big companies, have become much more skilled in developing memory devices, and it is possible that two or three different 4,000-bit, or 4K, devices may dominate different segments of the market.

"We're probably reaching a major milestone now," says Noyce. "Any time there is a generation jump, it's a new ball game. The score you racked up before doesn't count. The experience your players got in the earlier game is still valuable in the new one. They work together as a team and don't make too many errors. But at the 4K level we're starting in the first inning again—and somebody else may win. It could be anybody—Mostek, TI, Fairchild. Everybody has gotten into the act this time," adds Noyce. "In fact, Texas Instruments, ourselves, and ten others have announced 4K chips."

Texas Instruments took an early lead with a fast 4K chip it started making available in sample quantities in August 1973. Intel had announced its 4K chip about a month earlier, but its circuitry operated more slowly than TI's model. It was fast enough for peripheral computer equipment but too slow to be a successor to the 1103 in computer main memories, the biggest market. With his customary frankness, Noyce called the early TI device "a major threat to us."

Intel soon countered, however, by deciding to make its 4K chip compatible with the one introduced by Texas Instruments. This, of course, was a tacit admission that TI's device is more advanced technologically. But Intel still counts on beating TI at volume production. This confidence is based on the fact that Intel has a better delivery record for its highly complex circuits than many industry giants have for simpler, long-established items. To bolster its bid in the 4K-chip game, Intel has continued development of faster 4K devices. In 1974 it came up with a chip that matches TI's in speed, so the two companies are competing for the same customers—computer main-frame manufacturers—and the firm that can deliver reliable components in quantity will win the major share of the market. The prospect makes TI a little nervous. Says J. Fred Bucy, group vice president in charge of TI's components division, "We've a high respect for Intel. They are always dangerous."

So fast is the semiconductor industry evolving that already under furious development are successors to the 4K—16K chips that contain up to *four* times the number of the minuscule components. In any case, Intel now appears to be firmly entrenched in the memory field. The 1103 chip accounts for only 20 percent of sales and the company offers a large number of other memory components for computers as well as calculators. Lloyd, the ex-chairman of Advanced Memory Systems, says, "They've got so much momentum, so much success, so much profit, and the microcomputer is opening such a big area that I hate to say it, but I look for them to keep growing."

To Noyce the future of Intel looks just as exciting as its past. The trap he wants to avoid is to become so engrossed in existing profitable products that he neglects new opportunities. Accordingly, Intel has been diversifying. For $2.8 million worth of common stock, the company in 1972 acquired Microma, Inc., which makes electronic watches that use Intel's chips. Recently Intel has also begun making add-on memories for computer users.

Intel's pioneering of the remarkable computer-on-a-chip, or microcomputer, has enabled it to capture about 90 percent of that burgeoning business. It is the fastest-growing segment of the semiconductor industry, faster even than memory and doubling every year. Microcomputers also offer new opportunities for entrepreneurs—not to make the devices but to put them together into brand-new products or to advise large users how to apply the new electronic brain power in places where computers are too expensive to use. As Noyce puts it, microprocessors offer people who want to start new companies "the power of going into advanced technology without a huge investment."

The beauty of the microcomputer for Intel lies not only in its apparently almost unlimited range of applications but also in the fact that it creates a potentially huge market for memory chips. Gelbach says that, for every dollar's worth of a microcomputer's logic circuits, Intel sells $5 to $10 worth of memory components. So great is the interest in microcomputers that their sales continued to increase even during the recession in 1974–75. What's more, Texas Instruments, the industry giant, once again became a backstop for Intel by announcing in the spring of 1975 that it would "second-source" Intel's principal microprocessor. This move, of course, enhanced Intel's already entrenched position in the field.

Microcomputers are beginning to extend the range of electronics into all sorts of unusual places. Noyce sees the telephone— "a phenomenally obsolete piece of equipment"—as the next big consumer item likely to switch to semiconductor innards. He visualizes a day not far off when office equipment, home appliances, games, cars, and many other products will come equipped with memory chips or microcomputers. For example, some automobiles already are built with microcomputers that can take over control of the brakes if the vehicle goes into a skid. An Intel microcomputer is being used to monitor the physical stresses in a loaded supertanker. This smallest of computers assures that the largest of all ships afloat can travel at a maximum safe speed under all ocean conditions. In another application, a system based on an Intel microcomputer performs a complete eye refraction in thirty-five seconds. It then prints out any required eyeglass prescription, freeing the opthalmologist of routine measurement tasks. This allows mass clinical eye examinations at a greatly reduced cost. Having led the way in putting the computer on a chip, Noyce is confident that Intel will play a big role as tomorrow's consumers reap the benefit of that accomplishment.

CHAPTER EIGHT

Zoecon Turns Bugs Against Themselves

In 1968 a tiny new company darted into an arena dominated by giants, seeking to produce safe and superior insecticides that would imitate a growth-regulating hormone naturally present in insects. Since then, Zoecon Corporation, of Palo Alto, California, has drawn nearer the goal than its much bigger rivals, which include Hoffman-LaRoche, Ciba-Geigy, Sandoz, and Stauffer Chemical. A significant step came early in 1975, when the Environmental Protection Agency gave Zoecon a permit to begin unlimited marketing of Altosid, a compound to keep pupae of mosquitos and barnyard flies from maturing into adults. This was the first time that a regulatory agency has allowed the sale of a product that depends for its effectiveness on deliberately planned molecular interference with the insects' own physiology. Older conventional insecticides were usually discovered in a hit-and-miss fashion. Now Zoecon is preparing still other remarkable hormonal insecticides to control pests that attack both ornamental plants and food crops.

Still a little enterprise, employing only about 100 people in its central operations, Zoecon is another of those pioneering companies started by businessmen-scientists who hope to cash in on new technologies. Its products are chemical mimics, or analogues, of a hormone—known as the juvenile hormone—that retards an insect's development. Applied at the right time, these synthetic imitators of natural secretions can disrupt the insects' growth, trapping them in a developmental dead end, creating tiny mixed-up mon-

165

sters with both mature and immature parts—insects destined to die because they can't feed or mate.

Another class of Zoecon products are chemical copies of the insect sex attractants known as pheromones. They lure unsuspecting male insects from miles away to rendezvous with dummy females, only to have the males perish on sticky cardboard traps.

These new insecticides are unlike any that came before them. They appear to be safe for other types of life, including man, other animals, and even insects of other species that live on the same plant and prey on the target pests—a big advantage over conventional chemicals that indiscriminately kill insects good and bad. Furthermore, these novel insecticides do not persist in the environment but are quickly degraded—another big plus over conventional insecticides. And while insects eventually might be expected to evolve resistance to the new compounds, they could have some difficulty in coping with copies of the molecules of their own internal secretions. In fact, their defense might prove suicidal.

There are many reasons Zoecon surged far ahead of its big competitors. It has some of the best scientists in the field, operating from a cleverly constructed financial base. Its president and chairman, Carl Djerassi, is a famous chemist, a principal developer of the birth-control pill, and a whirlwind of highly productive activity. But the main reason for Zoecon's advance—it has many other hormone analogues in field tests and laboratory development—is similar to the reasons for success of other pioneering companies discussed in this book.

Like other pioneering new companies, Zoecon is unencumbered by any need to protect existing products or by a big-company bureaucracy that could hinder the assembly of an efficient team of scientists from different disciplines. Furthermore, as Dr. Djerassi puts it, an independent company as small as Zoecon has "no insurance policy"—nothing to fall back on. This realization, he says, spurs its researchers to work with greater determination than they might in a larger company. Innovative small companies based on bright ideas create an atmosphere full of challenge, excitement, and the promise of big rewards and generate a momentum that big, more cumbersome corporations can't match.

The Entrepreneurs

In bringing juvenile-hormone analogues to market, Zoecon achieved the transition from the laboratory to application with dazzling speed. The structure of the natural juvenile hormone, vital for creating synthetic analogues, wasn't even known until 1966. And Zoecon didn't set up a product-development department until 1971.

Djerassi is no small reason for Zoecon's success. A chemist with a worldwide reputation, Djerassi leads two lives—as a professor of chemistry at Stanford University and as an industrial executive. He has done so many things so well that his friends never cease to marvel at his abilities and stamina. "I think of him as one of the wonders of nature," says Joshua Lederberg, the Stanford Nobelist and one of the "fathers" of molecular genetics.

To the consternation of some of his graduate students, Djerassi is the only chemistry professor at Stanford who schedules classes at 8:00 A.M. He spends the noon hours at Zoecon, eating lunch in his office to save time. (But it's no sandwich-at-the-desk ritual; a cook on the company's staff prepares and serves his meal with great care.) In the afternoon, Djerassi is usually back in his Stanford office.

Since he got his doctorate at the University of Wisconsin in 1945, he has written six books, contributed more than eight hundred papers to scientific journals, and has made major discoveries in steroid chemistry. He has also developed some novel molecular-instrumentation techniques. On weekends he can often be found on his big cattle ranch near Palo Alto. There, as elsewhere, his friends have trouble keeping up as Djerassi bounds up and down the hills and through redwood glades, even though he limps slightly because of a fused knee—the aftermath of a skiing accident. He has since designed a special boot and continues to ski with zest.

To his job at Zoecon he brings a feel for both the risks and the payoffs of research as well as knowledge of how research scientists think and work—insights gained in his years as a principal research executive at Syntex Corporation. Djerassi was born in Vienna of a Bulgarian father and an Austrian mother who were both physicians. After coming to the United States in 1939, he got a chemis-

167

try degree from Kenyon College in 1942, at eighteen. The following year, working for Ciba Pharmaceutical, he participated in the discovery of the first antihistamine.

The excitement of that discovery fired the young scientist to progressively greater achievements. As part of his Ph.D. thesis at Wisconsin, Djerassi attained the difficult technical feat of converting the male sex hormone testosterone into the female sex hormone estradiol.

Later Djerassi joined Syntex Corporation, then a small company in Mexico that was trying to develop new means of synthesizing cortisone and other steroids. He led a team at Syntex that produced synthetic cortisone from Mexican yams, bringing down sharply the price of this important hormone just beginning to be used in treatment of arthritis and other major diseases.

That achievement led to what may be considered the apex of Djerassi's career, the synthesis of an analogue of progesterone, a female sex hormone that could be taken orally to treat menstrual disorders. From there it was just a short step for researchers to figure out that a compound of that type could be used as an oral contraceptive. Djerassi's compound, norethisterone, is still found in more than half of all oral contraceptives in use in the world today.

For this achievement Djerassi is still acclaimed as a hero. When the president of Columbia University presented an honorary degree to Djerassi in 1975, he was interrupted by thunderous applause and cheers in the midst of his reading of the citation for Djerassi when he came to the sentence: "You were the prime mover in the introduction of the first widely successful oral contraceptives."

Djerassi has received dozens of other American and international honors, including the National Medal of Science and the American Chemical Society's Award for Creative Invention. He has also been elected member of the academies of science of a large number of foreign countries.

Djerassi continues to be intensely interested in the development of improved means of contraception. (He is even interested in a contraceptive pill for cats and dogs; in 1973 with two collaborators he wrote an article for the *Bulletin of Atomic Scientists* entitled

"Planned Parenthood for Pets?") But he views as his most satisfying scientific achievement still another of his contributions: the application of an analytical technique called optical rotatory dispersion to chemistry. In conjunction with other advanced methods it has made it possible to resolve in weeks chemical questions that used to take years, even lifetimes, to answer. Without those techniques, in fact, the existence of Zoecon would not have been possible. The new means have allowed the detection and elucidation of the structure of substances such as the juvenile hormone that occurs in minute amounts in insects.

As a company, Zoecon had its genesis in Syntex Laboratories, Inc., the Palo Alto–based subsidiary of Syntex Corporation. Zoecon's technology came out of an imaginative postdoctoral program started at Syntex by Djerassi, then vice president for research. Under this program, top professors at various American and European universities who were advisers to Syntex sent some of their best graduates to the company. Among them was a British-born chemist, John Siddall, who led a pioneering effort to synthesize ecdysone, a chemically complicated insect-molting hormone.

Syntex chemists became galvanized by ecdysone because it turned out to be structurally similar to steroid hormones, in which they had great proficiency. But an important adviser, a Harvard biologist named Carroll Williams, who has played a leading role in insect-hormone studies, convinced the Syntex scientists that they should abandon the work on ecdysone because of its great structural complexity and concentrate on the simpler juvenile hormone instead. Williams back in 1956 had made the first public suggestion that the juvenile hormone could be turned into an effective insecticide. Syntex followed Williams's advice.

The idea of what Syntex would try to do in the insect-hormone field crystallized, too. Originally the Syntex chemists were simply looking for new steroids with possible medicinal applications. But now they could see the intellectual beauty of turning an insect's key regulatory molecules into a potent weapon against that insect. For the first time the new approach would introduce a rational biochemical basis into the search for new insecticides, replacing the old-fashioned and not-so-intelligent random screening of

169

chemicals in the hope of hitting upon one that for some reason proved fatal to insects.

Syntex's decision to heed Williams's advice proved auspicious. Almost all researchers in the field since then have concentrated on the juvenile hormone. Aside from its complexity, ecdysone contains the stilbestrol molecule, which is suspected of being carcinogenic. Researchers therefore have shied away from introducing a synthetic molting hormone as an insecticide, but they are seeking an antiecdysone agent which would be an effective insecticide. Juvenile hormone occurs only in insects and holds no cancer-causing potential, as ecdysone appears to do.

As the research effort at Syntex grew, the company faced a decision on how best to proceed. Early in 1967 Syntex contacted about a dozen big manufacturers of pesticides to gauge their interest in a joint venture. While their research men were interested, their marketing executives were concerned about the possible impact of such research on their existing products. Syntex then took a different route. It decided to set up an independent company. The two top men at Syntex in the United States, the executive vice president, Alejandro Zaffaroni (see Chapter 6), and Djerassi, then vice president for research, both believed strongly in advancing new technology by forming new companies. A Syntex consultant—and having first-rate consultants was another strength—suggested a clever way of financing the new venture. Why not, he asked, make a stock offering that would retain a significant investment for Syntex stockholders in the new venture yet allow the venture to proceed independently by raising capital for it? The idea was accepted and executed in steps.

First, Zoecon was formed in 1968, with Syntex transferring to the new company its knowledge, rights, and patents in insect control as well as rights to the services of certain scientists and executives. Zoecon's three principal executives came from Syntex. Djerassi became president and chairman, in addition to his many other activities. Daniel Lazare, a chemist and research manager, became vice president for administration. British-born Lazare gave Zoecon its name: *zoe*, from the Greek for "life," and *con*, a con-

170

traction of "control." John Siddall became director of research; now still in his thirties, he is vice president for research.

Syntex kept 907,365 shares, or 49 percent, of Zoecon's stock and offered its shareholders the right to subscribe to the remaining 51 percent at the rate of one Zoecon share at $11 for each ten shares of Syntex held. The offering was made in 1968, just before the stock market began its big slide, and brought Zoecon about $10 million. This was the amount Syntex management had estimated would be needed for a five-year effort to determine if commercial insecticides could be developed from the juvenile hormone.

Syntex's interest in Zoecon has decreased to 44 percent and eventually may go down to 20 percent if all of the five million authorized shares are issued. It no longer takes an active role in Zoecon's management. Says Djerassi, "As far as I'm concerned, Syntex is a separate company that chose to invest in our place, and that's it."

Somewhat unexpectedly, Zoecon soon became listed on the Pacific Coast Stock Exchange; the exchange itself suggested the listing after trading in rights proved so popular. Zoecon stock zoomed to $60 a share at one point in 1969, riding the crest of the market boom in entrepreneurial high technology.

The stock's high price in 1969 led Djerassi and Lazare to think about acquiring a marketing capability by buying an established— and profitable—insecticide company. Djerassi is an exceedingly forward-looking scientist but a conservative in financial matters. He was eager to build a solid financial and marketing base for Zoecon as quickly as possible and did not want to repeat at Zoecon an error he had seen Syntex make. That company had been first to have an oral contraceptive ready for market, but it lacked a sales force at the time. As a result Searle moved into the market ahead of it.

Searching for a suitable match, Zoecon surveyed about two hundred firms before settling on Thuron Industries, Inc., of Dallas. Thuron operated outside the mainstream of the insecticide business; it made and sold chemicals to control insects that plague

171

farm animals. But the company was well managed and profitable, having registered a pretax profit of $671,000 on sales of $4,826,000 in 1969. Its owners, two brothers who had started the company on $2,000 in 1949, agreed to merge into Zoecon, in return for 289,098 Zoecon shares, worth about $10 million at the time. Since Zoecon acquired it, Thuron's sales and profits have increased significantly, with sales rising to $16 million in 1975.

The acquisition of Thuron turned Zoecon into an operating company, enabling it to write off its research and development expenditures against current income. Research spending in 1972 reached $2.9 million, about what a $100 million company might be expected to spend. Thuron's earnings have also enabled Zoecon to postpone the time when additional financing will be needed.

When hormone analogues begin to reach the general market, Thuron will sell those that fit its lines. Zoecon will sell the others itself, with the help of the marketing expertise that Thuron can supply. Zoecon has already established its own marketing network abroad, by taking different routes in different places. In Japan and Scandinavia it set up a joint venture with local companies and is doing the same thing in Italy and Greece. In Switzerland it established a subsidiary. In Spain it acquired a farm-chemicals company. In Czechoslovakia, where the Academy of Sciences was a pioneer in insect-hormone investigations, Zoecon made a short-term reciprocal agreement under which the academy assigned its patents to Zoecon for use in the Western world in return for use of Zoecon's patents in Eastern Europe.

Zoecon has found that both the Chinese and the Russians are very much interested in hormonal insecticides. In 1973, at the invitation of the Chinese Academy of Sciences, Djerassi lectured in China on birth control and insect-growth regulators. At the same time Zoecon's vice president of product development was visiting the Soviet Union. Since then, Zoecon has sold its products to both China and the Soviet Union.

The international scope of Zoecon's activities reflects the international nature of the original research that began in the 1920s and finally led to the juvenile-hormone analogues, or insert-

172

growth regulators, as Zoecon scientists prefer to call them. Researchers in Poland, England, Japan, West Germany, and many other countries contributed to the base of knowledge.

Scientists had long been fascinated by the carefully programmed course of cell and tissue division in insect development. The stages of development are punctuated by precisely timed periods of differentiation that lead from the eggs to the strikingly diverse forms that appear progressively as larvae, pupae, and adults. The remarkable metamorphosis that turns a dowdy caterpillar into a brilliantly hued butterfly is directed by the genes in the insect's cell nucleus. The chemical structure of this program is still little known, but it is clear that its forward progress is stimulated by the steroidal hormones, ecdysones, while the magnitude of change in the structure of a developing insect is governed by the amount of the juvenile hormone.

Juvenile hormone thus puts a brake on ecdysone to prevent an insect from maturing too soon. It is, in fact, a status quo hormone that keeps an insect in a state of eternal youth if there is an overdose of the substance. An insect has a high level of the hormone during its larval, or nymphal, stage but destroys most of it internally before metamorphosing into a pupa or adult. The juvenile hormone appears to prevent the expression of genetic information needed to take an insect into its next stage of life.

Into this chink in the insects' armor enter Zoecon's analogues. When insects are sprayed with the synthetic juvenile hormone at the susceptible stage in their development, their orderly growth is disrupted. Unable to undergo metamorphosis, the insects emerge as crippled intermediates between larvae and pupae, or pupae fail to develop into adults.

In the beginning, it seemed to Zoecon and almost everyone else doing research with hormonal insecticides that the primary target should be the major pests attacking big cash crops—cotton, potatoes, corn. To protect those crops, American farmers spend at least $100 million a year on insecticides. Accordingly, Zoecon scientists in 1969 began testing a large number of juvenile-hormone analogues on such insects as the tobacco budworm, which despite its name is a major cotton pest, and the corn rootworm.

It soon became evident, however, that there was no easy way to deliver hormone analogues to some of the major pests. The tobacco budworm, for instance, develops inside a cotton boll, while the larva of the corn rootworm matures underground. Besides, some of the most destructive insects cannot be directly and effectively attacked with juvenile-hormone analogues because they are most sensitive to the substances only at the very end of their larval stage. By that time, the larvae, or caterpillars, may have devoured most of the crop. In fact, in one grotesquely science-fiction-like test, experimenters with bad timing sprayed a potato patch with juvenile-hormone mimic and produced hordes of giant Colorado potato-beetle larvae that voraciously attacked the crop. Obviously, that's not what the farmer needed. Zoecon therefore began to shift its emphasis to pests that are easier to control. "After screening analogues for about eighteen months," recalls Siddall, "we recognized that there was a small number of insect types that were going to be susceptible to our compounds, and we saw clearly that some others wouldn't be susceptible. And that's still true today." Since perhaps $500 million a year is spent on conventional insecticides in the United States alone, Zoecon still has a sizable market to shoot for.

Zoecon was able to adjust to this changing situation because its researchers discovered how to derive a whole class of hormone analogues from a readily available compound made from turpentine. They were at once much more potent and stable than the natural juvenile hormone and much less expensive to make. It was no easy task to arrive at these analogues, of course. Siddall and his team, for instance, had to synthesize about fifteen hundred variants of Altosid before they finally came up with an analogue about two thousand times more potent and five times more stable than the natural juvenile hormone. This development dramatically improved Zoecon's outlook. Its scientists could now predict how analogues would work in the field. As Siddall puts it, "We arrived at the structure [of analogues] by a combination of witchcraft and intuition, with a lot of guidance from the basic principles of medicinal chemical modification."

To figure out the structure of analogues that would work, Zoecon scientists had to bridge some big gaps in knowledge. So minute are the amounts of natural juvenile hormone in insects, so fleeting is the nature of the hormone once it is exposed to air and sunlight, so difficult is the collection of sufficient amounts of the hormone for analysis that so far the hormone has been detected only in certain moths and one type of grasshopper. Scientists aren't even certain whether there is one juvenile hormone or more. They have found so far three similarly acting substances but two of them may be precursors of the third.

The Zoecon scientists, however, were going on the reasonable assumption that all insects, in one way or another, need juvenile hormone for normal development. The empirical nature of the research so far hasn't stopped them from developing analogues active against insects in which juvenile hormone has not yet been detected.

Testing the analogues, Zoecon scientists found them to be effective against a long list of insect pests, including aphids, scale, whiteflies, leafhoppers, and mealybugs. Zoecon already is trying out a number of the compounds as possible commercial products. "What we need to control those insects in a practical and economic way," says Siddall, "is proper formulation of the compounds to increase their stability."

It was Zoecon's special packaging of its antimosquito Altosid analogue that boosted the substance's stability in the field from about thirty-six hours to as much as ten days. If a raw chemical were sprayed in a swamp, it would degrade fairly rapidly and there would not be enough of the substance around to affect the mosquito larvae. Zoecon scientists therefore put Altosid into microscopic polymer capsules that slowly release the compound as they degrade. This slow-release packaging is something that other companies were not able to offer.

Since some of the insects that succumb to analogues attack both cash crops and garden flowers, Zoecon has a dual marketing opportunity. Its initial applications will be for use of analogues on ornamental and other nonfood plants. This could be a big market that would include home owners who grow flowers in their backyards as well as greenhouse and nursery operators. It is also a fairly accessible market because regulatory approval can be obtained more readily for substances that are not used on food crops. Nevertheless, regulatory agencies obviously have to be extremely careful in approving large-scale use of substances that have never been used before. A lot of testing has already gone into proving that juvenile-hormone analogues are not toxic to other kinds of life if used in prescribed amounts.

Agricultural uses will expand before long, however. Zoecon is already putting Altosid into cattle feed. The substance is consumed by the cattle and passed through their intestines into the manure to kill the pupae of flies that infest cattle feed lots and barnyards. Zoecon scientists have shown that the structure of the Altosid molecules prevents their absorption into the tissues of cattle.

Altosid also has been found to destroy fire ants, possibly because it disrupts the complex chemical communication system in an ant colony. This is important for farmers because in heavily infested areas fire ants may build as many as fifty mounds per acre, interfering with cultivation. The ants have a fierce sting and frequently make their homes in bales of hay; farm workers understandably dislike handling infested bales. Unless brought under control, the Department of Agriculture fears that the fire ant—now confined mainly to the South and Southeast—may spread as far as New Jersey and California. Present-day ant killers are potent poisons.

The analogues' lack of toxicity could be employed to great advantage in another important agricultural application: protection of stored grain. Conventional chemicals, because of their high toxicity, have to be used in such small amounts that they don't quite do the job.

Any resemblance the analogues have to conventional insecticides, which usually kill on contact, is superficial. That is why Zoecon likes to refer to its products as "insect-growth regulators." The slow and seemingly devious ways in which analogues dispose of insects can best be seen in the action of Enstar, an analogue the company is now testing. Enstar is active against aphids, the tiny, ubiquitous, and voracious devourers of garden plants and food crops. Gerardus B. Staal, Zoecon's Dutch-born director of biological research, found that Enstar kills aphid embryos, which are carried to maturity inside the female aphid. Subsequently, the mother aphid is killed, too, possibly because she is poisoned by the dead embryos.

But it takes a few days for the aphids to die, and farmers accustomed to the instant killing power of conventional insecticides are apt to get impatient. One Zoecon scientist recalls that a farmer on whose plants the antiaphid hormone analogue had been sprayed was upset the next morning at seeing the aphids just as frisky as they had been before spraying. The farmer then did what most others would do; he sprayed the aphids with a conventional insecticide that kills on contact, spoiling Zoecon's experiment.

The slow action of products like Enstar obviously has a marketing disadvantage that can be overcome only by an extensive educational effort. Zoecon scientists think, however, that they can effectively explain the importance of timing to users, through illustrated product literature, lectures, and advertising.

The complexities of analogue action may well be outweighed by the advantages offered by the substances, especially their relative specificity. A selective attack against target pests has been difficult with conventional insecticides because they generally kill indiscriminately. But analogues devised by Zoecon are more potent against certain insect pests than they are against their predator insect enemies, which are usually of a different species. The compound that kills aphid embryos, for instance, leaves such aphid enemies as ladybird beetles and predator wasps largely unaffected and fully active. When pests are attacked with specific analogues, says Staal, "the predators are going to help you, because they will be desperately looking for the few survivors."

The introduction of these promising new insecticides comes at a highly appropriate time not only because of widespread concern about the damage to the environment by the persistent conventional insecticides but also because superpests have emerged, so resistant to present-day insecticides that in some areas farmers have been forced to abandon cotton fields, for instance. Many types of mosquitoes are also becoming resistant to standard sprays. Among them is the dangerous *anopheles* mosquito, which transmits ma-

177

laria, still the most serious disease in terms of the number of people afflicted. Some insects have become so adept at coping with the conventional chemicals that they even seem to thrive on them. Some of the conventional insecticides, such as DDT, have already been largely banned or face a legal ban, and effective and safe substitutes are badly needed.

The arrival of juvenile-hormone analogues does not signal a sudden end to conventional chemicals, to be sure. Without these insecticides and pesticides, the practice of agriculture as it has evolved in the developed world would be difficult. Conventional insecticides, furthermore, will continue to be used for a long time to come, but in smaller amounts and in conjunction with other methods. Integrated techniques are now being developed in which many factors, such as crop rotation, the use of predator insects, and control of pests with viruses and with juvenile hormone analogues, are incorporated into a single powerful weapon.

Zoecon is pioneering another class of insect substances called pheromones that fit well into the new approach to insect control. Some pheromones are sex attractants. Probably the most potent biological molecules known, pheromone sex lures are released by female insects in minute amounts and can be detected by males miles away. Zoecon's synthetic preparations, now selling at the rate of a few hundred thousand dollars' worth a year, imitate the natural pheromones. They draw the male pests to sticky cardboard traps hung in orchards and fields to monitor the emergence of such pests as the codling moth, red-banded leaf roller, and various fruit flies. Conventional insecticides can then be employed more judiciously than in the past. A later step will be to use the pheromones in conjunction with hormone analogues. To start with, Zoecon is successfully marketing a housefly attractant, Muscalure, by adding it to a sugar bait manufactured by Thuron.

Insects release a large number of other pheromones—to call their friends to a choice food source, for instance, and even to warn of approaching predators. The effect of one such "alarm pheromone," discovered by Zoecon and its collaborators at the University of Massachusetts, is to make aphids, in Siddall's words, "run like crazy or drop off the leaf." The congregation pheromones, on the other hand, are being tested to lure insects into traps.

Zoecon's future will depend to a large extent on how successfully it can balance the scientific realities against the grower's needs. Djerassi is certain that his company's decision to concentrate on fairly small markets first and even to create brand-new markets will pay off fast. "We are going to become a very significant company much earlier than anyone assumes," he predicts. This will happen, he hopes, in part because of Zoecon's strategy of relying on sales of established and improved insecticides by Thuron and other subsidiaries.

At least in the beginning the new insecticides will sell for about as much as farmers and mosquito controllers now pay for the most expensive new conventional insecticides. But the per-acre cost of control is what really counts for the field users. And analogues such as Altosid may be the only workable insecticide for certain specific applications. Because some species of mosquitoes have become resistant to conventional insecticides, the alternative has been to use oil to stop the larvae from developing. Altosid arrived just in time to help divert oil to more pressing uses. It takes only three fluid ounces of Altosid to control mosquitoes on one acre of water.

If insects should develop resistance to the analogues, Zoecon's long-term prospects obviously would become clouded. Only a few years ago some scientists said flatly that insects would be unable to evolve a defense against their own internal secretions or their analogues. But they are no longer so sure. Siddall and most other chemists now believe that natural juvenile-hormone molecules are attached to bigger protein molecules. The analogues, lacking a protein partner, are much smaller molecules than the natural substance and therefore might be subject to easier destruction by the insects' own enzymes. It is also possible that the insects may evolve tougher skins that would prevent analogues from penetrating their bodies. So far, however, no sign of developing resistance has been seen.

It remains to be determined, too, whether long-term use of hormone analogues on a large scale can damage other life. In laboratory and field tests, the hormone analogues have appeared to be remarkably nontoxic compared to conventional chemicals. Tests on animals for possible cancer-causing effects also have been negative.

With conventional insecticides under increasing pressure—an almost total ban on the use of DDT went into effect in 1973 in the United States—Zoecon's success depends to a large extent on how fast it can develop a market for its analogues. Not only are new and safer conventional insecticides being developed, but there will also be competition from such nonconventional insecticides as bacterial and viral agents.

Getting a product from the laboratory to the market is always a tricky business, and in Zoecon's as in any other insecticide manufacturer's case, the difficulties are compounded by the need to meet the requirements of the regulatory agencies. It took the company five years to get the final approval of Altosid by the Environmental Protection Agency.

Djerassi and his colleagues are highly optimistic, however. Djerassi believes that the molecular attack on insects is just beginning to gather speed. If other kinds of hormonal weapons can be developed, he thinks products of this kind might eventually capture perhaps as much as 30 to 50 percent of the worldwide market for insecticides, which at present amounts to about $1 billion a year. Efforts will be made to apply existing analogues in new ways, broadening the market for them. For example, analogues could be sprayed in the winter in places where insects hibernate or undergo a diapause; this would fool the insects into thinking spring had come, and they would perish because of their untimely emergence.

One promising addition to the arsenal of hormonal control weapons would be an anti-juvenile-hormone agent. Work on this kind of agent, which would vastly increase the scope and range of hormonal insecticides, is now in progress at Zoecon and elsewhere. Such a chemical would gum up the molecular machinery inside an insect, blocking the manufacture of the natural juvenile hormone. As a result larvae would precociously develop into micropupae and then into miniature, and probably deformed and ineffective, adults. "If this didn't solve the insect pest problem," says Carroll Williams, the Harvard biologist, "it would certainly make it smaller because of the microminiaturization of insects."

This approach, of course, would finally open the big agricultural crop market that Zoecon had aimed at originally. To control major caterpillar pests, it might be easier to try to interfere with their development at two or three stages—the egg stage, the larval stage, and the female adult stage.

While keeping that long-range goal in sight, Zoecon scientists hit upon a new class of nonpersistent chemicals that kill mites by inactivating their eggs. The chemicals are not related to the juvenile hormone but their development was suggested by the research into those insect substances. Mites destroy crops and garden plants; the miticide market amounts to a $100 million-a-year business.

Many additional facets of the hormonal method remain to be worked out. Siddall expects, for example, that probably half a dozen more kinds of insect hormones will be discovered. Among them should be sex hormones; once these are isolated, it will be possible to seek out antagonists that will block the reproductive drive of various species. Other weak spots in the insects' defenses will surely be found. Williams thinks it will be possible to manipulate by chemical means the behavior of insects in such a way that moths, for instance, would behave as if they were still larvae and die as a result.

With much still to be learned, Zoecon's translation of the purest kind of pure research into a marketable product in just five years already ranks as an impressively rapid application of science to the solution of an urgent need. This is the fastest ever that a major basic scientific discovery has been transformed into practical application. Djerassi, who has long been concerned about the impact of science on society, is particularly pleased with the apparent safety of the new compounds. He says, "It is not often that you can combine great scientific excitement and profit potential with genuine social responsibility."

CHAPTER NINE

Thermo Electron Corporation: From the Moon to the Steam Engine

The area of energy generation and conversion has been one of the least successful of man's technological enterprises. The steam engine, developed two hundred years ago, freed man from his dependence on the power of human or animal muscle and on wind and water power. Since then, only one really new way of generating power—nuclear reactors—has been added. Even the harnessing of the atom, however, did not change the basically backward methods of transforming energy into useful work or products. There has been surprisingly little improvement in many industrial processes where energy use is concerned. It still takes two hundred tons of water and a ton of fuel to make one ton of paper—the same as at the end of the last century. In terms of utilization of energy, the paper industry rather typically is operating at an astounding *0.2 percent* efficiency.

Into this static, wasteful world in 1956 barged George N. Hatsopoulos, a quiet-spoken, young thermodynamicist intent on revolutionizing the field. He employed as his vehicle a company he calls Thermo Electron Corporation, based in Waltham, Massachusetts, along Boston's famous Route 128, home of many other high-technology enterprises.

Approaching sales of $100 million a year, Thermo Electron has emerged as a quintessential example of how high technology can be applied to technologically impoverished fields. Few companies have utilized new technology as successfully in such diverse

183

places. Thermo Electron has sent its novel energy-generating devices both to the surface of the moon and into the kitchens of fast-food chains. It has built home furnaces smaller and more efficient than any that existed before, again employing space-age technology. Under intensive development in the company laboratories is an implantable artificial heart powered by a tiny steam engine that runs on a single drop of water. That's just a small sampling of Thermo Electron's work in energy conversion and generation.

In an exceedingly timely development, furthermore, the techniques being developed by Thermo Electron conceivably could help the United States attain energy independence. This could be achieved by applying existing as well as novel devices to industrial energy generation. A mere 1 percent increase in energy conservation in industrial processes, Hatsopoulos calculates, would save the United States more than a million barrels of oil a day. He even thinks that the American industry could generate enough electricity to meet the country's needs as a by-product of these improved approaches.

Thermo Electron's cornerstone is thermodynamics, the branch of physics that deals with the relationships between energy and heat (*therme* is "heat" in Greek, and *dynamis* stands for "power"). Hatsopoulos, now one of the world's foremost thermodynamicists, as well as business innovator, had been bothered by gaps in thermodynamic knowledge ever since he was a college student in his native Greece. These gaps in part account for the amazing industrial inefficiencies.

He grew up in a family of scientists and engineers. His father was both a mechanical and electrical engineer. One of his father's cousins presided over the National Technical University in Athens, informally known as the Athens Polytechnic. In the clannish, close-knit Greek manner, the youngster was groomed to become a professor and eventually president of the country's best technical university.

Hatsopoulos's preparation for a scientific career began of his own volition when he was still in the first grade of grammar school. "I was always, as far back as I can remember, extremely interested in anything mechanical or electrical and was always the fixer-upper of the whole neighborhood," he recalls. "When I was about eight years old, I set up my own laboratory in the basement and that's where I spent all my free time. I didn't participate in sports or anything else."

In the busy brain of the fledgling technologist also burned an entrepreneurial urge. He used his lab as a commercial venture even as a teenager. When the Germans occupied Greece in World War II, the young Hatsopoulos not only put together illegal radio transmitters for the Underground for free but he also made and sold equally illegal receivers to the public at large. "I loved enterprise," says Hatsopoulos, "so the idea of having my own technical company, or creating a company, was my desire as far back as I remember."

But Hatsopolous didn't fall in love with thermodynamics at first sight. In fact, when he took a course in thermodynamics in his second year at the Athens Polytechnic, he disliked it. He was intent on becoming an electronic engineer. Thermodynamics seemed dull by comparison.

Often an exciting teacher ignites a student's interest in a field. In Hatsopoulos's case, a fairly dull teacher did the job. The elderly professor who taught thermodynamics became so exasperated with his curious student's difficult questions that he finally forbade him to ask them. Hatsopoulos, however, persisted on his own. His interest was now aroused by what seemed to him to be gaps and inconsistencies in thermodynamic theory. He sought answers in the library and from other professors to no avail.

Hatsopoulos had intended to do graduate work at MIT, but when an opportunity came in 1947 to go to MIT on a scholarship even before he had graduated from the Polytechnic, he took it. He knew that there were world-renowned thermodynamicists at MIT and he hoped they would answer his burning questions. He sought a description of thermodynamic events on the molecular level. At MIT he discovered soon enough that those questions concerned some of the world's major physicists, from Einstein on down. Undeterred, Hatsopoulos engaged in a dialogue with MIT thermodynamicists, including Professor Joseph H. Keenan. They assured him there were no definitive answers to his questions. Continuing his quest, Hatsopoulos eventually wrote a definitive textbook on thermodynamics, with Professor Keenan. But he continues his ceaseless search for better definition of thermodynamic theory even today.

During his studies at MIT Hatsopoulos became convinced that heat generation and conversion was a badly neglected but potentially enormous field waiting to be tapped commercially. He could see that after World War II many industrial areas—electronics, drugs, chemicals, plastics—had transformed themselves into fast-growing, technologically oriented industries. But the field of energy had hardly been touched by innovation.

Hatsopoulos could see clearly that energy-conversion efficiencies obtained in industrial processes were far below the limits imposed by the laws of thermodynamics. The processes of steel, paper, and cement making, among others, were developed at the end of the nineteenth century and had changed little since. Whatever progress had been made was achieved by squeezing an existing fixed process to near perfection without changing the nature of the process itself.

Even such a relatively efficient technique as conversion of steam into electricity in power stations reached its upper limit at about 40 percent efficiency. That was by far the highest efficiency achieved in any industrial process—most others had attained a mere fraction of that—but Hatsopoulos knew that the thermodynamic limit in energy conversion in burning fuel is about 96 percent.

The answer was clear: start thinking of new processes with a higher upper limit. That's precisely what Hatsopoulos did during 1953–56 while a graduate student and instructor at MIT. He began investigating more direct means of transforming heat into electricity.

At the same time Hatsopoulos started thinking about starting a company that would embody his ideas. The concept of the company was broad. Thermodynamics would serve as his company's conveyor belt to develop new products. It would be the currency that could be applied anywhere there are energy transactions.

That was the concept Hatsopoulos sold to his good friend Peter Nomikos and later to Laurence Rockefeller, who became another important backer. Nomikos was then a student at Harvard. Being the heir to a Greek shipping fortune, Nomikos could afford to invest $50,000 in Thermo Electron to start with, and by 1960 a half million dollars to help the company expand. The Rockefeller family later put in $750,000.

In the traditional manner, Thermo Electron began in 1956 in a garage in Belmont. The garage was below street level, so when it snowed and the snow melted, the floor would be covered with about two inches of water. "We had to build the equipment above the water level," says Hatsopoulos. He continued at the same time as an assistant professor at MIT, drawing no salary from Thermo Electron to help the young company conserve its resources.

Although Hatsopoulos's idea for company foundation was broad, the firm had to start with something specific. This happened to be a device that attracted worldwide notice, a thermionic energy converter. Thermionics is direct generation of electricity from heat—a dramatic shortcut over the "normal" process. Normally, heat is converted into electricity by using it to boil water. The steam that is generated is employed to drive turbines. Efficiency of generation of electricity with steam has an intrinsic limit, however. The upper bound is imposed by the temperature of steam. Even though combustion temperature is typically about 3,000 degrees Fahrenheit, a steam power plant is limited to a working temperature of around 1,000 degrees. "The moment you limit your acceptance of heat to 1,000 degrees," says Hatsopoulos, "you have established an upper bound of efficiency of about 40 percent."

So the trick to getting more efficiency is to utilize heat at a higher temperature. But this can't be done with steam because pressures become too high and corrosion too dangerous. The need thus arises for a new working fluid.

Hatsopolous asked himself an intriguing question: Why not use a flow of electrons as a kind of a working fluid? He knew electrons could withstand any temperature. The idea of doing away with moving parts in energy-generating devices and thus achieving far more efficient production of energy had intrigued scientists ever since the phenomenon of thermionics became known at the end

187

of the nineteenth century. What could be a more modern working "fluid" than matter itself, in the form of electrons?

As a heat source for his thermionic device, Hatsopoulos had in mind both fossil and nuclear fuels. Since fossil fuels are easier to handle and can generate sustained combustion at about 3,000 degrees Fahrenheit, Hatsopoulos calculated that thermionic conversion could yield efficiency of approximately 60 to 90 percent—half again as good as the best power plants operating on steam alone.

Hatsopoulos was the first scientist to build a working thermionic device in 1956. In its simplest configuration, a thermionic converter is similar to a diode electron tube. It consists of a heat source (which could even be solar energy), two metal plates, or electrodes, and a heat sink. The electrodes are sealed in a chamber containing electricity-conducting gases. Heat is supplied at high temperature to one electrode, the "emitter" from whose surface electrons are forced to evaporate and flow to the cooler "collector" electrode, situated only a fraction of an inch away. There the electrons condense and enter the "electrical load"—say, a light bulb in an experimental device—and then return to the emitter electrode via electrical leads.

Since the electrons don't burn up in the process, high theoretical efficiency becomes possible. Hatsopoulos's pioneering thermionic converter was a rudimentary experimental device, of course. Even so, its electric output ran a tiny electric fan. Hatsopoulos knew, of course, that tremendous obstacles stood in the way of practical commercial thermionic converters. High temperatures, he knew, would require major advances in metallurgy, in heat transfer, in combustion, in electron emission from metal surfaces, and in insulation, among other areas.

"When we started," Hatsopoulos recalls, "we said let's set a goal for ten to twenty years from now to have the process developed. We planned to take the problems areas more or less simultaneously and try to achieve breakthroughs in each. As advances would occur, we figured that we could utilize these findings in other areas, even before thermionics had a chance of being put together."

Thermionics indeed proved to be the seed from which flourished the Thermo Electron tree. Its branches thrust out in completely unexpected directions.

Before that expansion became possible, though, Thermo Electron had to cope with the unexpected competition it had created. The infant company had only five employees—two engineers, two technicians, and a bookkeeper—two years after it was founded. But its successful production of the thermionic converter created a worldwide commotion. Now giant companies—General Electric, General Dynamics, North American Aviation, Martin-Marietta, and others—all rushed into the field. The startling beeps of Sputnik I had just signaled the start of the space age and scientists could clearly see a use for compact energy sources promised by thermionics.

By 1961 Hatsopoulos could count no fewer than twenty-seven companies working in thermionics. The entry of the huge firms made life difficult for Thermo Electron. Although Thermo Electron was recognized as the inventor, when it came time for the government to hand out contracts, officials felt that big concerns such as GE and RCA were better equipped to pursue research in thermionics. Such blind trust in big companies, often unjustified, hinders small companies in other fields, too.

It would have been easy for Thermo Electron to give up or reduce its goals in order to cash in on the aerospace bonanza. There were attractive offers from big companies. One, Martin-Marietta, offered to buy 51 percent of Thermo Electron stock and to double Hatsopoulos's salary while retaining him as president.

Hatsopoulos stubbornly held on to his long-range goals. It took some years before the government became convinced that despite its limited size Thermo Electron was far in the forefront of thermionics. Now the government began to award important contracts, including work on components for the generators, to the tiny company. Out of this work grew the development of thermoelectric generators to power recording instruments installed on the moon by United States astronauts.

But practical-minded Hatsopoulos never intended to make Thermo Electron dependent on aerospace contracts. In fact, in the early 1960s, after the Atomic Energy Commission had started a major research effort in thermionics that it oriented toward space applications, Hatsopoulos tried to convince the AEC that space was only one of potential applications. Says Hatsopoulos, "The potential of this device is for generating electric power on earth."

The Thermo Electron tree really began to grow, however, when the company began solving the fundamental problems that stood in the way of commercial thermionic power. It was one thing to develop nuclear thermionic generators for the space program. Money was no obstacle in those programs. As Thomas H. Widmer, Thermo Electron's vice president for engineering, puts it, "Problems were trampled to death." Widmer himself led the development of the nuclear generators for space applications while working for GE before joining Thermo Electron in 1968.

To develop such devices for the commercial market was something else again. Obviously, commercial customers couldn't pay millions of dollars for a single energy generator the way Uncle Sam did. Thermo Electron had to evolve economic ways to make thermionics work.

In Hatsopoulos's scheme, thermionics was to be only an element in the whole process of rigorous application of thermodynamic principles to improvement of energy generation and conversion. His interests start with the fundamental and extend all the way to a practical product that's salable. "I have deliberately pushed the whole company always thinking in terms of products that someone would need and not just fun things to do."

Hatsopoulos's strategy from the start was to build manufacturing facilities if Thermo Electron could afford them or to acquire companies that had production facilities in the fields of interest or to license a product or process to a larger company.

But even the fertile brain of George Hatsopoulos could not visualize in advance the remarkable ricocheting of Thermo Electron's research results into ever new applications. As early as 1963 the company began to commercialize its products; it started metallurgical services and began to manufacture rare metals, an outgrowth of its research on heat transfer at high temperatures. Soon thereafter, Thermo Electron scientists spotted an invention that they applied in many imaginative ways. This was the so-called heat pipe that had been invented by AEC scientists. It seemed particularly well suited to make thermionic emitters yield electrons at a constant temperature.

One of the embodiments of the heat pipe as a practical device is a tube of tungsten with boiling lithium inside it. The boiling metal forms a vapor that condenses, transferring the heat through the pipe walls. Aside from using the heat pipe as a component of thermionic converters, Thermo Electron could see many other uses for it. One such application, still evolving, is to employ the heat pipe as a heat source for vacuum furnaces that are used for heat treating high-grade steels and other metals. The normal way of supplying heat for such furnaces is to use electrodes, but that's wasteful. First, heat must be turned into electricity, and then electricity back into heat. "If we could put a heat pipe in the wall of a furnace, we could transfer huge amounts of heat down the heat pipe, instead of heating the furnace electrically," says Widmer. Thermo Electron has now completed an experimental model of such a furnace, which is undergoing tests.

That and other furnaces Thermo Electron has developed have gained from research on thermionics in still other ways. As part of its work in heat transfer, Thermo Electron developed a process it calls "jet impingement" in which hundreds of small combustion jets transfer about four times as much heat as is available in a conventional furnace. Jet impingement, too, has found its way into Thermo Electron products.

To run a thermionic converter at nearly 4,000 degrees Fahrenheit, Thermo Electron needed a new type of insulation. Existing insulation had ten times the heat leakage rate that a thermionic device could tolerate. Thermo Electron needed the seemingly impossible: one hundred insulation layers in a space one-eighth of an inch wide. The problem was how to separate the layers in that small space. Thermo Electron engineers overcame the obstacle by making very thin rows of tungsten foils. On these foils they spread insulating microspheres so small they are invisible to the naked eye. This is somewhat equivalent to taking two plates of metal an acre in area each and keeping them a foot apart. The plates,

1/1000 of an inch thick, transfer heat by radiation. This insulation, Thermo Electron scientists feel, is ten times better than any that existed before. It enables the new furnace to operate efficiently at 4,000 degrees Fahrenheit, with an electrical power requirement less than one-tenth of conventional furnaces.

Another clever application of these seemingly esoteric devices is in the mundane field of cooking griddles, where Thermo Electron applied both the heat pipe and jet impingement. Instead of liquid metal, an organic—that is, carbon-based—fluid is used. In this case, a small, compact gas burner warms up the lower surface of the heat pipe. The upper surface is the grill. It produces highly uniform temperature. "You don't get burning fat at one point because you've got the right cooking temperature in the middle but cooler temperature at the edge," says Hatsopoulos. "You've instead a uniform surface that heats up in a few minutes as opposed to an hour or so for a regular griddle." All around, the heat-pipe griddle is a striking example of how sensible use of energy can cut waste. The wasted energy that is now produced in restaurant kitchens has to be taken out with air conditioners or fans—a second price for excess energy use. The heat pipe griddle not only uses about 40 percent less gas than a conventional griddle but it also eliminates that waste.

The heat-pipe griddle is now being tested by a fast-food chain. Thermo Electron has also applied the heat-pipe principle to deep friers and frozen-food warming ovens. All these devices have been licensed to be manufactured by the U.S. Range Company.

So far, the novel griddle is too expensive for the average home. One home that will boast the new device, however, will be Hatsopoulos's new house being built in Lincoln, Massachusetts, not far from the company headquarters. Cooking is among the versatile scientist's many interests.

The thermionics tree has nevertheless thrust out a branch into the home. Thermo Electron has applied jet impingement to compact furnaces for homes and apartment buildings; this cuts the furnaces' fuel consumption by about 15 percent.

In trying to market the novel furnaces, Thermo Electron ran into the limits that a small company must often face. It licensed

Rheem Manufacturing several years ago to make the furnaces, but that large manufacturer at the time was selling all the conventional furnaces it could make. Understandably, Rheem had little incentive in taking something of a gamble on a new furnace, even if it was more efficient. Then the economy went from boom to near bust and demand for furnaces fell off sharply. In 1975 Thermo Electron was still waiting for its novel furnace to reach the consumer market.

As this case shows, there's often an inherent difficulty in bringing new technology into a mass-production environment. "It can be a long step between laboratory demonstration of a device," says Hatsopoulos, "and its demonstration in the hands of the public." He thinks that where energy conservation goes, it may be up to the federal government to apply pressure on manufacturers to make sure the equipment they sell is more efficient in energy use. Tax credit to consumers who buy such equipment may be still another way of encouraging the use of more efficient energy devices.

Thermo Electron's research has been so impressive that the natural-gas utility companies have been supporting it to the tune of about $1 million a year since 1964. Out of this support evolved Thermo Electron's industrial and commercial furnace division. One of its most recent products is a gas water heater for homes which incorporates jet impingement and is only about one-fourth the size of a conventional high-powered gas burner. Thermo Electron has been far more successful in selling industrial furnaces. Among other things, it has opened up a substantial market abroad. The Soviet Union's showpiece Kama River truck plant, for instance, is being equipped with Thermo Electron's process furnaces.

Through the years Thermo Electron has expanded in other directions by nourishing other unexpected offshoots of the thermodynamic tree. One day in 1964, for instance, during a brainstorming session on future energy-conversion needs, a company engineer asked: "How about an old-fashioned steam engine? What's wrong with it?" Hatsopoulos asked the engineers to come up with a list of shortcomings of the conventional steam engine and for ideas how it might be modified.

193

The engineers soon decided that water would have to be replaced as the working fluid by a carbon-based substitute. Water is corrosive; what was needed was a good lubricant. Thermo Electron engineers decided that the class of fluids that offered the most flexibility were organic compounds. The malleability of the carbon molecules that make up these compounds would allow them to connect these molecules into any desired configuration. They settled on a fluid called trifluorethynol, which is similar to the fluids used in refrigerators.

For four years Thermo Electron carried on research on the modified Rankine-cycle steam engine with its own funds. In 1968, however, Ford Motor Company became intrigued by the work and entered into a joint venture with Thermo Electron to explore the capabilities of organic engines.

The plan called for Ford eventually to manufacture the new engine in its existing facilities. The new engine promised to reduce greatly the emission of pollutants into the air compared with an internal combustion engine. Its combustion was so complete that very few contaminants escaped from the engine. The engine was hermetically sealed, compact, and lightweight.

In the excitement that accompanied this news, Wall Street traders ran up Thermo Electron's stock in 1969 to the highest point it has ever reached—137½ per share. This was a rather spectacular rise for a company that had gone public only a year earlier at $15 a share.

A conservative man with a long-range view, Hatsopoulos was not too happy with all the outside attention centering on the modified steam engine. He kept telling everyone that the engine was only one aspect of the company's work. In the end, Hatsopoulos was proved right. When the energy crisis came in the early 1970s, emphasis shifted from pollution control to fuel efficiency.

Ford dropped its support of the Thermo Electron engine in 1974. But in Thermo Electron's unique scheme, the Rankine-cycle engine served as still another seed that set off a whole series of new product development. First, the engine itself is far from dead. A small, two-cylinder version is being tested as a power source for indoor industrial vehicles, as well as golf carts, lawn and garden tractors, and a variety of pumps, compressors, and refrigeration systems. Recently Thermo Electron acquired two manufacturers of marine engines with the idea of equipping boats with the new steam engines. Since Thermo Electron had to keep track of the engine's exhaust components, it developed a line of instruments to measure nitrogen oxides and other gases. Instrument sales now comprise a good part of the company's business.

An even smaller version of the original engine is being tested in a stationary mode in tandem with a Mack truck diesel engine. The work is being supported by the Energy Research and Development Administration, the successor to the AEC. Heat from the diesel exhaust drives the smaller steam engine, imparting an additional 40 horsepower to the 290 h.p. diesel power plant by recovering energy that is now wasted in the exhaust gases. The fuel consumption of the big diesel engine is this cut by 15 percent. "You get something for nothing," says Tom Widmer. When the system runs on the highway for the first time, in 1976, it is hoped, it will be the most efficient truck power plant ever designed, yielding overall energy conversion efficiency of well over 40 percent.

The principle of using an add-on vapor engine tailored to run on the hot exhaust of a "mother" engine is not applicable to automobiles because the system works best where work loads are large. But Thermo Electron is investigating its application to diesel locomotives, ships, and to stationary power plants. The advantages to power stations should be even greater than to moving vehicles. In all these cases, the modified steam engine would operate on the low-quality heat that now goes to waste.

The engine's most surprising application, however, will be inside the human body. In the late 1960s Thermo Electron became this country's principal contractor for the development of a complete implantable artificial heart system. The work is being supported by the National Institutes of Health and involves the collaboration of a number of companies and medical institutions, including the Harvard Medical School.

This version of the steam engine will be a tiny one, powered by a capsule of plutonium that has a half-life of eighty-nine years. The minute, single-cylinder engine will run on a single drop of water that will be alternately turned into steam and back into water.

In a closed room at Thermo Electron dozens of heart pumps clatter like castanets as materials for the artificial heart are being tested. Work has progressed so well that the the first implant in a human may be tried in 1976 by the famous Texas heart surgeon, Donald Cooley. The heart has already been successfully tested in calves. During the initial trials, the heart will be implanted as a temporary assist and will be left in the patient's body for weeks or months. It will take many more years of experimentation before the mechanical heart is fully developed for routine implantation for total replacement of failing hearts. But its development already signals the dawn of a new day in medicine, for the mechanical heart will allow heart patients to return to normal lives.

Development of the mechanical heart has not been easy. But in its unique fashion, Thermo Electron has turned problems into products. At one point, its scientists found that while the heart pump worked, it was clotting the blood that passed through it. A Thermo Electron scientist devised a way of establishing a permanent electrostatic charge on plastic films called "electrets." Lined with this material, the artificial heart no longer formed clots; the charge repelled the passing blood corpuscles.

In an imaginative extension of the use of electret plastic, Thermo Electron scientists applied it as a filter material to electrostatic precipitators. Soon they also hit upon the idea of making microphones about the size of a capital letter on this page. The electret microphones, with their high fidelity, quickly attracted the attention of the hearing-aid industry. Thermo Electron now makes the tiny microphones at the rate of 10,000 a week and sees a huge market opening up as telephone companies gradually begin to shift to all-electronic telephone systems. Hatsopoulos thinks that the electret will become the most widely used microphone in two-way radios and in all types of sound reproduction and recording equipment.

In fact, Thermo Electron executives now feel that they entered the market too soon with the revolutionary microphone. Thermo

Electron created a market it couldn't fill—always a hazard for a small company. Bigger corporations have now jumped into the field. Thermo Electron still keeps the electret production process secret but others have guessed correctly that the job was done thermodynamically and they have begun making their own electret microphones.

All through Thermo Electron's growth—the company now employs 1,300 people and has plants in four states and four foreign countries—Hatsopoulos has emphasized careful selection of people. "It's relatively easy to find brilliant technical people," he says. "On the other hand, it's very hard to find people who combine technical ability with an ability to handle people. The moment you combine intelligence, good judgment, and ability to deal with people, you have a very successful leader who can build up an enterprise."

Hatsopoulos feels that a company is a living organism and that the spirit that unites its people is foremost. Part of this spirit is an uncompromising emphasis on excellence. This, plus Thermo Electron's pioneering, plus the fact that it was a tiny underdog competing against giant corporations, helped the company attract first-rate scientists from aerospace research who normally would not think of going to work for, say, a furnace manufacturer.

If any single year stands out in Thermo Electron's history, it is 1968, when it began commercializing its products in earnest. That year, to make and market its novel industrial furnaces, Thermo Electron bought Holcroft and Company, a Livonia, Michigan, furnace maker. Holcroft at that time was selling furnaces principally to the automotive industry in Detroit, but Thermo Electron's novel products have now expanded its markets worldwide. That same year, Thermo Electron bought the Lodding Engineering Corporation, of Auburn, Massachusetts, and went to work improving the paper-making process.

Inside Thermo Electron, Hatsopoulos has encouraged development of new product ideas by having Thermo Electron act as if it were a venture-capital firm helping to set up new enterprises. Thermo Electron has encouraged initiative and rewards it financially.

197

Thermo Electron has been profitable every year since 1962. In fact, the company has been so well run that the late Charles Smith, a well-known partner in the Rockefeller family venture-capital operation, was fond of referring to Thermo Electron as the best-managed company that the Rockefellers had ever put their money in—and their investments include such giants as Eastern Airlines and Exxon.

Hatsopoulos keeps going at a steady pace. He is unhappy when not intensely occupied. He can't sit long in one spot and can be frequently spotted strolling through the company's sprawling laboratories and manufacturing facilities. The busier the place, the easier he finds it to solve a problem preoccupying him at the moment. He lives in nearby Lincoln, only ten minutes from work, and spends about fifty hours a week on company matters.

Hatsopoulos feels that there is a tremendous amount of "fun things" to do in science—but in his view, that is not the function of a company. "That's a function of a scholar or a professor or someone who wants to advance knowledge. I like to be involved in that, too. But that has to be separate from the company." Hatsopoulos continues basic research in thermodynamics on his own time and even today remains a part-time senior lecturer at MIT. Senior lecturer was a title MIT created and awarded to Hatsopoulos first when he resigned as full-time professor in 1962. He still hopes to publish a treatise on a unified quantum theory of mechanics and thermodynamics. But he also plays tennis, cooks, has lately developed a great interest in economics, and is busy designing his new house that will include, naturally, heating devices such as infrared lamps to heat food from above to keep it warm, as well as one of the advanced heat-pipe griddles.

Twenty years after thermionic converters gave birth to Thermo Electron, the devices are not yet here except as experimental tools. Thermo Electron has been laying the groundwork, of course, and continues research on thermionic converters. Hatsopoulos's invention set off active research in many countries, with the Soviet Union establishing the biggest program of all. In 1965 the Soviets started a whole institute devoted to thermionics, with about five hundred scientists on the staff. "They are now building their third

198

thermionic reactor," says Hatsopoulos. "They are way ahead of us. And yet I remember in the sixties they were coming here to Thermo Electron. This was a great surprise to the State Department because in their list of about a dozen companies a Soviet scientific delegation included Thermo Electron along with GE and other giants."

The Soviets had read all of Hatsopoulos's articles and subsequently invited him on a lecture tour sponsored by the Soviet Academy of Sciences. Hatsopoulos went in 1969. "I have some very good friends there working in this field."

Now as the energy shortages continue, interest in thermionics has picked up again. Hatsopoulos has been doing his share of proselytizing in Congress and in federal energy agencies. There is continuing interest in thermionic generators as space-borne energy sources; the West Germans, for instance, are interested in using thermionic converters to power direct-broadcast communications satellites. More importantly, Hatsopoulos finally seems to be winning his argument that thermionic converters belong on earth as well as in space. Now the Energy Research and Development Administration is supporting research at Thermo Electron into improved efficiency of thermionic converters. The converters are getting closer to the point where they look more and more attractive technically and economically. In another year or two Thermo Electron hopes to design a pilot thermionic power generator to be used by industry.

The great interest now centers on the use of thermionic converters in conjunction with steam boilers in conventional power plants. From the beginning Hatsopoulos had visualized such employment of his brainchild. A thermionic converter could take the combustion gases at high temperature, generate electricity, then release the heat to generate steam. The turbines would run on this steam to generate still more electricity. This use of the so-called topping cycle could boost power-plant efficiency from the present 40 percent to between 50 and 60 percent.

The other Thermo Electron device, the modified steam engine, could be employed to produce additional energy at the "bottoming cycle"—from the lower-temperature exhaust gases of turbines and

199

other conventional generators. By fully exploiting such energy-saving techniques, Hatsopoulos thinks that American industrial plants could not only meet their own energy needs but also "generate a large part of the electricity the country needs."

Thermionic converters may not become a commercial reality for another decade; the add-on steam engines will come earlier. With all these exciting developments, Hatsopoulos expects Thermo Electron eventually to become a billion-dollar-a-year company. "We feel that we are among the companies best situated to help through our products and equipment to improve the effectiveness of fuel utilization in this country," he says. "This retooling, or reequipping, the country will take anywhere from ten to fifteen years and will mean a total market on the order of twenty-five billion to fifty billion dollars, and possibly more, over the next decade. I think we can contribute in revamping the whole U.S. industry in making it more efficient." He sees the vast flow of wasted steam and exhaust gases as a major untapped resource and believes that there will be increasing emphasis on this aspect of energy conservation in the years to come.

An interesting study by Thermo Electron scientists in collaboration with the Ford Foundation, completed in 1974, showed that even with presently known technology, United States industry could upgrade its equipment and practices to reduce fuel consumption by more than 30 percent without decreasing total output. Long-term, even larger savings could be achieved through the development of entirely new industrial processes.

The study disputed the widely held view that fuel is efficiently utilized by industry. It found that thermodynamic principles are grossly misused in determining process efficiency. One government report, for instance, said that American industry effectively utilizes almost 70 percent of the energy supplied. Thermo Electron found, however, that the effectiveness of a large segment of industry is an average of 11 percent. The study attributed the large discrepancy to gross errors in the use of the laws of thermodynamics.

As applied by engineers, thermodynamic rules always seemed satisfactory on a large scale but they could not be used on the microscale of one or two molecules. In this context, Hatsopoulos's

200

continuing quest for the elusive answers about the basics of ther-modynamics has been far from esoteric. Thinking in mechanical terms about active, moving thermodynamic systems, says Hat-sopoulos, has led to those striking misconceptions about efficiency of energy use in industry. "You can arrive at a conclusion that an industrial process is 80 percent efficient while it's only 10 percent efficient.

"There has been neglect of something as fundamental as motion and force fields—something that has not yet been understood—a quantity called entropy. Everybody thinks of energy per se and in mechanical form but there is another property inherent in matter and it has very subtle connotations. What exactly entropy is has not yet been deciphered but it has been demonstrated from our work that entropy has to do with built-in uncertainties that exist. That is, there are two aspects of natural phenomena. One is the molecules and particles—their motion and the forces that exist. Another aspect is that all these materials have inherent uncertain-ties in them. Not uncertainties created by lack of knowledge or lack of measurements, but uncertainties that are fundamental to the nature of things. To say what energy is is not sufficient. You have to say what dispersion, what fuzziness it contains. Disregard-ing entropy leads to wrong conclusions. There are built-in uncer-tainties that molecules have about their locations; they don't have exact locations, only average locations. Entropy is built into the molecules."

Another reason for errors often made in calculating energy use, adds Hatsopoulos, is that the value of energy, not only its amount, is important. Insidious losses can occur in terms of quality of energy, for instance, when in an industrial process 3,000-degree-Fahrenheit energy is transferred to 500 degrees. Hatsopoulos likens the value of energy to the value of money. Energy at high temper-atures is worth a lot more than energy at low temperatures. In monetary terms, high-temperature energy is a dollar's worth in gold while low-temperature energy is a dollar's worth of land in Australia. Says Hatsopoulos, "Energy at higher temperature is like sound money."

Thermo Electron scientists further calculate that the United

States could use its financial resources much more effectively by investing them in such devices as recuperators that recycle waste heat rather than spending the money to search for new oil deposits. It now requires up to $14,000 in new investment to find, process, and distribute an additional barrel of oil per day, according to Thermo Electron calculations. Controlling furnace operations with recuperations and other devices, on the other hand, could save the same barrel for $2,000. But they fear that without government encouragements, such as tax credit to companies using fuel-saving devices, the spread of recuperators will be slow.

Although industry is becoming increasingly aware of the new means of saving fuel, one big obstacle to wider use of such devices has been a great shortage of capital. Another reason is that when energy was cheap, there was no real incentive to conserve it. Consequently, American industrial processes—cement making, for instance—have fallen far behind their European counterparts. Now with demand for their products slack, such industries find it difficult to experiment with brand-new processes.

Other processes, such as paper making, were originally devised without taking into account the underlying thermodynamic principles. It takes two hundred tons of water in present paper making to dilute one ton of paper fiber. On top of that, it takes a ton of fuel to make a ton of paper. Yet thermodynamic properties of fibers are completely different from those of water. This was not taken into account in the standard process, which, not surprisingly, is less than 1 percent efficient in energy use.

A way to boost this efficiency sharply, Thermo Electron scientists believe, is to go to a dry paper-making process. But it might cost as much as $40 million to build a demonstration plant. This seems to be beyond the means of even big companies. Thermo Electron executives think the government should start supporting the development of such advanced processes, the same way it has supported the development of such energy sources as nuclear reactors. This support could come through tax credit to companies employing such new energy-saving processes.

Some industrial production techniques are fairly efficient compared to paper making, the study showed. The steel industry, for instance, operates at 20 percent efficiency. "The blast furnace that is the core of the steel industry is based on sound thermodynamic processes," says Widmer, "while grinding up a tree and mixing it with water isn't."

Thermo Electron's contribution to more efficient paper making is a machine that uses only half the energy and one-fourth the amount of water normally consumed. The device employs the principles of fluid flow and microturbulence—probably the first time basic science has been applied to paper making.

Hatsopoulos feels that "we are still down on the bottom of the stick" in efficiency of energy production and conversion. "The best we've ever done has been about 40 percent—converting heat into electricity. We already see our way clear, by combining these engines with thermionic devices, of getting 50 to 55 percent efficiency." The theoretical limit of efficiency that can be achieved with present materials that could be used in thermionic converters lies in the 70 to 80 percent range.

Thermionics, of course, had never been Hatsopoulos's sole idea. Back when Thermo Electron was started, Hatsopoulos and his associates worked for a year on an idea that didn't get far—storing energy in a flywheel. The plan was to try to power a car as this stored energy was released when the wheel was made to rotate rapidly. Hatsopoulos and his colleagues abandoned the idea after they found out that the amount of energy that could be stored would propel a car for only about ten miles without recharging. More recently, as the energy shortage began to hurt, the idea has been resurrected by others.

In the end, though, thermionic converters may turn out to be Thermo Electron's biggest contribution. One day thermionic generators will no longer be used as add-on devices but will replace present generators in electric power plants. They may even run automobiles. That would mark the ultimate success of the energy revolution started by George Hatsopoulos.

CHAPTER TEN

Sam Wyly Builds a
Highway for Computers

Sam Wyly, an engaging and boyish-looking computer-technology
pioneer, unlike the other innovators portrayed in this book, is not
a scientist or engineer by training. He studied accounting and
business administration at a small college in his native Louisiana.
Yet Wyly not only introduced the concept of a "computer utility"
to the business world and built his successful University Computing Corporation on it, with headquarters in Dallas, Texas, but he
is in the process right now of creating another pioneering concern.
This second company is Datran (Data Transmission Company), a
classic entrepreneurial venture intended to become a telephone
company for computers.

Until Wyly came along with Datran, computers, the electronic
marvels of our age, were forced to communicate in a costly and
convoluted way over old-fashioned telephone wires designed for
the human voice. Signals carrying voices travel over the wires as
undulating "analog" waves; computers speak an entirely different,
machine-gun-like, digital "language" of "yes" or "no" pulses. The
two don't mesh. To be transmitted over facilities designed for a
slower, simpler, precomputer age, digital data has to be laboriously
encoded with expensive electronic devices to fit the analog facilities and then decoded at its destination to be comprehensible to
computers. It was as though the digital data "bits" (short for "binary digits") were being lugged along jungle trails by native carriers
as freight added to their normal burden, after being fitted to the

205

carriers' backs at the beginning of the journey and carefully re-molded to match the computers at the end. In between, errors easily occur, data "bits" get lost or "damaged," and the circuits, because of added work, become overloaded. As Wyly once told a cheering national conference of computer specialists, "The computer industry has dialed into a busy signal."

Wyly boldly proposed to build an electronic highway through this jungle where the "bits" would speed along effortlessly like closely spaced cars. His microwave highway would link United States cities from coast to coast with radio transmitters atop towers beaming the "bits" across open spaces and delivering them to their specific destinations in cities via special wire links designed for data flow.

By any measure, the task of building such a network seemed overwhelming, even foolhardy to some. To begin with, that mammoth of monopolies, the American Telephone and Telegraph Company, or AT&T for short, strenuously opposed Datran's application to federal authorities to enter the field. It claimed there was no need for Datran's separate digital network. In doing that, AT&T was only reflecting the fact that when companies that once might have been innovators themselves grow big and fat, they often are reluctant to change the profitable status quo. Typical of this attitude, Western Union Corporation in the late nineteenth century turned down the chance to buy for $100,000 the rights to a device invented by Alexander Graham Bell. Western Union officials were convinced that few, if any, people would ever want to use the strange new contraption. It was the telephone, of course. So a group of enterprising men formed AT&T to cash in on Bell's invention.

A century later, AT&T had grown to one of the world's most powerful monopolies, protected by the United States government. When Wyly started spending millions on Datran, there wasn't clear assurance that federal authorities would allow any competition against the Bell System. Besides, just as Datran was getting started in 1968, the stock market, source of financing of dreams, began its long downslide. Wyly had hoped to finance Datran through a public offering. But Wall Street suddenly lost interest in high-technology companies, no matter how solid the idea behind them. The market, as Wyly puts it, went from "too much enchantment to too much disenchantment." In the ensuing years, it became difficult to get bank financing as well, as interest rates soared and much bigger and better-known companies vied for loans. The original cost estimate for Datran called for expenditures of an astounding $375 million. Venture capitalists don't have that kind of money. Yet despite financial and technical obstacles Sam Wyly today is well along on his road to success with Datran. In the breadth of its vision and its cost Datran comes close to matching ventures such as Comsat (Communications Satellite Corporation). Except Sam Wyly built Datran without the benefits of public financing or certainty of regulatory protection by Uncle Sam that Comsat had.

Datran's technology, furthermore, will do much more than tie together computers in a more efficient way. It will open up new vistas for expanding man's mind, just as the introduction of the telephone brought with it a new level of efficiency and convenience to social and business transactions. The incredibly rapid access to information—the Datran network even now can transmit the equivalent of 25,000 words, or about one-third of this book, across the country in one second—is bound to enlarge our educational, entertainment, and business horizons. Not only computer-generated information but all written and pictorial data, as well as voice and video signals, will eventually be transmitted in digital form because it's the most efficient way of putting electronics to work. One early benefit for businesses and later for everyone will be "electronic mail," the sending in seconds of whole pages of text across the country at exceedingly low cost via digital facsimile. The emerging technology of digital data transmission, specialists predict, will create a giant new industry in the decades to come.

Wyly's achievement is all the more impressive because it came at a time when mere survival was considered a great feat for many one-time *wunderkinder* of the computer age. During the heyday of high-technology company creation in the 1960s, some companies blossomed suddenly only to wilt like exotic short-lived flowers a few years later. Too preoccupied with the present, young technologists tended to neglect the future, to buy more new businesses than they could digest, or branch out into such unpromising fields as manufacturing computers in direct competition with IBM. Mohawk Data Sciences, Memorex Corporation, Viatron, LTV Corporation, and Cogar Corporation are a few of the many high-technology firms that streaked across the Wall Street sky only to nose-dive dramatically.

Some crashed. In Dallas, fast-talking Jimmy Ling, whose lightning mind and remarkable talent for financial dealings enabled him to build up Ling-Temco-Vaught into the marvel conglomerate and fourteenth-largest company in America in the late 1960s, was forced out of LTV. Ling later failed at a comeback with another concern he called Omega-Alpha. H. Ross Perot, another Wyly contemporary operating out of Dallas, whom *Fortune* once called the "Fastest Richest Texan Ever," found his paper fortune melting rapidly after an injudicious purchase of a Wall Street brokerage firm that resulted in a big loss. Ironically, Perot once gave Wyly a stock certificate which hangs behind a glass frame in an anteroom to Sam's office. It reads: "Electronic Data Systems Corp. 10 Shares to S. Wyly from Ross Perot. In case of emergency break glass. September 1968."

Wyly successfully avoided such pitfalls as buying Wall Street firms, even though he did not escape the financial roller-coaster ride. He was smart enough, however, not only to cope with the tough new business environment in preserving University Computing but also in raising nearly $100 million during these economically turbulent times to get Datran going. In doing that, Wyly has shown a lot more business acumen than many of his contemporaries. Yet Wyly doesn't fit the stereotype of a tough business tycoon. Blond and blue-eyed, attractive and short-statured, still in his early forties, he has a sometimes self-deprecating "Oh, shucks," country-boy manner and his speech is softened by the musical notes of Louisiana. Wyly is so unprepossessing in appearance and bearing that when he was meeting with *Fortune* magazine's editors for lunch in New York once, Robert Lubar, the managing editor, not knowing Wyly by sight, kept surveying the room in puzzlement upon entering, looking for the touted tycoon.

The Entrepreneurs

Behind the deceptive appearance is a fluid, creative mind with an ability to grasp concepts, see the future, and the courage to act. "Sam Wyly," says an associate, "is an entrepreneur's entrepreneur." Even during his childhood in Delhi, Louisiana, a tiny town in the northeastern part of the state not far from Vicksburg, Mississippi, his contemporaries looked up to Sam for leadership. He was a game captain of his high school's football team and helped lead it to winning the state championship in his senior year, playing at guard.

Aside from an intense interest in football during his childhood and adolescence, Sam Wyly acquired from his parents a voracious appetite for reading. He wasn't particularly interested in science or in mechanical things. His father had originally operated a four-hundred-acre cotton plantation at Lake Providence, Louisiana, on the shore of the Mississippi River, where Sam was born on October 4, 1934, the second of the two Wyly boys; his brother, Charles, Jr., was born the year before. The Great Depression dropped cotton prices to five cents a pound and forced Sam's father to look for other employment. He had studied journalism at Louisiana State University, worked as a reporter on the Lake Providence paper, and always wanted to be a writer. But when a friend was appointed by a new reform governor to be the superintendent of the state penitentiary and offered Sam's father a job as an administrator, he took it. He wasn't too happy, though, about being a cog in a big civil-service machine. It was here that Sam says he "got a flavor from both my parents about being deeply concerned about being an individual in the grip of a big institution where you really don't control your own destiny." What better place than a state penitentiary to instill a yearning for independence?

Sam's father soon bought the *Delhi Dispatch*, a small weekly. Sam and Charles helped out with all kinds of chores: writing stories, selling advertising, setting type, laying out pages, folding the papers, and addressing them. The deadline was midnight on Mondays, and Sam learned the importance of setting benchmarks for accomplishing specific tasks.

From his parents he also inherited a deep interest in politics. Being a local editor, Sam's father was visited and courted by different politicians. While he steadfastly opposed Huey Long for what he felt were his dictatorial tendencies, he was always on one or the other side of every political race. Sam's interest in politics carried over into his school and later business life. Sam was always a president of something: of the student body in high school, his freshman class, student senate, and business and scholastic fraternities in college. He wound up in positions of leadership partly because of ambition and partly because "others looked around for me to give the answers."

Reflecting Sam's interest in politics and also his long-standing fondness for American history, today the walls of the big anteroom to his office on the fifteenth floor of the UCC Tower in Dallas are decorated with original letters by George Washington, Sam Houston, and Jefferson Davis.

Enrolling in Louisiana Polytechnic Institute (now Louisiana Technical University) in nearby Ruston, Sam first majored in journalism. He then decided that the tiny *Delhi Dispatch* could not support all of the family; in fact, Sam's father also had a fire-casualty agency and the local Western Union franchise in order to make a living. Sam asked around what would be the hardest subject he could major in. He was told it would be engineering or accounting. Not caring for engineering, he took accounting.

Armed with his new knowledge, on a visit home once he looked at his father's ledger books with a new eye. He saw that his father spent only five or six hours a week on the insurance business and yet the time was more profitably spent than the many more hours devoted to the newspaper. The budding tycoon then asked his father why he didn't give up the newspaper and concentrate on the insurance agency instead. His father replied: "Son, the first thing you need to know is that as a sophomore in college you are at your peak—this is as smart as you'll ever be. It's all downhill from here. Secondly, I like putting out this newspaper." Says Sam, "That wasn't real easy for me to understand then, but I've thought about it a lot since."

In college he began to get intrigued with business subjects. "I enjoyed the problem solving. I liked to do what a lot of other students seemed to do with great agony." He did so well that he

210

won a graduate scholarship to the University of Michigan Business School. He also had the chance of going to work for IBM in Dallas but opted for additional schooling.

His brother, Charles, who had also studied business at Louisiana Tech, had in the meantime gone to work for IBM in New Orleans. Charles did so well that he earned $12,000 in his second year with the company. This looked awfully impressive to Sam, who was considering offers less than half that amount as he got his M.B.A. from Michigan.

Sam decided to take the dormant IBM offer and went to work for the company's subsidiary, Service Bureau Corporation, as a sales trainee in Dallas early in 1958. IBM was then just beginning to introduce computers, and since tests showed that Sam had good technical ability, his boss suggested he should go into technical work instead of sales. But Sam resisted; selling appealed to him more. The Service Bureau was beginning to provide programming and computing services to corporations.

A little later, though, he did wind up operating a computer in Fort Worth; the recession of 1957–58 was hurting and IBM decided to suspend sales training temporarily. In the end, says Wyly, "it was the best thing I could have done because I had to learn to operate the machines, program them, and do some beginning systems analysis."

Within a year he was back in Dallas with his own sales territory and in both 1959 and 1960 made IBM's "100 percent club" for top salesmen. Two and a half years after starting with IBM, Sam was offered a bigger job with Honeywell: to become their first area sales manager in Dallas. His mission would be to sell Honeywell computers in northern Texas, Arkansas, and Oklahoma in competition with IBM and other manufacturers.

Sam took the job because he was curious to find out whether he could be a manager. It was "a tough, tough job," he recalls, because IBM dominated the market so much. But he made an impressive record, attaining sales with five salesmen as high as some other Honeywell offices had with thirty.

Sam was doing well but was becoming impatient. "I was probably in a typical entrepreneurial spot," he recalls. "OK, I can stay

211

with this corporation and progress in it. But I would always have a whole chain of command above me and I won't have my arms around the whole business. I won't really know what the engineers are doing up there, or the people who create the software. I don't see the whole business but just my little piece of it."

He not only had a yearning for independence but, as he puts it in his succinct way, "At the beginning of 1963 I began to feel that if I can put Honeywell into the computer business, I could put Sam Wyly into the computer business."

This he did later in 1963 with a used computer housed on the campus of Southern Methodist University in Dallas. He had saved $10,000 but in the end needed only $1,000 of his own money to start the company. He left Honeywell and began to pound the hot pavements of Dallas "looking for a banker with some imagination to finance the purchase of a used computer." He didn't find a receptive banker. Instead he worked out a deal with two potential customers. With SMU he negotiated an agreement under which he would supply the university with computing time in exchange for housing the computer on the campus. SMU was only too glad to push aside an ancient Univac in favor of a much newer machine Sam planned to get. To the research department of Sun Oil Company he sold a five-year service contract for a lower than normal price and Sun Oil in return prepaid the contract. This way, Sam recalls, "I had about $250,000 cash in the company although I didn't have any net worth."

The money equaled twenty-three months' expenses if Wyly found no other customers. But he was certain of signing up a big third one, Texas Instruments. He found a leasing company that would buy a used Control Data computer for $650,000 and lease it back to him. The deal was guaranteed by a Dallas company named Diversa, with which Sam's father-in-law had dealt in the past. The guarantee was made in exchange for a 49 percent interest in Wyly's company. "All I had to do is make monthly payments," says Sam.

It was Wyly's wife, Rosemary, who suggested the company's name. Sam was thinking of calling it the Mustang Computing

212

Company—the mustang being the SMU athletic mascot. Rosemary wondered whether the wider-ranging name "University" should not be used instead since the company would be likely to serve other universities and businesses. Sam liked the suggestion.

University Computing was off to the business sweepstakes. From the beginning Wyly concentrated on big companies as customers. He was convinced that his customers should be able to tap computing power with the ease one uses electricity or the telephone. At that time the idea of a "computer utility" was bandied about only by academics in universities. With University Computing, Wyly brought it to the world of business. Farthest from Sam Wyly's mind was the idea of a computer utility being a monopoly. He visualized it rather as a series of specialized "utilities" consisting of the most powerful computers available and serving specific industries and scientific specialities. Vital to the whole concept was the ease of communicating with computers from great distances, thousands of miles away if needed.

Wyly felt that users would also find the economies of a computer utility attractive. Since the cost of giant computers would be borne by hundreds of users, it would be less expensive to tap the utility's computing power than for each user to own a big computer which they would be running only a fraction of the day anyway. Sam felt that most companies would no more buy their own huge computers than they would acquire their own electricity-generating plants.

In some ways this was like offering efficient public transportation to a nation of private automobile owners. Wyly had pitted himself against empire building in data processing where, as one of his associates says, "you have a chrome-plated floor with fancy colored machines with whirring tapes and a whole bunch of people running around. There's a big glass window where everybody can look in and say, 'Isn't that great.' "

But the concept of the computer utility caught on fast with knowledgeable users. Sam had recruited his brother to work with him, and while Charles stayed in Dallas, Sam spent a few months in Tulsa, Oklahoma, opening a branch office this time with a new

213

Control Data computer. In 1963 University Computing recorded sales of $70,000, but in its first full year, 1964, sales jumped to $692,954 with a net of $136,057.

At the end of 1964, the first substantial equity investment in the company ($100,000 for 9 percent of the stock) was made by Ben Voth, a retired Tulsa businessman who owned the building where Sam located his Tulsa computer center. Voth had sold his insurance company and saw in UCC and Sam Wyly an exciting investment opportunity; he served as UCC's chairman for several years.

Sam's aim all along had been to provide programs and computing equipment that a user would have trouble finding elsewhere. "A business," says Sam, "exists to serve customers. You must deliver a value. If a customer does not perceive your service as having a value, it doesn't have value."

University Computing started implementing the utility concept as early as its second year when its salesmen began to offer customers the total company abilities and services without regard to where a given piece of company equipment was located. Rapid expansion followed; by 1966 University Computing had customers in twenty-three states. The company began to grow through acquisitions as well, buying smaller computer services and research, engineering, and consulting firms.

Wyly had chosen a good time to enter the computer-services business. "Successful innovation is a question of timing, a question of competition, as well as a question of the man," says one of his associates. There was some competition in the field, but it was far from a well-developed industry. Day after day new companies, big and small, discovered the value of computers and new applications were being thought up rapidly.

University Computing derived most of its revenues from its utility function as well as by providing programming services and acting as a client's computer department, supplying all equipment and staff. It offered services in both scientific and business applications. Scientific uses accounted for the greater portion of its revenues. Even in its earliest years the company successfully handled a wide range of scientific and technical applications, including sim-

214

ulation of oil-field reservoirs, control of petroleum refineries, design of optical instruments, automatic control of factory machine tools, and calculation and graphic display of geophysical data. In business applications, the company offered a wide range of services such as inventory control, accounting, billing, and personnel record management.

By 1968 University Computing had become a multinational company when it acquired Computer Services Ltd. in England and Computer Bureau Ltd. in Ireland, the largest independent computer service firms in Europe. It also opened branch offices in Australia, Venezuela, and the Netherlands.

There seemed to be no limit to University Computing's growth or the adulation that was developing around Sam Wyly. He was twenty-eight when he started the company; two years later he was a millionaire. (His wife noted with a lot of common sense, however, "It's all on paper, so what does it matter?") Wall Street had less common sense. In all its history the stock market had never shown quite as much enthusiasm about an industry as it did about the computer business in the late 1960s, and University Computing was one of its biggest stars. Its sales had soared to $57 million, with a net of more than $5 million, in 1968. Its stock rocketed to its all-time high of 187¼ a share. The company had gone public at $4.50 a share in 1965; the stock had been split three-for-one before the big advance. The high of 187¼ was equivalent to a remarkable $561 a share before the stock split. Put another way, an investment of $9,000 in University Computing in 1965 would have become worth more than a *million* dollars in 1968.

Sam refers to those heady days as times when it was "hard to get a benchmark on values." The young man from rural Louisiana was suddenly being showered with tons of paper that looked like gold. Wall Street said Wyly personally was worth more than $100 million and his company nearly one *billion*.

"When our stock went sky high," says Wyly, "my first thought was, my Lord, how can we be worth that much money? And then I did the same thing I guess the other fellows did. I looked around at my competitors and saw the prices their stocks were selling at

215

and I said, well, we are as good as they are and probably better. I guess we sort of rationalized it that way. I really hadn't set out to personally get rich—I just wanted to work for myself."

A master of understatement, in an interview with *Fortune* in 1968 Wyly offered this modest explanation for his company's spectacular success: "You find a little bitty thing you can do, and you keep on doing it." He was pictured standing proudly in front of a not-so-bitty skyscraper with big letters proclaiming it to be the home of "UCC Computer Utility." Actually, by that time Sam was in a lot of good-sized things such as making computer terminals, running a chain of computer-programming schools, even designing a supercomputer "to meet the exact requirements of the computer utility operation."

Reaching outside the computer field, Wyly took advantage of the lofty Wall Street valuation of his stock and acquired Gulf Insurance Company by issuing 306,000 shares of University Computing for it. Gulf had $5 million in cash on hand and owned stocks and bonds worth $60 million; it had judiciously invested long ago in such innovative companies as Xerox. Wyly's aim was to use Gulf as a kind of a bank to underwrite the growth of University Computing subsidiaries.

The deluge of money set off by University Computing stock not only enabled Wyly to buy out Diversa's interest in his company but personally he was also able to branch out into new fields, too. Trying to prove to himself that University Computing wasn't just a fluke and that he could start a brand-new company again if he had to, he did just that by buying an oil refinery in Memphis, Tennessee. He used it as a seed for a concern he called Earth Resources Company. He bought a small exploration company as well and applied profits from oil refining to finance a search for copper, silver, gold, and other metals. Earth Resources now operates gasoline stations in the South and is building a refinery in Alaska. In terms of sales, it has been the most successful of all Wyly ventures, reaching $250 million in 1975.

Another investment during that period took Wyly into the restaurant business. Sam was out for dinner one night with his father-in-law at a small Dallas eatery where steaks sold for $1.29. The

216

father-in-law was impressed. He suggested to a friend who was looking for something to do to start a chain of Western restaurants; the result was Bonanza International. Sam wound up as the chain's owner when a $1 million loan he guaranteed to the chain could not be repaid; he and his brother still own 40 percent of Bonanza. Bonanza operates 200 restaurants and has franchised 350 others; total sales were expected to top $200 million in 1975.

Those other businesses have been kept separate from the Wyly Corporation. But when added up, all these ventures make Sam Wyly one of the most, if not *the* most, successful post–World War II entrepreneurs in the United States.

It was only a short step from Wyly's heavy involvement in his computer utility concept to his own data-transmission company. The whole idea of a utility depended on efficient communications between users and the company computer centers; early in its history University Computing had pioneered so-called remote batch processing. This is a procedure similar to a customer sending in his laundry and then receiving it back washed and pressed.

But transmitting data over telephone wires, Wyly could see even when he started the company, was a lot harder than taking a load of wash to the laundry. The computer industry was then still an infant; the telephone company not only didn't have the right facilities but often didn't want to bother with the tiny upstart customer. For a long time the telephone company wasn't attuned to the needs of the computer-data users. It kept charging them, for instance, for a minimum three-minute call as it did all other customers, regardless of the duration of the transmission. But the computer operates in fractions—billionths—of a second. Three minutes is an eternity for a computer and presents a big unnecessary expense for the user.

Trying to change that, Wyly in May 1968 made a tender offer to acquire about 10 percent of Western Union's stock. He figured that even a partial ownership of that carrier would give University Computing a voice in Western Union's policy making. He was turned down. Undaunted, he set out to build his own national communications network.

He was floating high. The future looked bright for University

217

Computing—so bright that Wyly went on to forecast that the company would have $1 billion in sales in 1975. In light of its previous advance from sales of less than $700,000 in 1965 to $108 million in 1969, that might not have been such an outrageously optimistic prediction.

Being human, Wyly and his associates had become overconfident. "Probably part of our euphoria was based on having done more than we ought to have been able to do," says Wyly. "We had forecast the doubling of sales and profits each year during 1965–70 and that came true. We probably didn't realize the amount of luck that had been with us and also the amount of leverage we had gotten from the euphoria in the stock market."

Bad economic weather came as suddenly as one of those devastating hurricanes that hit the Gulf Coast. "We got caught in the 1969–70 money crunch and then in the recession. We thought we were invulnerable to it—and we found out we weren't," says Sam. There was another difficulty; University Computing had grown helter-skelter. "In retrospect," says Sam, "it's clear that we went into more businesses than we could effectively manage or finance."

Not all those purchases were bad. The most important one, Gulf Insurance, was a good company, and all along Sam had been upgrading its stock and bond portfolio so that Gulf could pay higher dividends to the parent corporation. Gulf was contributing millions of dollars each year to the effort to build a worldwide computer utility.

In 1970, however, the fire and casualty insurance business fared badly not only because of the economic downturn but also because of natural disasters. A vicious hurricane leveled most of Corpus Christi, Texas, and a tornado severely damaged Lubbock. Gulf sustained the largest underwriting loss in its forty-five-year history.

That wasn't the only problem. The network of programming schools had to be drastically scaled down because the activity wasn't paying off. Large after-tax losses were incurred by sold or discontinued operations. And University Computing and its divisions found themselves revaluing downward certain accounts receivable, inventories, computer equipment, and even that nebulous and subjective quantity known as a corporation's "goodwill." All this led University Computing to report a staggering $18 million loss on sales of $114 million for 1970. The year before the company had reported a *profit* of nearly $17 million.

In light of the new unpromising economic climate, Wyly's efforts to get a huge new venture off the ground may seem quixotic. The cost of the Datran network was estimated at a staggering $375 million. But Wyly wasn't flying blindly. As a star salesman for IBM and Honeywell, he had learned that success in making a sale lay in absolute mastery of a client's business. To find out all about Datran's potential business, he had a team of financial analysts from two New York investment banking firms and a major commercial New York bank carefully examine Datran's cost and operations assumptions. They concluded that the project was financially feasible.

Behind Datran also lay a lot of technical planning. Wyly had assembled a big team of outstanding scientists and engineers, rate specialists, economists, and legal experts to prepare the case for Datran. When University Computing filed its initial applications with the Federal Communications Commission in November 1969, the application consisted of a stack of documents six and a half feet tall—the biggest document ever submitted to the FCC in a single filing. The FCC was sold, but not until the middle of 1971 when in a landmark decision it ruled that competition in data transmission was practical and desirable. AT&T retained its monopoly over toll voice messages, although new carriers such as Datran could now send voice messages over private lines. Among its competitors Datran was and is the only carrier whose sole mission is digital-data transmission.

By the end of 1970 Wyly had invested $6.6 million in Datran. He found out that it would be almost impossible to bring out Datran as a public company; Wall Street's ardor for new stock offerings had cooled to the freezing point. Wyly's assistant, Ray Hannon, recalls trying to cope with a backlog of more than one hundred telephone inquiries from analysts in a single day when Wall Street bulls were on a stampede. Now the analysts had stopped calling; in fact, many of them had lost their jobs or moved on to other things.

Luckily, through the years Wyly had assembled or started from scratch some basically sound components of University Computing. He aborted such schemes as the planned "supercomputer" and began "cannibalizing" in a fashion similar to that of KMS Fusion (see Chapter 5), selling off less-promising components of the parent company in order to keep Datran going and to pay off large long-term bank debts.

In addition, during University Computing's expansion into Europe, Wyly had met Walter Haefner, a wealthy Swiss entrepreneur who had made his fortune importing Volkswagen and Chrysler cars and General Electric appliances into Switzerland. In 1975, Haefner's various enterprises had revenues of nearly $400 million. Haefner had earlier sold his ten computer service centers in Europe to Wyly. Now he became highly enthused about Datran and began a series of major investments in the new company. His Datran investments amounted to $40 million through 1975.

"Without the Haefner investment," says Wyly, "there would have been no Datran. When I read of bills being introduced in Congress to limit foreign investment in United States companies, I marvel at our natural desire for self-punishment. What could be worse news for American consumers? What could do more to preserve monopoly and business inefficiency in the United States?

"In Datran's case, Wall Street was obsessed with its fears of industry shakeouts, liquidity crunches, whether our technology would work, and whether we could compete with the world's largest corporation. No venture capital was available to us except from Walter Haefner who had faith in United States data markets and in our ability to manage our way through these stormy seas and had the courage and the resources to act upon his convictions."

Wyly himself continued to seek funds for Datran with a missionary zeal. He could divert some Gulf Insurance and University Computing profits into the new venture as things looked up in 1971. University Computing reported a $2.6 million profit on sales of $128 million. Gulf achieved a small underwriting profit and realized $8.5 million from capital gains. Wyly was able to invest another $5 million in Datran.

University Computing had by then become one of the world's largest independent computing service organizations and a substantial manufacturer of auxiliary computer equipment. It was employing more than 5,000 people.

The roller-coaster car dipped down precariously in 1972, however, as University Computing reported an even bigger loss than in 1970. This time it lost $83 million on sales of $101 million. Gulf's best performance in its history, an underwriting profit of $4.1 million, hardly offset the big loss.

To a significant extent, however, that big loss occurred mostly on paper. It included, for instance, big losses on sales of unprofitable components of the company—sales from which University Computing actually gained millions of dollars. It got $20 million for its computer-terminal-manufacturing subsidiary, for instance. But in accordance with accounting practices, since the terminal company had a higher "book value," its sale resulted in a recorded loss.

Wyly had realized for some time that his remaining companies needed strong managers. The computing division, for instance, had gone through five presidents. When Wyly ran it himself, it was profitable, but with technical men in charge, the computer services operation began to lose money.

To bring that operation back to profitability, Wyly sought out Donald Thompson, who had acquired a reputation at International Telephone and Telegraph Company as a skilled "turn-around" man. Thompson had made it his profession curing "sick" companies. In the process he employed some clever techniques. At ITT World Communications, for instance, he discovered that the real decision makers on whether ITT or its competitors got the business were teletype operators, usually unattractive girls who sat in the back rooms where few visitors ventured. In long-distance communications, who got the business depended on whether an operator pressed an ITT, RCA, or other button. ITT's share rose significantly after Thompson reduced the average age of his salesmen to twenty-eight—to match the girls' average age—from the mid-forties.

Unlike his predecessors, Thompson brought only one man with him to Dallas. The assistant's sole duty was to invite employees to air their complaints. Thompson then reshaped University Computing to make it even more of a utility than it was; he moved eight big Univac computers, then scattered around the country, to Dallas. Next, he concentrated on money-making businesses, such as banks, as customers. Results were rapid: a year later University Computing was making a good-sized profit.

Wyly's deft handling of the situation enabled him to reduce the parent firm's long-term bank debt by $62 million and at the same time to invest $18 million in Datran by 1972.

To run the accelerating systems and design development at Datran, Wyly brought in as the new company's president Glenn E. Penisten, a young electronics engineer who had risen to a vice presidency of Texas Instruments, the huge technical conglomerate headquartered in Dallas. Still in his early forties, Penisten had spent ten of his fifteen years at TI managing the creation of new businesses as well as heading up the semiconductor research laboratories and worldwide TI supply company. Penisten's job was to take a market need, tailor technical capability to it, and build new businesses that way. He had successfully engineered TI's entry into antisubmarine warfare, missiles, and ordnance, organized TI's worldwide semiconductor business objectives and strategies, and initiated TI's highly successful entry into the consumer electronics market with its hand-held calculators.

The first thing Penisten did at Datran was to install TI-type management discipline. To start with, he trimmed the network's projected size to a realistic level. This reduced the financing requirements to a more manageable $100 million from nearly $400 million. Penisten recalls telling his new colleagues: "It's fine to think that we're going to build a national network and turn it on like a Christmas tree one Sunday morning, and on Monday morning the world will line up to subscribe to our services. But it won't happen that way. The network is too complicated—you have to build it one step at a time. And we're going to have a long, painful job of conditioning the market."

Penisten's experience in semiconductor technology and his setting of tough construction standards enabled Datran to cut sharply the cost of electronic instruments that were being manufactured for the company. And before Datran broke ground for its first transmitting site—visible in the distance from Sam Wyly's office— its engineers had effected broad cost reductions through new approaches, such as the design of a new type of radio tower. By a simple expedient of having three legs instead of the usual four, Datran's towers saved the company half a million dollars on steel— some of the towers are 450 feet tall. Curiously, Datran engineers also found that the three-legged towers withstand high winds better.

To reflect University Computing's wider scope of activities, the company was renamed Wyly Corporation in 1973. But it continued to lose money; in 1973 it lost nearly $5 million. To continue to invest in Datran and repay debts, Wyly mortgaged the stock of Gulf to secure a $30 million loan and a $20 million investment by Haefner. The goal seemed within reach.

Excitement reigned at Wyly Corporation on December 1, 1973, when Datran's first test message was flashed from Houston to Dallas. It was a remarkably complex message, lasting an hour and a half and designed to bring out errors—yet none were recorded. The first segment of the digital network worked flawlessly. First customers were signed up soon thereafter and found they could save almost half on their data-sending bills.

Wyly Corporation lost money again in 1974—$9 million mainly because Gulf Insurance experienced record losses. That year Sam thought he had successfully negotiated a $50 million bank loan to take Datran over its last hump. But the deal fell apart as the prime rate soared to 12 percent and banks found themselves short of cash. That was a dark moment. Wyly faced the problem of either shutting down or selling Datran. He faced that question again in May 1975, when inflation caused Gulf Insurance underwriting losses to soar and dividends from Gulf to Wyly Corporation had to be discontinued. Both times, a combination of company sales by Wyly, and Haefner's help, rescued Datran.

Over these troubled years Wyly managed the prodigious feat of paying off $120 million in long-term debt and investing $40 million in Datran. Haefner had contributed another $40 million and a $5 million investment came from Bechtel Corporation, the construction company.

223

Despite its financial tribulations, Datran scored a big *coup* early in 1975 when it put into service most of its novel network. To be sure, the company had to compromise on the original plan. Its fifty-nine microwave towers so far march only along the Houston-Chicago segment. To reach the West Coast, Datran subleased microwave circuits from the Southern Pacific Communications Company, a subsidiary of the Southern Pacific Railroad. To reach the East Coast, Datran will be leasing bandwidths from AT&T and possibly locating some of its equipment on Southern Pacific's sites that link St. Louis with Boston. Southern Pacific, on the other hand, extended its network from St. Louis to Chicago by utilizing the Datran-engineered sites. Southern Pacific transmits voice, facsimile, and video over its facilities.

For local, in-town connections, Datran for the time being decided to rely on the telephone company, but with the enhancement of the quality of these wires with special electronic devices. This unexpected collaboration was made possible by AT&T's belated entry into an improved data transmission service. The FCC was backed by the courts when it required the telephone company to make these local loops available to other carriers.

Despite such compromises, Datran still arrived with the most impressive, fastest, and least expensive to use data network. Its heart is a unique electronic switch, a technical marvel that consists of a room full of computers that can handle eighty thousand calls an hour for more than ten thousand subscribers. It switches high-speed computer data circuits in half a second, connecting any two computers or terminals anywhere on the network. This isn't possible on the analog network unless a customer leases a point-to-point private line—and pays for it whether it's in use or not, at a cost that's huge compared with Datran's.

Datran thus employed advanced technology to multiply and leverage its capital. With less expense and equipment, it has built a network that is ten times more efficient than any analog transmission plant in existence.

The sharp reduction of the connect time between two computers miles away—to half a second from an average ten to twenty seconds—on the face of it may seem trivial. But a big user of data transmission, say, a department store chain with each store querying a central computer thousands of times a day, can benefit significantly from the faster speed.

The speed of the switch, furthermore, permits Datran to replace the telephone company's one-minute minimum rate with a *one-second* minimum. This allows occasional users to become customers, without the need to rent expensive private lines. A customer can send a burst of 9,600 bits of data—equal to about 2,500 words—to a terminal six hundred miles away and be charged only three cents for the ten-second transmission. The existing telephone system does not permit transmission that fast. Sending this data at available lower speeds and paying the one-minute charge would cost forty-nine cents.

The Datran system is almost completely error free, avoiding costly retransmissions frequently required on the conventional telephone network. The Datran network is under constant electronic surveillance of the type that enabled the United States to launch faultlessly the giant Saturn 5 rockets that carried astronauts to the moon.

At Datran's headquarters in Vienna, Virginia, just outside Washington, D.C., an elaborate, computer-controlled sentinel system checks the status of the whole network every five seconds and displays the results on a TV-like screen. Irregularities in the lines and at unmanned transmission sites are instantly detected. Maintenance crews are immediately dispatched by radio from the nearest Datran office, if needed. The surveillance system keeps track of about 450 functions at each site. If an unauthorized person breaks a lock on a wire gate at a transmission site thousands of miles away, or even if the red aircraft warning light atop a radio tower goes out, the information is immediately displayed in the control center. At 8:00 each morning Datran management gets a twenty-four-hour trouble report. This kind of innovative automation, far ahead of any other civilian communications network, will allow Datran to spend less than half of what carriers spend on maintenance.

After Datran began large-scale operations in 1975, signing up business customers at a fast clip, the skeptics began to see the possibilities. Although compared with AT&T Datran is a mosquito buzzing around an elephant, the elephant has become concerned. Reversing its previous stand, AT&T entered the field with an upgraded data transmission service which it offered at a low price in five cities. Can AT&T force Datran out of business? The FCC now seems inclined to encourage regulated competition; in 1975 it restricted AT&T from offering its service at the low rates in other cities, thus increasing Datran's survival chances. Furthermore, Datran reached agreement to lease bandwidths from AT&T at wholesale rates, thus making its expansion easier.

There are other big entrants eager to jump into what now looks like a lucrative field. Since the market for digital data already amounts to nearly $1 billion—with AT&T accounting for the overwhelming share of it—and because it is expected to grow to $5 billion or $6 billion by 1980, such giants as ITT and IBM have become interested. Wyly and Penisten are certain, however, that Datran can stay ahead by remaining technically flexible; they expect Datran to be a $200 million-a-year company in 1980. Their optimism is echoed by Sol Linowitz, former chairman of Xerox Corporation, who became a Datran director "because I regard it as undertaking a very exciting, innovative program in an area of immense potential."

Another prominent Datran director is Dr. Glenn T. Seaborg, Nobel Prize–winning nuclear chemist and former chairman of the Atomic Energy Commission. He feels that "digital data communications will, over all, expand into a huge business—this seems inevitable in view of our societal march toward a future based so largely on data and communications. The question with Datran, of course, is whether an emerging company based on brains and daring can carve out a substantial share of the market. If Datran can survive the next year or two, I believe they will succeed in doing this."

Datran's future will not be fully assured until the company starts recording significant sales and banks begin to lend it money to expand into such promising fields as digital transmission of voice. Wyly says he may be forced to sell Gulf Insurance to keep Datran going, or even sell a majority interest in Datran, although he feels that's unlikely. "We've brought it this far," he says, "and we think we can carry it the rest of the way."

Wyly remains firmly convinced as ever that we are in a transition stage toward "knowledge work—working with your head instead of your hands. Knowledge," says Sam, "rather than capital, labor, or raw materials is now the major source of industrial growth. The computer is a revolutionary tool like the steam engine that changed the way man worked." The computer's product, information, he is convinced, is the intellectual equivalent of energy. With Datran, he feels that the twentieth century's counterpart of the steam engine now has a railroad network all its own to open up new frontiers of the mind.

Wyly is supported in his views by the ever growing, pervasive use of computers and computerized equipment. The list is impressive. Retail point-of-sale terminals are moving into the stores, electronic transfer of funds by banks is catching on, more insurance claim adjustments are being transmitted over long distances, law enforcement agencies need to exchange information fast, and there are myriad demands for fast data transfer in business.

The number of big computers is expected to more than double to 162,000 from the present 80,000 in this country by 1980, while the number of computerized terminals is expected to soar to nearly three million from the present less than one million. More and more, these devices are being oriented toward telecommunications, or distant data transmission.

Wyly starts out each day, month, and year with a list of objectives to accomplish, written down on a lined yellow pad. Some of these goals may look grandiose to an outsider. But Wyly quietly goes about his business, removing the obstacles one by one. He finds that clearly crystallizing a matter and setting a date for a decision galvanizes him and his associates into action. "I go home and sleep well every night," says Sam, who most of the time is as serene as an astronaut landing on the moon. "I don't chew my nails."

"He moves with great acumen and confidence in that strange

227

labyrinth of the financial world," says Glenn Seaborg. "He has tremendous courage in the financial field and is willing to risk a good part of his fortune on Datran."

Sam thinks that data processing remains an excellent field for entrepreneurs. Personally, he would like "to get back into producing good report cards again—after five years of lousy report cards. Not so much that it matters whether I'll be richer because I'm rich enough now, even at the lousy prices my stocks command right now." (Wyly Corporation dropped to its all-time low of 1¾ in 1975.)

"I'm well ahead of the $10,000 a year I thought I'd ever have to earn when I was in college. I wouldn't want to live in any bigger house than I'm in right now; I don't need a bigger car. I have no particular buzz about having a bigger bank account—it probably wouldn't matter. I'd just do what I've done before—give it away." He has contributed heavily to churches, schools, and helped get the educational TV channel going in Dallas. A sixteen-story Wyly Tower graces the campus of his alma mater, built in part with funds contributed by Sam and Charles, who is now chairman of Wyly Corporation's executive committee. The Charles Wyly, Sr., Tower of Learning was named in memory of Sam's late father, who always strove for knowledge. About the Wyly Tower Sam says with a laugh, "It's the tallest building between Shreveport and Vicksburg, Mississippi." Appropriately, on its first floor it houses a computer center while full nine floors are occupied by the university library. Several hundred youngsters have gone to Louisiana Tech on Wyly scholarships. Sam has also been actively involved in helping start minority businesses and has served as the national coordinator of the federal effort in that field.

"I really like my job and I like it a lot better than I did when the market said I was worth $100 million more," he adds. "I feel a lot more satisfied with the things I've accomplished. And if the report card doesn't say so now, it really doesn't bother me because I keep my own score card. The public score card will catch up. It may be a year or two away but it will be there."

INDEX

INDEX

Index

Index

233

Index

Index

235

Index

236

Index